D1300480

# PRINCIPLES AND METHODS
# IN SECONDARY EDUCATION

# PRINCIPLES AND METHODS IN SECONDARY EDUCATION

## Second Edition

**Robert C. McKean**
*University of Colorado*

Charles E. Merrill Publishing Company
*A Bell & Howell Company*
Columbus, Ohio

International Standard Book Number: 0-675-09237-X

Library of Congress Catalog Card Number: 77-149005

1 2 3 4 5 6 7 8 9 10/75 74 73 72 71

Printed in the United States of America

To Lora

# Preface

Education occupies a position of crucial and strategic importance in the determination of the future of the American society. Classroom teachers, aware of their vital role, seek to remain sensitive to the insistent demands of the culture within which they work and continue to improve the effectiveness of their central task, the teaching of youth.

Secondary school teachers, especially, face profound changes requiring mastery and perspective of the knowledge in their teaching areas, knowledge which is growing at a fantastic rate. They must gain a deep understanding of new and more valid insights into the processes of learning, child growth and development, available materials and resources, and instructional procedures. They are the professional workers who accept all youth and provide constructive, helpful guidance to students in the search for excellence.

Great changes are under way in the role of the classroom teacher in the modern secondary school. New and different relationships among teachers, supervisors, and administrators have developed so that the direct instructional personnel have become more truly participants in the decision-making activity of the schools. Accordingly, they need to develop an understanding of the responsibilities of the secondary school and a perspective of the complex curriculum with which it seeks to fulfill these expectations.

Principles of secondary education cannot be separated from instructional practices within an acceptable curriculum; therefore, this book combines the essential aspects of both areas. Practical, tangible illustrations, examples, and real situations are provided as bridges to reality. Specific suggestions are carefully integrated throughout.

The first three chapters are intended to be foundational. They seek to (1) deepen the basic objectives of education, (2) systematize vital concepts, and (3) build a modern interpretation of secondary education upon which common agreements can be structured. The following chapters are detailed discussions of essential topics. Considerable effort has been made to cover the wide range of significant material as concisely as possible without unnecessary overlap, repetition, and verbiage.

This volume is written for those who are interested in improving instruction in the junior and senior high school. The author's experience as teacher, supervisor, curriculum consultant, and college professor has led inexorably to the form and substance of this book. If such a work, born of reflection upon experience and research and tempered by the realities of the classroom teacher's task today, contributes to the continuing advancement of learning, its purpose will have been fulfilled. This Second Edition has been revised and updated to reflect the emerging realities of teaching in the 1970's. While not quite a revolution, the changes may be characterized as undergoing evolution at a pace seldom seen in an institution of this magnitude.

The author wishes to express a full measure of gratitude and appreciation to his students, teachers, colleagues, and family for their assistance and stimulation. Particular thanks goes to Bob Taylor, Hazlett Wubben, Calvin Grieder, Harl Douglass, Hubert Mills, and Stephen Romine of the University of Colorado for their continuing support and wise counsel.

*Robert C. McKean*

# Contents

# Introduction

Today the American junior and senior high school is an exciting place to be. A galaxy of changes large and small are underway. Teachers in every subject area and grade level are feeling the effects of these changes.

Some observers have characterized the events as a "revolution in American education." Others note, however, that, even in the 1970's with a climate remarkably hospitable to educational change, we are moving at glacial speed. Probably neither of these views is entirely accurate. The real truth of the matter is that we are undergoing evolution, continuous evolution, of this institution so vital to the welfare of our nation and our culture.

Actually, American public education, almost by definition, is an enterprise which is nearly immune to real revolution. For example, consider the following characteristics:

1. Our decentralized school system places decision-making in the hands of many different school districts controlled by part-time, non-professional board members.

2. The professional personnel—teachers, administrators and supervisors—are faced with job demands which make it difficult to organize and utilize the considerable talents and resources available and which inhibit opportunities for unhurried reflection and cogitation essential to the best use of reason and wisdom in decision-making.

3. Even given consensus among teachers for a rapid change along some front, local resistance slows it down. Parents and taxpayers feel secure with schools which look like the ones they attended.

4. In large school districts, especially, the momentum of change is slowed by the friction of bureaucracy.

5. The very nature of education as a highly complex enterprise presents many and varied needs all of which demand attention and divide our energies.

6. We have somehow developed a role for our educational leaders, particularly principals and superintendents, which requires that they assume personal responsibility for all manner of things. Revolution is unlikely when self-survival is likely to be a daily concern.

7. Finally, it is difficult for school districts to develop functional objectives which provide direction to educational change.

Certainly there are revolutionaries and militants on the educational scene. However, the objective observer is often disturbed by their activities. They sometimes present the image of a rather motley group of academic Don Quixotes charging wildly about, riding their hobby horses, lances at the alert, helmets flamboyantly askew, tilting at windmills.

Actually, revolution would seem most often to be a process of the few, while evolution is likely to involve the many. Evolution is a balancing of forces—a strong, ground swell desire for change pitted against the enormous force of inertia and resistance. Such is the nature of enduring change in the schools.

Educational evolution is bringing profound changes in the approach to teaching and learning, in the instructional resources available to teachers, in the organization of educational personnel, in the nature of the physical environment for teaching, and in the very role of the teacher himself. The teaching profession needs people who are able to deal realistically with the tensions and anxieties of the present and who can look to the future with anticipation and interest. If you are intelligent, alert to new ideas, naturally curious about a multitude of things, and thoroughly committed to the future, not to the past, your services will be needed in the exciting, challenging years ahead.

## Perspective In Education

Right now the major task confronting you is to prepare yourself for teaching in the modern secondary school. This is a highly complex task, largely because teaching itself is a highly complex process. The essential function of the teacher is performed in the context of the teaching-learning process which involves you, a highly complicated human personality, and a group of students, each of whom is a unique, equally complicated personality.

As you pursue your training and develop some perspective toward teaching, certain ideas will become clear.

*Teaching, a Practice*

Teaching is not a science; it is a practice, or, if highly developed, an art. The truly fine teachers are artists. Most of them are gifted intuitively. They are highly sensitive to the developing relationships between teacher and students and to the shifting pattern of relationships among the students themselves. Thus, they are able to operate within this complex of variables with the sureness of an expert golfer stroking a long putt over an undulating green.

The practice of teaching calls for a high degree of flexibility, adaptability, and nimbleness of mind that goes far beyond the mechanical application of step-by-step procedures. Therefore, the beginning teacher who is looking for a set of "100 per cent guaranteed or your money back" blueprints for teaching is doomed to the unhappy realization that there are few really final answers in education. Until psychologists are able to reduce human behavior to a formula, the successful teacher will continue to be eclectic and pragmatic in his approach to his job. That is, he will pick and choose among various methods and materials and through trial and error adopt certain ones according to their worth as demonstrated in use.

*Teacher Education*

The teacher is a product of the whole college or university, not just the school of education. The entire range of resources of the institution of high learning is available to help you become a successful teacher. It seeks to build upon the background of experience you bring with you through (1) general education, which gives you some of the breadth and scope necessary to a well-rounded person; (2) subject matter preparation, which provides you with depth and mastery sufficient to teach these subjects to others; and (3) professional training, which offers specific vocational preparation for the job of teaching.

At this point you are likely to be involved largely in the professional phase of your training. Although this varies from state to state according to state teacher certification requirements, the number of course credits taken in professional education to qualify for a secondary school teaching certificate tends to be only about 20 per cent or less of the total required for your bachelors degree. In this phase the school of education seeks to achieve certain essential objectives. Broadly stated they include the following:

1. Professional courses are planned to give you an understanding of youth and how they learn. Your students make up the other half of the teaching-learning relationship. Thus, a knowledge of them and the pro-

cesses by which they learn is essential to the task of setting up situations in which the most desirable and effective learning may occur.

2. The education faculty seeks to deepen your knowledge of the modern American society in which you will work. Teachers need to know the common expectations and demands made upon the school.

3. An essential part of the teacher's preparation involves the development of insight into the role of the teacher in the modern high school. This normally includes job conditions, employment opportunities, and the nature of the profession of which you are to be a part.

4. Professional training provides an understanding of the nature and functions of the public secondary school as it has evolved in America. If you are to be a successful teacher you need current information regarding the educative institution in which you will work and its relationship to the other educative agencies which share the task of the total education of youth.

5. Courses in the field of education offer a body of instructional resources and teaching procedures which successful teachers for years have used and refined in the classroom. In addition, guiding principles and processes are presented by which you can develop and adapt teaching methods to fit your personality and your situation.

6. Professional preparation includes observation and actual teaching experiences with the guidance and assistance of a classroom teacher and a college supervisor. This on-the-job training, which normally makes up about one-third to one-half of the required professional work, is designed to provide an opportunity for you to try out methods and materials in an actual classroom situation.

*Commencement*

Upon graduation you will be ready to *begin* to learn to be a teacher. As in other professions, such as law and medicine where students are prepared for their practice through years of training, you will be prepared to begin to practice teaching. At the end of your pre-service training it will be up to you to take advantage of the resources available in order to further your development as a teacher in service. The administrator of the school, supervisors, department heads, experienced teachers, and your college professors all want you to succeed and will offer help and guidance when you need it.

At present you are well on your way toward your goal of becoming a teacher. You will find it exciting, challenging work. As the vista of the future unfolds you can have a vital and influential part to play. Good luck!

# one

# The Setting
# for Teaching

The high school teacher of today is a member of a large and influential group of professional workers. He is a participant in a huge educational enterprise and he works in an educative agency of impressive dimensions.

Over the years, education has been important to the American people. They hold powerful and insistent beliefs regarding the nature and amount of educational opportunity which should be available to all boys and girls. Today's junior and senior high schools differ considerably, however, from the first Latin Grammar School established in 1635 in Boston. The colonial secondary schools, which were upper class, college preparatory, narrowly humanistic in emphasis, have been replaced by an institution which enrolls a broad cross section of American youth, offers a wide range of subjects, and seeks to prepare boys and girls for college and for life. The public high school of today has developed an orientation and configuration characteristic of the society in which it exists.

Youth are necessarily interested in the schools because compulsory attendance laws force them to enroll. In addition, many of them see education as requisite to vocational and social success. Parents are concerned because many of their hopes and dreams for their children depend upon educational achievement. Taxpayers focus attention on the schools because they must pay more for the continued support of these schools. Governmental leaders are sensitive to the needs and the results of the educational system because of its importance to the nation's future. You as future teachers are bound to be concerned with the high school, for this is the setting in which you will work.

You are likely to require information regarding the following areas.

1. The status of secondary education. What are some of the important quantitative dimensions? How is secondary education organized?

2. The climate of opinion surrounding the schools. How well does the public support its schools? What attacks and criticisms are prevalent?

## THE MODERN SECONDARY SCHOOL

The public high school is an American development. In the United States, graduation from high school is the common expectation for all normal youth. No other nation has asked its secondary schools to implement the goal of universal secondary education. Influenced by parental pressures, compulsory attendance laws, employer requirements, and general public sentiment, the American high school of today is attempting to meet society's demand that it provide all youth with an appropriate education.

In the process, our total public school system has become an enterprise of gigantic proportions in which, it is safe to estimate, at least one-fourth of our population is directly involved. Actually, the schools have become big business. A great many systems have annual multimillion dollar budgets. In most communities, the school payroll stands among the largest in town. Value of school buildings, equipment, and land places education high on the list of important business and industrial activities.

## FACTS AND FIGURES

Secondary education in the United States is impressive by sheer size alone. Literally millions of students jam the many buildings. Fleets of buses are needed to transport them and hundreds of thousands of trained teachers are required to educate them. Complex problems of operation demand a corps of professionally trained administrators and supervisors. Some of the more important facts and figures will help describe this educative agency in which you will work.

*Students.*     Attendance in the junior and senior high school has become the accepted "job" of the adolescent. Compulsory education laws and insistent pressures by parents and society in general act to encourage all youth to attend and, if possible, to graduate. Estimates[1] for the mid-1970's place the number of boys and girls enrolled in the public junior and senior high schools at more than twenty and a half million and non-

---

[1]*Projections of Educational Statistics to 1975–76* (Washington, D.C.: Government Printing Office, 1966), 1–3, 23.

public high schools 1.6 million. All secondary schools in the United States are estimated to graduate about 3.4 million young people at the end of the 1975–76 school year.

*Schools.* Today there are considerably more than thirty thousand secondary schools as contrasted with about six thousand in 1900. These, of course, range in size from a few one- and two-teacher high schools located in remote areas to huge urban complexes of five thousand pupils or more. At present, the average size secondary school may be estimated at close to 450 students.

*Teachers.* An estimated[2] one million plus classroom teachers are required to staff these schools and to educate this great student body. On the basis of present trends, the secondary school teacher can count on teaching an average of five class periods each day with an average of twenty-six pupils in each class. He will spend about forty-eight hours per week in direct instructional duties and school-related activities such as lesson preparation, paper grading, extra-class responsibilities, and the like. His school year is likely to include at least 180 classroom teaching days plus five to six days of non-teaching duties.

## ORGANIZATION OF HIGH SCHOOLS

Public high schools are organized into a number of different patterns. The early pattern was an 8-4 plan with an eight-year elementary school and a four-year high school. Early in the twentieth century, a movement toward reorganization emerged which led to various plans including some form of junior high school or middle school. For example, the 6-6 or 7-5 plans involve a combined junior-senior high school. The 6-3-3 and 6-2-4 organizations have a separate junior high school building with an administrative head of its own. More recently, there has been a growing interest in plans which provide a middle school in such patterns as 5-3-4 and 4-4-4. At the present time, the great majority of public school systems have adopted some reorganization of secondary education, notably the 6-6 and 6-3-3 plans. However, the non-public schools have overwhelmingly retained the traditional 8-4 pattern.

*The junior high school.* Significant factors, such as concerns about accomplishing a downward extension of the high school and building

---

[2]*Ibid.,* 37.

shortages in the light of greatly increased secondary school enrollments have led to a vision of a new kind of education for the early adolescent. Ideally, the junior high school should span the gulf between elementary school and senior high school. It seeks to provide transition in methods, curriculum, and activities. It aims to offer opportunities for pupils to explore their interests, aptitudes, and emerging abilities and to give them a foundation for future decisions. It is set up to offer specialized guidance and it is especially planned to take into consideration the characteristics of boys and girls from ages thirteen through fifteen.

From the teacher's point of view, the junior high school, in comparison with the senior high school, tends to be characterized as more consciously concerned with general education for all youth, having more required courses and fewer electives. Its students are in an awkward period of early adolescence when special understanding is needed. It is a school which is often staffed by teachers who have elementary training and experience as well as teachers with secondary preparation. Having less tradition behind it, the junior high school frequently is the exciting scene for educational innovation. It is most often thought of as comprising grades 7, 8, and 9.

A few school systems look at the junior high school as a sort of academic "minor league"; that is, the administrators try to hire new teachers when possible at this level and, if they prove themselves in the first year or two, they may be asked to move up to the senior high school. However, a great many teachers have discovered that they much prefer to deal with youngsters of junior high age, and they wouldn't consider leaving. Many beginning teachers now have completed college programs tailored for the preparation of junior high teachers and look to junior high school teaching as a career goal.

*The senior high school.*     The comprehensive senior high school attempts to enroll young people who have a wide variety of interests, capacities, educational and vocational aspirations, and backgrounds of experience and seeks to provide them with an appropriate education. It is at the senior high level that students are becoming conscious of the apparent gulf between themselves and their parents; they require special assistance in relating constructively with the adult world. Most are caught up in their fascinating peer group culture, but in the background lie thoughts of college, jobs, marriage, and possibly the military service.

The senior high school program of studies must include the subjects which will prepare some for college and it must offer others (the majority of the students) the courses which will be helpful in preparing for work. Increasing opportunities, therefore, are provided for electing a variety of different classes. Teachers work with youth at a more mature level and are able to teach more specialized courses than in previous grades. Most prize the satisfaction that comes through their graduates' successes in further education and life.

At whatever level you decide to teach, there are satisfactions and rewards. It is wise to visit both junior and senior high schools, observe students, and talk to school personnel; this may help you decide the level at which to teach.

## LIMITATIONS WITHIN WHICH THE SCHOOL WORKS

The public junior and senior high schools operate within some very real limitations. The expectations of society, the aims of the school, as well as the actual achievements and failures of the secondary schools must be considered with these limitations in mind. They tend to affect the nature and extent of experience which students may receive.

*Universal education.* The ideal of universal education in the United States presents a challenge to the secondary schools which is unprecedented in history. It means that public school educators have accepted the responsibility for enrolling and educating the wide diversity of high school age youth. In some nations, secondary education caters to a rather select minority privileged by position, wealth, or aptitude. However, in America, the high school classroom teacher accepts all the students who happen to reside in the district and seeks to provide a program which will be helpful and constructive for all. Thus the curriculum must be adaptable and flexible; the teacher cannot plan for a fairly homogeneous group, but must prepare a variety of materials, activities, and approaches in order to teach effectively a complex heterogeneity of pupils.

*Compulsory education.* The realities of compulsory secondary education (boys and girls are required by law to attend school until age sixteen in most states and until age eighteen or graduation from high school in an increasing number) force the classroom teacher to accept an instructional imperative. If all youth are forced to attend, then the school must somehow provide them with at least some experiences which they will perceive to be satisfying and rewarding. Moreover, every boy and girl who works diligently should be able to find some kind of success regardless of his intellectual aptitude. If the school does less than this, it indicates that it has not fulfilled the mandate given it by society.

The very fact that young people are forced to attend school has some interesting implications for teaching and learning. A group of high school juniors was asked this question: "What would happen if the state legislature passed a law which read that students could leave school upon completion of the eighth grade?" After some discussion, the consensus of the members of the group was that many of their friends would leave school tomorrow, they would probably stay away for a couple of weeks, but that most would dribble back but with an entirely different attitude. The students would feel that they were in school because they wanted to be—not because they were compelled to attend. This group felt that school was probably more attractive than other things available to them at that age. For many, compulsory attendance laws fostered a feeling of resignation to the inevitable, for some an attitude of hostility. Classroom teachers ought to understand and plan their teaching with this in mind.

*Mass education.*     The secondary schools in the United States patently are engaged in mass education. All students must somehow be transported to school, brought into contact with highly competent teachers and appropriate instructional materials, fed and protected from the weather, and returned home at the end of the day.

School administrators rightly are concerned with such complicated problems as bus routes and schedules; insurance coverage; purchase and maintenance of school buses; hiring, training, and supervision of drivers; and special uses of the buses for field trips and travel to other communities by athletic teams, spectators, and band members. These concerns are related, of course, to the transportation services provided by the school district. However, it is also clear that decisions made here may have important curricular and instructional implications. For example, in a district where a large proportion of the students are bused to and from school, the bus schedules which bring the boys and girls to school a few minutes before the opening bell and take them away right after the last class surely will affect the opportunities for interested students to use the library, to meet after school in social and subject-matter clubs, to practice for the coming speech contest or dramatic production, to work on the school paper or yearbook, to utilize the language lab or science facilities for independent study, and to participate in intramural games.

With the increase in enrollment and growth in school size, the logistics of grouping and moving students from room to room, distributing textbooks and supplementary materials, providing lockers for coats and miscellaneous possessions, and organizing the parking of bicycles, motorcycles, and automobiles pose immediate and pressing problems for the principal. Moreover, the teachers often complain that somehow the central work of the school—teaching and learning—sometimes takes second priority to class schedules, hall supervision, smoking control, attendance reports, and administrative efficiency.

*Big business methods.* In the process of developing secondary education on a mass scale, some big business methods have been adopted. School board members, many of them successful businessmen themselves, and trained school administrators have sought to utilize or adapt for school use a number of the systems and procedures which have proved to be useful and efficient in American industry. The present bookkeeping practices, pupil personnel accounting, school budgets, inventory control and reports are greatly influenced by the procedures and motives of successful business.

These practices undoubtedly have contributed to the orderly and efficient management of the school, yet, in some cases, they have operated to limit the instructional adaptation possible. For example, small classes are expensive and "inefficient" therefore, a fifth-year Italian class is not offered for it would only attract six students. Other small classes planned for the very bright students, or the slow, or for some with special interests and needs are not likely to be approved in many schools because the enrollment would be too small to justify them. This quantity, production-oriented conception of education is often in conflict with the aims of individualizing instruction and the notion of the teacher-scholar.

In all these and similar characteristics of the modern junior and senior high schools represent the realities within which those schools must operate today. On one hand they serve to give American secondary education its distinctive character and to suggest the enormous task which it has undertaken. On the other hand the very nature of this responsibility and some of the steps taken in order to fulfill it serve to limit its effectiveness. The fact is that professional teachers and administrators are doing a rather remarkable job in meeting this challenge.

## CLIMATE OF OPINION

Teachers in the public secondary schools must work within a climate of opinion. This climate is highly important because the public schools are subject to local control and therefore must be sensitive and responsive to the ideas and opinions of the lay public. Classroom teachers find that they can more nearly achieve the goals of education if they have the freedom to teach the material they consider important. They have this freedom, however, only if they also have the assistance and confidence of parents. Teachers secure the materials and equipment to enhance learning through the support of an interested public. Thus the nature and degree of confidence, interest, and support invested in the schools by the community may facilitate or inhibit the work of the teacher and the resultant learning of the students.

*Situations*

Teachers often find themselves in situations where they must represent their high school in particular and public education in general. The following examples represent some situations which classroom teachers have had to face recently. Place yourself in the position of the teacher. What would you say? How could you answer helpfully and validly?

> *Situation one.* You are sitting at your desk after school grading a set of student papers when Mrs. Brand comes in to see you. As you ask her to sit down, you think rapidly over her son Tim's recent work. He has been doing well; he is at least a solid "B" student as nearly as you can recall. "What can I do for you?" you ask.
>
> "I'm disturbed about what an atomic scientist said in a TV speech last night. He said that our schools are not tough enough. He said, too, that boys and girls today have too many electives and are not required to take the solid subjects which will best prepare them for college. Is this true?"

What exactly is this parent asking? What would you say to her? What are the facts?

> *Situation two.* You have been invited to attend a meeting of one of the local service clubs. About half-way through the luncheon, and right in the middle of the creamed chicken on toast, someone says, "I read an article the other day which said that the private high schools are far superior to the public high schools. With all the money we spend on education, why can't the public schools do as well as the private schools in preparing our kids for college?"
>
> Suddenly conversation ceases, all eyes move in your direction, and everyone awaits your reply.

What is the answer? How *do* the public and private high schools compare in the preparation of top students for college work?

> *Situation three.* You are pushing a grocery cart in a local supermarket, leisurely doing your weekly shopping, when the manager rushes up to you

excitedly. "Last night," he says, "someone left some mimeographed materials on my front porch which claim that the schools are brainwashing our youngsters. It says that the textbooks are subversive. It even quotes parts of some social studies and English books which are socialistic and maybe even communistic. What about this?"

What would you say to him? How would you answer his question tactfully and validly?

*Situation four.* You and several of your colleagues are attending a P.T.A. meeting. At the conclusion of a lengthy business session, a parent stands up and says, "I would like to address a question to some of the teachers who are present tonight. Is it true that you are neglecting our gifted children? Is it true that we are wasting this valuable resource? What are you doing for the gifted and how can we help?"

How would you reply? Within what limitations do the schools work to help gifted children? How can interested parents help?

## *Implications*

These four descriptions are a small sampling of the kinds of situations in which a teacher may find himself. They seem to suggest some important implications.

1. Parents and the general public are usually concerned about school problems. They are caught in the crossfire of conflicting criticisms and attacks on public education, and quite understandably may become confused and anxious about today's school conditions.

2. Parents and townspeople may approach teachers and administrators with questions on school affairs, which of course should be welcomed. Through the examination of these questions, the public can be apprised of the real situation in the schools.

3. Teachers are liable to be asked to serve as representatives of their profession at any time. They may be required to interpret the work of the public high school, its aims, and the kind of progress being made toward achieving those aims to parents and to the general public. This does not seem to be an unfair demand.

4. Classroom teachers must know the facts about the current status of the school program. They should keep themselves informed about recent changes or developments in the total school picture.

5. Teachers should keep posted on the attacks and criticisms of public education. What is being attacked and who are the attackers?

6. Teachers cannot ignore public relations. If the schools really belong to the public, if public understanding, interest, and support are necessary for progress in education, teachers must help parents and townspeople know their schools.

## ATTACKS AND CRITICISMS

Certainly today, public education is under heavy attack and persistent criticism as never before. Most educators would be the first to assert that the public secondary school is far from perfect. In fact, they are its most insistent and perceptive critics. However, it seems clear that the anxiety and fear which plague the American people in a period of international tension and unrest also contribute to the volume and intensity of these attacks and criticisms. In such a state, the public is impelled to critically examine many of its basic institutions. Of these, the public school is especially exposed.

There is a fundamental difference between criticism and attack. Criticism is welcome for it is constructive in intent. Criticism attempts to point out shortcomings so that they may be corrected or improved. Attack is destructive in intent; it attempts to destroy all or part of public education as we know it. Attacks on the schools may result in one or more of the following unfortunate effects:

1. Teachers may become defensive in the face of unfair attacks and react negatively toward any suggestion for improvement. They may even resist efforts to revise the curriculum which come from their own staff.

2. Teachers may become fearful. Today in some communities they are afraid to deal with controversial issues or to use unconventional instructional materials and procedures.

3. Public confidence may be shaken. Attacks on the schools can cause the public to withdraw its support, can reduce or eliminate lay participation in the maintenance and improvement of the high schools.

4. The separation between teachers and students may widen. If student demands for more involvement in decision-making are ignored, the resulting conflict will drive a wedge between the two first-hand participants in the teaching-learning process.

### What Is Being Criticized?

Education is a highly complex activity; therefore, it is to be expected that criticisms and attacks will be infinitely varied. However, most of these cluster around the following six areas: (1) goals of the high school, (2) methods, (3) curriculum, (4) gifted students, (5) the disadvantaged, and (6) teacher training.

*Goals of Secondary Education.* The conflict over the goals of secondary education is an old and continuing dispute. It arises from a difference in concept of the role of the secondary school as an educative agency. One substantial group has long believed that the high schools ought to be highly selective, admitting only those who have the ability and resources to go on to college. The central task of the secondary school would be to prepare these boys and girls for college or university admittance. Some critics in this group assert that we must take the dullards out of high school and provide them with suitable vocational training. This group calls for tougher education and demands that high minimum standards be set up and enforced. A high school diploma should indicate that the youngster is ready for college work.

The other group feels that secondary schools should be open to all youth because, in fact, the very basis of our democracy rests upon an educated electorate. Compulsory attendance laws and general public sentiment are concrete indications of this attitude. This group believes in universal secondary education, by which all boys and girls attend high school and receive some constructive, helpful education there.

It seems clear that the great bulk of classroom teachers accept the second point of view, even though there is little doubt they would prefer to teach the better, college-bound pupils. However, they accept the goal of universal secondary education as the will of the people and attempt to meet this great challenge as best they can. If society wishes to modify this mandate, then it is for society to decide.

The central point of this dispute lies in the choice between selective, college preparatory education and education for all youth. The former represents the European attitude toward secondary education and contrasts sharply with the current American trend.

Another aspect of this conflict in the goals of secondary education is in the difference of opinion regarding liberal education as opposed to practical education. Secondary education has been the battleground for this dispute during practically the entire history of education in the United States. The Latin Grammar School was supplanted by the academy because of sentiment in favor of a curriculum somewhat more practical than one which provided training only in Greek, Latin, and religion. When the academy no longer provided the practical education that was demanded by the rising middle class, the public high school appeared and the academy was gradually replaced.

One point of view asserts that certain liberal arts subjects have the power to liberalize the student. According to this view, the best approach to a secondary curriculum lies in utilizing a certain pattern of courses modeled after the curricula of liberal arts colleges. Supporters of this type of education consider it as the best preparation for all youth no matter what their future area of special interest may be.

Opposing this is the demand that, if the secondary school is to enroll all boys and girls, it must prepare them for life; it must provide practical education. As a result, such practical courses as home economics, shop, business, driver education, distributive education, and the like have been included among the traditional subjects.

*Methods.* The critics of methodology tend to frame their protests in terms of progressive education, with its soft teaching, lack of competition in the schoolroom, and easy discipline. The schools, they say, misled by the writings of John Dewey and his disciples, have retreated from the traditional standards of secondary education. Children are encouraged to study what they please; the elective system in high school allows students to take courses which do not demand real effort; competition has been minimized so that boys and girls are not motivated to their best efforts; schools no longer demand intellectual excellence. These critics insist that the secondary school must furnish the mind of the student with the academic information indispensable to thinking and problem solving. Teachers must help youth to discipline their minds through rigorous intellectual training. The schoolroom must no longer be a playroom, but rather a place concerned with serious scholarship.

Opposed to this view are psychologists, mental hygienists, and educators, who point out that research in psychology and instructional procedures demonstrates the fallacy of this point of view. "Discipline the mind," "furnish the mind," "rigorous intellectual training," and "intellectual excellence" are simply modern, euphemistic terms for the old, fallacious concept of mental discipline. The mind was thought to be like a muscle which had to be exercised and made stronger through tough, rigorous courses. This theory was exploded long ago,[3] yet many critics still cry for a return to a methodology which is justified on this basis.

Critics sometimes enlarge on their demand that the high school "furnish the mind." For example, one prominent critic of the schools has said that the educational process must be one of collecting factual

---

[3] The classic study which led the way in disproving the mental discipline theory was reported in E. L. Thorndike, "Mental Discipline in High School Studies," *Journal of Educational Psychology,* 15:83–98, 1924; see also C. R. Broyler, E. L. Thorndike, and E. Woodyard, "A Second Study of Mental Discipline in High School Studies," *Journal of Educational Psychology,* 18:377–404, 1927.

knowledge to the limit of the absorptive capacity. Yet modern research in learning has shown clearly that boys and girls do not soak up information like greedy little sponges. They learn and retain academic knowledge only if it is pertinent to their purposes, interests, and experiences. Students learn facts and skills while they solve problems, answer questions, and satisfy interests. Abstract, factual information is difficult to learn by rote for it has little real meaning and is quickly forgotten. In other words, "the idea that children master a predetermined mass of information and skills which they will naturally put to intelligent use when they mature is belied by a half-century of experience and observation."[4]

Another theory of learning which was popular a generation or so ago was that learning must be painful or unpleasant if it is to be effective. This has been disproven; in fact, the reverse is generally true. However, many parents and critics still cling to this old attitude. When parents ask their child, "What did you learn in school today?" he may reply, "Oh, lots of things, and it was really fun!" This reaction immediately begins to worry mother and father. There must be something wrong if school is fun.

Teachers generally recognize that students learn more readily if the classroom atmosphere is warm and permissive rather than harsh and repressive. The methods used must be consistent with good mental hygiene and valid principles of learning.

*Curriculum.* This area of criticism is broad and varied. Critics from all positions comment on parts of the curriculum which are objectionable to them. Small but highly vocal pressure groups attempt to prevent the public school from teaching about such diverse topics as consumer education, evolution, UNESCO, and labor unions. As a matter of fact, teachers in some schools today are reluctant to discuss the United Nations, even though the President of the United States annually proclaims a United Nations Week. Schools are accused of brainwashing American youth if a particular brand of Americanism is not inlaid into the curriculum. Some critics, with justification, have asserted that the schools have not adequately presented the contributions which minority races have made to our society. However, the great bulk of the attacks and criticisms are focussed on the controversy over so-called "frills" vs. "solids."

Critics charge that the curriculum of the public high school is loaded with frills, to the detriment of the solid subjects. Depending on the critic, a wide variety of courses, such as physical education, driver training,

---

[4] *Judging and Improving the Schools: Current Issues* (Burlingame, California: California Teachers Association, 1960), 12.

home economics, band, chorus, shop, journalism, and creative writing are said to be frills. Because of the elective system, these critics maintain, students are allowed to waste their time on courses of little or no substance rather than taking the solid subjects which are respected. The abstract, factual courses are somehow more preferable than subjects which provide occupational training, recreational satisfaction, social adjustment, and citizenship competency. In one community, the pressure of attacks became so great that the principal instructed his counselors to try to prevent the college prep students from taking such frills as driver education, vocational courses, art, music, and literature and to encourage them to take more solid subjects such as math, science, foreign language, and history.

In spite of the criticisms that students today have not mastered the fundamentals because of the frills in the curriculum, evidence[5] shows that the performance of students in the United States has improved consistently with each generation. For example, researchers have compared students with pupils of twenty to thirty years ago by giving the same examinations that were given then. On these tests the mid-century students demonstrated significant superiority, even though a much larger proportion of youth were enrolled and there were twenty to thirty years' more knowledge to learn. The students are not deficient in the traditional fundamentals. However, concern is being expressed in regard to what many educators[6] feel is a more important set of primary curricular objectives. Young people today need help from the schools in meeting their need to become more adequate individuals, to gain the skills by which they may adapt to and master their life situations.

Another aspect of this disputed point is the control over curriculum by the public. As a case in point, driver education seems destined to remain in the course of study of the American secondary school regardless of the opinions of critics, teachers, and administrators. High school teachers and principals are reluctant to spend the thousands of dollars required for the purchase of a set of "driving simulators" and to support the costly at-the-wheel instruction. (One driver training teacher can instruct only a car full of pupils at one time, as compared to a math teacher who teaches a full classroom.) Principals and teachers are likely

---

[5] For some of the details see "The Truth About Our Public Schools," *Changing Times, The Kiplinger Magazine,* June 1954; Harold G. Shane, "The Strength of American Public Education," *Educational Leadership,* 16:161–164, 182, December 1958; and Finis E. Engleman, "They Don't Like," *Nations Schools,* 70:61–100, October 1962.

[6] *See,* for example, *Life Skills in School and Society,* 1969 Yearbook, Washington, D.C.: Association for Supervision and Curriculum Development, N.E.A., 1969 and *Perceiving, Behaving, Becoming,* 1962 Yearbook, Washington, D.C.: Association for Supervision and Curriculum Development, N.E.A., 1962.

to suggest that this money be spent on library books, provision for a planning period for all teachers, additions to the staff in order to cut down the size of classes, or increases in salaries. However, the parents are convinced, and rightly so, that the schools generally do a far superior job in driver training than the parents themselves. Insurance companies, as evidence of their belief in this program, offer reduced rates to young people who have completed driver education courses. Thus the public has usually been instrumental in adding this course to the curriculum, and is solidly in favor of retaining it. In fact, the curriculum of the present secondary school is generally in accord with the wishes of the public which it serves. High school teachers accept the reality of local control and work within this principle.

*Education of the gifted.*    In a period of great international tension and anxiety, the society quite naturally looks to the schools for assistance. One aspect in an evaluation of the school's power to assist the people of a democratic society reveals the waste of our bright students' talents. It must be remembered, however, that the school in a democratic society, where the individual decides for himself, may be handicapped to some extent in competition, say, with a totalitarian nation, where the state decides for the individual.

In a democracy, the individual student has the right to decide which high school curriculum he will follow, whether or not he will go on to college thereafter, and what occupation he would like to enter. Of course, the secondary school offers its counseling services in these matters to assist the student to make decisions which correspond to his particular strengths and weaknesses. However, these decisions ultimately rest with the student and his parents, not with the school; whereas, in totalitarian states, these decisions rest neither with the student nor with the school, but with the state.

Nevertheless, because the gifted youth is recognized as a human resource vital to our continued freedom and progress, many critics have charged the public schools with wasting this resource. High schools, it is said, do not challenge the intellectual powers of these students. Some critics emphasize the need for training in science and math, even urging that special schools be set aside for the training of an academic elite. Current shortages of engineers, scientists, and other professional groups, says one critic, are the result "of inadequate pre-professional education— of time wasted in public school which somehow must be made up later on."

Yet critics who have taken the time to visit the public schools and to assess the situation first-hand are less certain that gifted youth are shortchanged. Conant has said "That the intellectually able student was receiving a satisfactory education in certain large suburban high schools has long been evident to all who were well-informed about school and college."[7]

One real and pressing problem which high school teachers face in connection with educating the gifted is the demand of our society that all normal youth be required to attend school. The great proportion of all adolescents do attend junior and senior high schools with individual student ability varying widely. The schools are engaged in mass education. In the press of such great numbers, the gifted child sometimes receives something less than individual attention. The classroom teacher is the first to admit that more could be done to help the gifted student if there were more time, if classes were smaller, and if teaching loads were lighter. On the other hand, a variety of procedures—acceleration, ability grouping, enrichment, and special classes—have been instituted to help provide a better education for the academically superior student. Generally speaking, courses and instruction are available which can contribute substantially to the growth and preparation of gifted boys and girls if they are motivated by parents and by society to take advantage of the opportunity.

*The disadvantaged.*     Growing out of a genuine concern by behavioral scientists and public school educators and spotlighted by demands made by some of the black and Spanish-American militants has come an examination of how well the public schools are providing the disadvantaged youth with an education appropriate to their needs. Certainly, these boys and girls come to the high schools in rather large numbers. They bring with them the differences in their backgrounds of experience, many of which become handicaps in competing and succeeding in a middle-class orientated school.

Criticisms have pointed up the fact that in spite of a number of special programs initiated in the latter half of the 1960's by some school districts and the provision of federal funds for the encouragement of curriculum and instructional modification, much more needs to be done for these disadvantaged youngsters. Somehow they must be provided success experiences, must receive help in revising and improving their self-concepts, must come to understand and prize many of the strengths in their backgrounds, must find success figures with whom to identify, and must be offered school experiences which they can relate to and perceive as being worthwhile.

---

[7] James B. Conant, "Some Problems of the American High School," *Phi Delta Kappan,* 40:51, November 1958.

Black parent groups have called for changes in the organization, administration, and staffing of urban core schools. Some want "black schools for black students." Others, in concert with white groups, have worked for enforced busing and boundary changes to secure a measure of racial balance in the interest of integration. Criticisms of textbooks have resulted in the comprehensive rewriting of historical materials to more nearly give an appropriate recognition of minority race contributions to the development of our nation. Literature materials now tend to include selections by non-white authors and other subjects have sought to recognize their cultural contributions.

*Teacher training.*    As a part of the total criticism of the public schools, the training that teachers receive has come under attack. By far the most common charge is overemphasis on the importance of methods courses. Knowledge of subject matter is said to be all that a teacher needs. Professional education courses, the majority of which are methods courses, are believed to bulk too large in the training of a teacher. Some critics assert that the teacher education program has emphasized the "know how" of teaching to the detriment of the "know what." Many of these critics would throw out all education courses with the possible exception of student teaching. They assert that, since college professors rarely have taken such courses, it is difficult to see why high school teachers need such training.

Many educators would rebut this criticism by pointing out that this lack of professional training is exactly what is lacking in some college teaching. They feel that students often learn in spite of the professor rather than through his help. These generally select, highly motivated, and academically capable pupils (at least when compared to the total high school student group), are usually able to learn with a minimum of assistance. One college professor of physics states candidly, "I have muddled along for forty years without the benefit of a course in education, but I am not as proud of my ignorance as most science teachers are."[8] Many college professors, through their performance in the classroom, reveal a lack of understanding of youth, of the principles of learning, and of the role of the teacher in the teaching-learning process.

Most high school teachers quickly discover through empirical means that mastery of subject matter is tremendously important; but it is not enough in itself. For example, some critics have suggested that the mere possession of a high degree of skill or facility in an appropriate area

---

[8] Paul Kirkpatrick, "On Colleagues and Clients," *Phi Delta Kappan,* 41:254, March 1960.

ought to be sufficient qualification for a teaching credential. Yet experienced teachers are quick to point out that there is a long and hazardous step between the mere possession, say, of a high degree of verbal and written fluency in a modern language and the ability to teach this to others. Could any upper-middle-class Frenchman who is likely to have moderately good language habits teach a beginning French class in an American junior high school? Could you, if you had the ability to read at 1200 words a minute with excellent comprehension, teach reading to five- and six-year-old children in the first grade? In spite of the probability of ridiculous consequences, some state legislatures have attempted to put this principle into law. Obviously, the utilization of sound methods of instruction is essential to success with immature pupils, with students who have average or lower academic aptitudes, and with boys and girls who are less than enthusiastic about compulsory school attendance.

The majority of states require about 18 semester hours of education for high school certification. A fairly general requirement by colleges and universities is 20 semester hours of education courses. Thus only about 17 per cent of the 120 semester hours usually required for college graduation consists of education courses. Of this 20, typically 6–8 hours are used for student teaching; only 2–4 hours consist of actual methods courses. Therefore, it appears that most colleges of education do not require an excessive number of methods courses, nor do they seem to demand an overwhelming proportion of the total requirements for graduation.

### What Should Be Criticized?

Of course not all is right with secondary education. In any complex operation there is room for improvement. In fact, classroom teachers, supervisors, administrators, and professors of education are the most insistent and perceptive critics of the schools because of their deep interest, insight, and experience in education.

According to these persons, an important conclusion regarding the attacks and criticisms of education is clear: Most of the critics and attackers are criticizing the wrong things. Actually, a careful appraisal of the public junior and senior high schools today reveals serious weaknesses which are seldom identified. These are the shortcomings of modern secondary education which are of great concern to those individuals who work with school problems firsthand—shortcomings which are seldom pointed out by persons less directly involved.

*High level abstraction.*    The present curriculum is too full of dry, isolated bits of academic information, stray facts, and abstract knowledge. Too seldom is course content related to the background and experience of the students. For example, a study of the geography of European countries is often simply a process of memorizing the names of the capital cities, the countries' principal imports and exports, and the various amounts of rainfall. Students never realize that they are studying the lives of real human beings living in a different geographical context and participating in an excitingly different culture. Typically, hyperabstract learning is not real, non-functional, and fleeting. It may provide practice in a sort of abstract, intellectual game of manipulating verbal symbols, but it seldom offers the opportunity to solve problems and answer questions which are real and important to students. This is what students mean when they say the curriculum is not relevant.

*Non-functional content.* Ever since the first public high school was established, we have been adding to the curriculum. Only infrequently have courses been dropped. Today many high school courses contain material which is repetitious, which does not prepare students for advanced study, or which can be justified only by tradition. At the same time, knowledge is being added at a tremendous rate. However, careful analysis could reduce overlapping, duplication, and non-functional elements in the curriculum. This is a task that calls for top priority.

*Rigidity.* The organization of the secondary school is rigid. It does not provide for the individual differences of boys and girls. Classroom teachers know that students learn in different ways, come from widely different experiential backgrounds, possess substantially different aptitudes for learning, and are moved by varying motives, interests, and enthusiasms. Yet in some schools all youth may be taught by the same methods, be held to the same minimum standards, and be required to take many of the same courses. The very bright student may not be able to take a senior course along with his regular ninth-grade work (even though the school counselor finds him qualified in every way), simply because there is no provision in the school policy for such a procedure. Arbitrary rules are established and enforced. Exceptions are difficult or impossible to secure.

*Conformity.* Mass education also produces conditions which foster conformity. Some teachers, overburdened with more students than they can handle, come to prize qualities of conformity. Students are rewarded for reliability, "self-control," amenability, and cooperation in "facilitating" class procedure. Boys and girls who ask probing questions and insist upon answers to these questions, who try approaches other than the one indicated in the textbook, and who question the teacher's explanation may be punished. Thus, in dealing with great numbers of students, the schools sometimes do not encourage creativity nor constructively handle non-conforming behavior.

*Poor mental hygiene.*     High school classrooms often are characterized by poor mental hygiene. In order to secure and retain control, some teachers resort to a great deal of ego threat. Students are subjected to vicious and unfair sarcasm. Group pressures are manipulated by the teacher to punish and isolate certain individuals. Savage competition is sometimes fostered in the classroom to enhance student effort. Under such conditions, the climate for learning is often harsh and unpleasant.

*Inexpert teachers.*     Secondary education today demands expert teachers. The high school instructor must have mastery of the subject he teaches. That a lack of this mastery of subject matter exists is most clearly shown in the average teacher's lack of perspective about his subject. Some high school history teachers confess that they are not sure why students should study history, except that it is traditionally done. What is even more significant, these teachers are unable to identify the important generalizations or concepts which students ought to gain through such study. English teachers want lists of the literature which they are expected to teach, for they lack the assurance and decisiveness needed to pick and choose among the writings which will be most suitable and helpful to their students. Math teachers follow the textbook, including everything in it in the mad effort to get through the entire book by June, rather than choosing the most essential material to emphasize. Teachers are indecisive because they lack real perspective of their subjects. These teachers need more work in their subject areas. Yet only seldom can they return to college and find a course which will provide this perspective. Typically, the further one advances in a study, the more highly specialized that study becomes.

Junior and senior high school teachers must be truly expert in the fields of instructional methodology, child growth and development, and principles of learning. Present teacher training programs offer little more than a good introduction to these fields. Yet, if teachers are to progress beyond an intuitive approach to making necessary improvements and innovations in methods of instruction, a sound mastery of these areas is indispensable.

*What Can Teachers Do?*

In the face of these criticisms and attacks what *should* the classroom teacher do? What *can* the classroom teacher do? The following suggestions are offered as a constructive approach to the many conscientious and dedicated teachers who must bear the brunt of these attacks.

1. Provide the highest level of teaching possible. Ultimately the superior quality of the public secondary school is the best answer to attacks and criticisms of all kinds.

2. Inform the community about the aims of the school, the instructional practices, the curriculum, and the results of the school's efforts. An informed public is likely to appreciate the work of its schools and participate in their improvement.

3. Make friends in the community. The most devastating reply to an attacker who claims that the local teachers are communistic and are engaged in brainwashing the students comes from the parent who says, "I know the teachers in our high school; they are my friends and they most certainly are not communists!"

4. Deal with attacks and criticisms like a professional educator. When parents come to you with clippings of controversial articles or reports of controversial speeches, deal with these parents as objectively and honestly as possible. Help them to understand your program and to appreciate the limitations within which you work. Help them to see the results of your efforts.

5. Know the facts. Know the nature and sources of current criticisms, and know your own school well in order to answer these criticisms effectively. Inevitably teachers are spokesmen for their own high school in particular and for secondary education in general everywhere they go. They should be able to refer interested persons to suitable sources[9] for further information. Classroom teachers have a responsibility to know the facts, admit the weaknesses, and stand up for the strengths of secondary education.

## REVIEW

The secondary school in America is a large and complex enterprise. A knowledge of its quantitative dimensions provides one important approach for the beginning teacher to use in developing understanding of the institution within which he will work. Today more than twenty-six thousand public secondary schools, staffed by more than half a million teachers, enroll over nine million boys and girls in grades nine through twelve.

The public schools are under continuing criticism and attack. Some writers argue that these criticisms and attacks are good because they

---

[9] For example, refer to some of the materials in the references at the end of this chapter.

impel the secondary schools to look carefully at their practices. To some extent this may be true; yet, as a consequence of the volume and intensity of the barrage, some unfortunate effects may result.

1. What are the important quantitative dimensions of secondary education? What proportion of high school age youth attend, graduate, enter college? What are the conditions of and reasons for the shortage of teachers? What is the average size high school and why is size a factor of some importance?

2. What is the nature of the climate of opinion surrounding the schools? What aspects of secondary education are criticized, and by whom? What measures should classroom teachers take in a period of attack and criticism?

# Selected References

Barrett, T. and DeVault, M. V. "Targets for Criticism." *Education Digest*, 29:14–16, January 1964.

Davis, E. W. "Extremists, Critics and Schools." *Educational Leadership*, 23:53–74, October 1965.

Douglass, H. R. *Trends and Issues in Secondary Education*. Washington, D.C.: The Center for Applied Research and Education, Inc., 1962.

*Education in America*. Washington, D.C.: Congressional Quarterly, Inc., 1968.

Eurich, A. C. *Reforming American Education*. New York: Harper & Row, Publishers, 1969.

French, W. M. *American Secondary Education*. New York: The Odyssey Press, Inc., 1967; Ch. 9 "The Contemporary High School."

Full, H., ed. *Controversy in American Education*. New York: The Macmillan Company, 1967.

Havighurst, R. J. "Requirements for a Valid 'New Criticism.' " *Phi Delta Kappan*, 50:20–26, September 1968.

Schrag, P. "Education's 'Romantic' Critics." *Saturday Review*, February 18, 1967, pp. 80–82, 98–99.

Stinnett, T. M. *Professional Problems of Teachers*. 3rd ed. New York: The Macmillan Company, 1968.

"Student Participation: Toward Maturity." *Educational Leadership*, 27: (entire issue), February 1970.

Taylor, B. L. "The Most Valid Criticism of Schools." *Colorado School Journal*, 80:24–25, February 1965.

# two

# Bases for Selecting
# and Organizing Content

Before you can begin your work in the classroom, an essential task must
be undertaken. Within the assigned subject area you must select and
organize a satisfying pattern of experiences for high school learners. All
teachers must face and, in some fashion, solve this problem.

Some attempt to avoid this responsibility by following closely the
adopted textbook. Yet they find they must continually make decisions
which affect content. The United States history teacher emphasizes some
events and dates above others. The English teacher, realizing that it is
impossible to cover all the literature in the anthology, assigns certain
selections and leaves out others. Regardless of the subject, every teacher
must pick and choose, organize and reorganize content to fit the needs
of his classes.

You are likely to express your concerns in such questions as: What
will we study? Where will we start? In what order will we proceed?

In order to answer these kinds of questions you need to look for
fundamental considerations upon which to base decisions. If the subject
matter is to be satisfying, it must take into consideration (1) the needs
of the learner, (2) the needs of society, (3) the needs of the community,
and (4) the subject matter itself. These, then, become the bases for the
selection and organization of content.

Within each of these four areas, certain understandings and competencies must be developed.

1. Adolescent needs are complicated and subtle. Thus, you should
strive, through study and observation, to know the general characteristics
of maturing boys and girls in America; you should seek insight into
need patterns by analyzing lists of needs formulated by adult observers

and expressed by adolescents themselves; and you should explore procedures by which you may become more sensitive to the interests and concerns of students in your classes.

2. The modern American society forms the general setting in which the public high school exists. The beginning teacher must understand the changing nature of this society and the tasks which it has assigned to the school as one of the many educative agencies in our culture.

3. Communities vary greatly from locality to locality. Therefore, you can best prepare yourself to deal intelligently with the needs and expectations of the community in which you may be teaching by developing a variety of community survey procedures.

4. Each area of knowledge has two important characteristics: (a) a body of acquired information and (b) a specialized strategy of acquiring and controlling that knowledge. Every subject-matter area in the junior and senior high schools demands some decision regarding what sort of balance is to be struck between the teaching of content and the teaching of process. You need to look deeply into the nature of your area of speciality in order to understand this basis for the selection and organization of curriculum.

## THE ADOLESCENT LEARNER

Probably the most fascinating and challenging facet of the high school teacher's job is the task of understanding the adolescent learner.

### Pupils Are People

Adolescents differ in many ways from mature adults; however, you must always recognize that they are moved by the ordinary human needs and emotions. The bizarre fads, incomprehensible teen-age jargon, and outlandish customs often make adults overlook the fact that these youngsters are, by and large, healthy personalities engaged in satisfying the demands of basic drives. These include: (1) approval from those persons whom they feel are important, (2) experience that represents success to them, (3) allegiance to a meaningful group, (4) new and interesting experiences, and (5) a sense of security and well-being.

The drives are common to all humans. However, the means to fulfillment are selected by teen-agers with limited backgrounds of experience and through still developing sets of values. Certainly, much assistance from parents and teachers is needed as adolescents face and make choices and decisions, often of great importance to their future lives.

### Adolescence: A Period of Adjustment

Teen-age boys and girls are engaged in the vital process of achieving adulthood. Adolescence, which may be roughly described as from the beginning of puberty to maturity, is not a period of sudden or abrupt change, but is characterized by gradual transition and considerable variation from person to person. The physiological changes, cultural pressures, and psychological changes present new and difficult problems in adjustment.

*Physical Changes.*    Probably the most dramatic aspects of adolescence result from a new cycle of growth and bodily development. For example, teen-agers find great difficulty in understanding and coping with the emergence of secondary sex characteristics. Changes, which have been developing gradually, suddenly burst forth upon the consciousness with great impact. Unless intelligent guidance is available, girls may react to the initial signs of menstruation with much fear and anxiety. Similarly, boys are likely to be disturbed over their first nocturnal emissions. Actually, the great need seems to be for reassurance that these changes are normal and are welcome as signs of approaching maturity.

As the body changes, young people must alter the way they look at themselves. Simple changes in height and size may cause significant adjustment problems. Girls, at one stage in their development, may find themselves towering above the boys in their classes. Some boys who have been looking up to adults may, in the span of a few years, grow so tall that they find themselves looking down on parents and teachers. Sometimes a youngster suddenly may stop growing. Picture the extremely difficult adjustment required in the following example.

In the elementary school years, a boy had been equal or superior to his age-mates in size and physical development. This factor, which is so important to pre-adolescent boys, made him a leader in athletics and provided him with considerable status. About the time he entered high school he stopped growing and soon found he could not compete on the same basis. He was forced to look for other ways to find success experience and finally earned his athletic letter as manager of the football team. A great deal of adjustment in self-concept was necessary.

Other evidence of adolescent development—change in voice, skin blemishes, awkwardness, initial growth of beard—are often the subject of much adult ridicule. It seems clear that the physical changes themselves are only a part of the problem; the larger part lies in the adolescent's perception of these changes and the reaction of others to them.

*Cultural pressures.*    Society places many demands upon the adolescent, and often these demands are inconsistent and seem almost irreconcilable. A large number of pressures exist which prolong dependency and actually prevent boys and girls from growing up. Family directives and community mores often keep adolescents from moving into situations which allow them to make meaningful decisions about important things. Other forces in society thrust young people into situations where they must accept responsibility for self-direction in vitally important areas (marriage, vocational choice, further education, moral and ethical decisions) without adequate practice.

Actually, adolescents have ambivalent desires; they want desperately to escape parental domination and yet they fear the loss of security that this represents. They need increasing opportunities to make decisions that are important to them and to face the consequences of these choices within reasonable limits. For instance, it would not be sensible to deliberately offer boys and girls with limited backgrounds of experience and immature value systems the choice of whether or not to try narcotics. Adults should allow maturing boys and girls to make choices within an ever-widening scope of importance, offer guidance and counsel, and insist that the privilege of decision making carries with it the responsibility of the consequences. In this way, adolescents are likely to be well prepared for the pivotal decisions they must inevitably make.

*Psychological changes.*    During this period, young people find themselves increasingly driven by what has been called the "need for personal significance." Intellectual and social horizons have expanded and adolescents find themselves looking for personal meaning in the world around them. They want to know how they will fit into adult society.

One evidence of this is seen in their interest in continually testing themselves in many different situations. The English teacher often performs a significant service in helping students to test themselves, to role play, through literature. High school students want to know how it feels to be married, a murderer, an advertising executive, a painter, a minister. They welcome all kinds of new experiences as opportunities to assess their developing powers.

In their search for the meaning of things and their own place in the society, adolescents begin to look closely at adult behavior. Typically, teen-agers are idealistic and what they see often shocks and repels them. They are confused by the inconsistency and the profusion of multiple standards in adult life. It is difficult for them to understand how persons can live with different ethical standards in work, play, church, and in personal life. They are concerned by adult moral values based on expediency and justified by rationalization. Boys and girls find it difficult to reconcile what they are told about adult life with what they see.

As young people approach maturity, they experience new and powerful emotions. Infatuation, sexual desires, open rebellion toward arbitrarily imposed authority, deep concern over apparent personal defects, and the like result in emotions that are awe inspiring and sometimes frightening. They need to grow in the ability to handle emotions at an increasingly more adult level. Symptomatic of wholesome emotional development are the sensitivity of the person to stimuli and the versatility of his emotional reactions. Adolescents begin to perceive emotional situations more clearly; they need to grow in their ability to "read" the situation for its emotional potentialities. Beyond this, they must learn to react in ways that are appropriate to the situation and conducive to better personal adjustment.

### Adolescent Needs

Adolescents are continually engaged in the important process of satisfying their needs. Some of these needs originate within the individual himself, while others derive from the pressures of the social milieu in which he lives. Thus, teachers must strive to understand and consider in their teaching the needs resulting from the learner interacting with his total environment.

*Patterns of needs.* As boys and girls grow toward maturity, their need patterns change. Many perceptive observers have attempted to analyze these changes and, with the same phenomena (that is, developing adolescents) as the basis, have formulated various lists of needs which are said to be of great concern to high school students.

The following "Ten Imperative Needs of Youth"[1] were formulated by the Educational Policies Commission of the National Education Association to describe the general needs which most youth face and to suggest aims of instruction.

1. All youth need to develop salable skills and those understandings and attitudes that make the worker an intelligent and productive partici-

---

[1] Educational Policies Commission, *Education for All American Youth* (Washington, D.C.: N.E.A., 1944), 225–26.

pant in economic life. To this end, most youth need supervised work experience as well as education in the skills and knowledge of their occupations.

2.　All youth need to develop and maintain good health and physical fitness.

3.　All youth need to understand the rights and duties of the citizen of a democratic society, and to be diligent and competent in the performance of their obligations as members of the community and citizens of the state and nation.

4.　All youth need to understand the significance of the family for the individual and society and the conditions conducive to successful family life.

5.　All youth need to know how to purchase and use goods and services intelligently, understanding both the values received by the consumer and the economic consequences of their acts.

6.　All youth need to understand the methods of science, the influence of science on human life, and the main scientific facts concerning the nature of the world and of man.

7.　All youth need opportunities to develop their capacities to appreciate beauty in literature, art, music, and nature.

8.　All youth need to be able to use their leisure time well and to budget it wisely, balancing activities that yield satisfactions to the individual with those that are socially useful.

9.　All youth need to develop respect for other persons, to grow in their insight into ethical values and principles, and to be able to live and work cooperatively with others.

10.　All youth need to grow in their ability to think rationally, to express their thoughts clearly, and to read and listen with understanding.

*Developmental tasks.*　　An especially useful concept developed by Havighurst describes the patterns of desirable growth in our society in terms of "developmental tasks of life."

> A developmental task is a task which arises at or about a certain period in the life of the individual, successful achievement of which leads to his happiness and to success with later tasks, while failure leads to unhappiness in the individual, disapproval by the society, and difficulty with later tasks.[2]

The developmental tasks[3] for adolescents are stated as follows:

1.　Accepting one's physique and accepting a masculine or feminine role.

---

[2] Robert J. Havighurst, *Developmental Tasks & Education* (New York: Longmans, Green & Co., Inc., 1950), 6.

[3] *Ibid.,* 30–65.

2. New relations with age-mates of both sexes.
3. Emotional independence of parents and other adults.
4. Achieving assurance of economic independence.
5. Selecting and preparing for an occupation.
6. Developing intellectual skills and concepts necessary for civic competence.
7. Desiring and achieving socially responsible behavior.
8. Preparing for marriage and family life.
9. Building conscious values in harmony with an adequate scientific world-picture.

*Problems of high school students.* A number of investigators have gone directly to adolescents to get information on student problems. One study[4] of school-related problems of junior and senior high school boys and girls grouped responses into four major problem areas.

1. The problem of self-understanding during adolescence.
2. The problem of developing new ways of relating to others.
3. The problem of teacher-student relationships.
4. The problem of the teaching-learning situation.

Much concern during the teen years is focused on the preoccupation with self. Physical, mental, and psychological changes call for constant readjustments in self-concept. Schools must seek constructive ways to foster this self-understanding.

Adolescents are engaged in the process of exploring and refining ways of interacting with others. The peer group relationship is overwhelmingly one of the most satisfying things about secondary schools, yet much trial-and-error activity goes on in somehow developing adequate relationships. A good deal of uncertainty exists in interaction with adults. In spite of the gap between generations, most youth seem able to interact satisfactorily with parents, teachers, first employers, and adults in the community.

Teachers are highly important in the lives of adolescents if for no other reason than the forced contact between them. Students react to the teacher as an authority figure responsible for the learning activities in class, but they also react to him as a person. Thus, the teacher's personality, attitudes toward subject, degree of respect and concern for individuals, and general philosophy of life may be as important as his knowledge of his subject in relation to many of the learning outcomes.

The classroom is the location where adolescents engage in their major work. Most recognize that, for now, it is their "job" to go to

---

[4] *Youth Education: Problems/Perspectives/Promises,* 1968 Yearbook (Washington, D.C.: Association for Supervisor and Curriculum Development, N.E.A., 1968), 7–8.

school. However, much of the problem in this area has to do with motivation. Boys and girls simply are not convinced that all of the subjects they are studying are really worthwhile. The classroom teacher seldom has been able to help them find convincing reasons for learning. In addition, difficulties of establishing effective and satisfying communication add to the student feelings of concern.

*Gifted and slow students.*    In a system of mass education, the pupils who are somewhat above and below the average in academic aptitude and scholastic achievement tend to pose special problems. Over the years, the schools have tried a wide variety of approaches to accommodate these students and some of the newer developments promise some benefits.

The most popular procedure is to employ some kind of homogeneous grouping. Criteria for grouping commonly include (1) academic aptitude, (2) academic achievement (tests and grades), (3) teacher recommendations, and (4) student and parent preference. Teachers quickly discover, however, that the resultant groups are not really homogeneous. There is still a significant range in ability. Great differences related to such characteristics as past experience, home and family background, interests and goals, and sex still exist. Actually, grouping just cuts down the ability range a bit.

Rather than skipping some students ahead and holding others back more than one year, more emphasis is being placed on adjusting content in classes, allowing students to "test" out of courses, and making provisions for some students to accelerate through materials at a faster rate.

Enrichment is a general procedure claimed by most secondary schools in adapting instruction to the needs of the bright student. Special planning is provided for him above and beyond the standard content of the course. Many top students complain, however, that much of what passes for enrichment is "more of the same old stuff."

Natural grouping takes place through the elective system, especially in senior high school. Honors classes and special seminars in a variety of subject areas are offered in many schools today for the bright pupils and special remedial and non-college classes for the slow pupils.

In addition, a well-planned counseling program is a vital part of the school's attempt to understand and deal with the problems of the bright and the slow. The slow student desperately needs to find some degree of success somewhere in his school experience and the gifted student seeks real challenge to his capacities and interests. Both groups must have some members of the professional staff who have a feeling for their special problems and who will work in their behalf.

*The disadvantaged.* Almost all schools enroll some youngsters who come from backgrounds which do not prepare them for satisfactory adjustment to the demands and expectations placed on them by the school and society. When many of these boys and girls get to the secondary school, they tend to read several years below grade level, often are older than their fellow students, typically have difficulty in abstract thinking processes, seldom have well-defined vocational goals, often are apathetic toward classroom activities, and may display hostility toward school authority. They are both white and non-white, they are found in the urban centers and in certain rural areas, and they bring with them the experiences of living in poverty, in slums, and in work camps. In the classroom, they need a teacher who understands their special characteristics[5] which must be taken into consideration in planning for their learning: (a) they tend to have a concern for the here and now, (b) they prefer the concrete and the functional rather than the abstract, (c) they have difficulty in seeing relationships, and (d) they greatly favor active learning activities over contemplative learning.

Some understanding of these needs and problems will be extremely helpful to you in your planning; however, you will be faced with a particular class containing a number of students, each a unique personality. They come to class with varying backgrounds of experience, from different socio-economic levels, with widely different sets of conscious needs and interests, and at various stages of physiological, emotional, and intellectual maturity. Teachers usually phrase this concern in the following kind of question: How can I become more sensitive to the changing needs and interests of my students in this specific class?

*Becoming sensitive to students.* If you are to become more sensitive to pupils, you need to provide situations whereby they are encouraged to express themselves in ways which will give clues to their problems and interests as they perceive them. Background information regarding their past experiences is needed to help interpret these clues. You also need to know a good deal about the out-of-school lives of boys and girls, for here is where many of their significant interests and most of their deepest concerns lie.

The following procedures have instructional value and may help you gain important insights.

1. Students may be asked to write *autobiographies*. These are valuable not only for the data they provide about past experiences, but also because they reveal the students' feelings about these experiences.

---

[5] Staten W. Webster, *The Disadvantaged Learner* (San Francisco: Chandler Publishing Company, 1966), 477.

2. *Diaries* which take the form of a running account of the out-of-school lives of pupils for a short period of time often show significant patterns of family relationships, friendship associations, and social roles. Leisure-time interests are usually clearly delineated.

3. *Open-end questions*[6] may be utilized to gain a variety of information. A well-formulated stimulus question allows the individual to structure his response according to his feelings and ideas. Students may respond to such questions as: What do you like most about your home? What things worry you? What would you like to do most? Describe the most serious problem of your best friend. What makes you angry? What do you want to be?

4. *Sample situations* may be discussed in class. A real life problem situation may be described and the students encouraged to identfy what is important in the situation. Their formulation of "the real problem" in the situation and their suggested solutions will give you real insight into the ways in which they perceive things, things they prize, maturity of judgment, and basic motivations.

The teacher who would become more sensitive needs to sharpen his powers of observation.

1. During the day-to-day class procedures, *surges of interest* should be noted. As certain topics come up in class, student activity quickens— questions are asked, discussion is stimulated, interest is apparent. What are the things in relation to the community, teen-age culture, and adult society which consistently stimulate interest? These "interest touch-stones" should be carefully gathered for possible future use in replanning content.

2. *Student feelings* will often be revealed in the classroom. What makes them laugh? What kinds of things gain their sympathy? What do they identify themselves with? What shocks and repels them?

3. The *non-verbal level of communication* in the classroom can provide new insights to the observant teacher. Watch for the messages delivered by the eyebrows, hands, eyes, shoulders, and tilt of the head. A whole covert system of intercommunication will be opened up.

4. *Out-of-class activities* of boys and girls are another rich source of information for the teacher. Observation of student activity in the halls, at athletic events, during dances, on the streets, and in the stores should be carried on. How do they act? What are they doing? Are they alone? With friends? How do they dress? How do they talk?

---

[6] For a discussion of these and similar procedures see Hilda Taba, *Curriculum Development: Theory and Practice* (New York: Harcourt, Brace and World, Inc., 1962); Ch. 16 "Informal Diagnostic Devices."

Knowledge of student needs is vital to the teacher's task. Boys and girls are impelled to action as they strive to meet their needs and solve their problems. These needs and problems are the stuff of which curriculum is made. All teachers must consistently strive to know more about the young people with whom they work.

## NEEDS OF SOCIETY

You are a member of modern American society. You probably vote regularly, keep up on current issues and civic problems, and otherwise participate as a good citizen should. However, when you become a teacher you will be placing yourself in a particularly strategic position to contribute to the welfare of society as you work with students in the secondary school. In order to do this intelligently, you need a real understanding of the various educative agencies in our society, the changing nature of our culture and, especially, the tasks assigned to the public school.

Any society has the fundamental need to perpetuate and improve itself. Thus, one of the deep concerns of modern, democratic America centers in the job of preparing American youth to take their places as productive members of the society. This implies a broad range of goals which must be accomplished in the total education of all youth. For this purpose, a number of educative agencies have evolved to which this task is assigned.

### Education: A Shared Task

The school is but one of the several educational agencies in our culture which operate to influence the total personality of youth. All of these agencies originally appeared and are maintained because they satisfy human needs in some way. Some of them may, as a central purpose, consciously attempt to transmit and interpret the cultural heritage; others, although having different aims, may be no less potent in influencing boys and girls in this same area. Actually, the educative agencies operate at times to complement each other and at other times in competition.

*The family.*    The elemental educative agency in society is, of course, the family unit. Here, most of the basic education of youth takes place. The individual, from the time he is born as a helpless infant until he attains sufficient mobility and maturity to move beyond the family circle to a significant degree, depends almost entirely upon his family for what education he receives.

Basic attitudes toward others, toward himself, and toward life itself are learned here. Fundamental value patterns are established; prejudices are absorbed uncritically at this early age. Social relationships—habits of responding to others—are begun within the family unit. Certain psychologists have long asserted that the foundational personality pattern is formed before the child has reached school age.

As the child matures, the family normally continues to remain one of the powerful educative agencies in his life. Thus, you will see in each of your pupils much of what his family is and has been.

*Friendship groups.*    Friends and playmates become increasingly important as the child grows older. The development of significant friendship groups produces a certain dilution or modification of the learning begun in the home. New interests are developed, new and different social relationships are initiated, allegiances are formed along different lines, and habits of work and play are modified.

As boys and girls approach adolescence, they naturally become caught up in the teen-age culture of their time. This peer culture often produces sudden changes in dress and behavior as fads and bizarre customs sweep their ranks. In addition, there are some authorities who feel that it increasingly is becoming an institution of fundamental value formation.

*The church.*    For the vast majority of American children, the church exists as a separate educational agency. This is consistent with our historical belief in the separation of church and school. Ecclesiastical institutions, through their religious education programs and religious services, seek to minister to the spiritual needs of the nation.

Recent concern regarding the response of youth to church offerings has led many churches to employ professionally trained educators. These persons help them revise their teachings, now largely geared to adult thinking, in the light of the immature values, motives, and interests of youth. It seems clear to many that the church must strive to regain the signal place it once held in the development of moral and spiritual values.

*Communication media.*    The great instruments of mass communication in America are important influences in the lives of boys and girls. Television, movies, radio, newspapers, magazines, and the advertising that comes with them are compelling teachers in a great variety of areas—from the simple presentation of facts (accurate and otherwise) to emotion-packed sequences which have the capacity to establish and modify interests and attitudes.

In regard to time, the mass media of communication appear to claim more than equal share with the school in the lives of young people; however, we have yet to really assess the competition that they offer to the other educative agencies in our society. The teacher in the classroom, striving to make his point, can hardly compete with the adman on television who utilizes a lovely model posed among multicolored props, an announcer with his mellifluous voice, and the music of the full studio orchestra swelling in the background to help him make his sale. And even more important, it would seem, the communication media are impelled by various motives (to sell products, to entertain, to propagandize, to sway votes, to inform, to increase circulation), few of which are consciously addressed at producing desirable future citizens.

*Military services.* At the present time, a considerable proportion of our American adult population has been exposed to military training and experience largely through mobilization efforts of World War I, World War II, and the wars in Korea and Vietnam. The continuing draft, enlistment programs, R.O.T.C., National Guard, and expanded reserve programs in all services seem to indicate that the armed forces will remain an important educative agency in our culture for some time to come.

*Public service institutions.* Certain institutions, established through governmental action, provide needed services to the public. Libraries and museums are two of these which are important educative agencies. Recently, libraries have effectively extended their resources to all but the most isolated communities through the establishment of branches and by means of mobile libraries or bookmobiles. Expanded services include the circulation of such items as paintings and phonograph records as well as such diversified activities as providing story hours for children, sponsoring discussions and talks for adult education, and setting up information services for the general public. Museums provide great storehouses of information about a variety of subjects. In many cases they sponsor lectures and exhibits for adult education and/or youth groups.

In addition, public service agencies such as law enforcement, public health, safety, and community improvement engage in considerable educative effort in an attempt to change the behavior of adults and youth.

*Youth organizations.* A large number of organizations exist in our society which attempt to enroll and influence the lives of young people.

The Boy Scouts, Girl Scouts, Campfire Girls, Y.M.C.A., Y.W.C.A., 4-H Club, and Future Farmers of America are but a few of these organizations. Again, the motives vary considerably; churches, political parties, labor unions, and police departments all sponsor youth organizations for a variety of reasons.

The above educative agencies are probably the most important of the hundreds of forces in our culture which affect the maturing adolescent. They have emerged by design and by accident to share the responsibility for the total education of youth with the institution most directly charged with this task, the school. An important future job for educators in general and teachers in particular is to explore the nature of this shared task. The school must strive to assess the quantity and quality of the contributions made by the non-school educative agencies and attempt to come to some agreement with them regarding the things each is best prepared to accomplish. For example, each of the three major institutions—the church, the home, and the school—can, by its very nature, be especially effective in accomplishing certain learnings. It seems clear that any progress made toward reducing competition among these institutions and formulating a truly working relationship would be beneficial.

*School and Society*

The relationship between American democratic society and the public secondary school has changed somewhat since the early days; however, two continuing principles exist which carry important implications for you as a teacher.

1. The public school exists primarily for the benefit of society and only secondarily for the benefit of the individual. Douglass states:

> Upon no assumption or premise other than that the school is a social institution established for common welfare and for the interest of society could we justify the practice of taxing, for the purposes of public education, individuals who have no children and individuals who send their children to nonpublic schools and of taxing individuals according to their wealth and income rather than according to the number of children they have in school.[7]

However, American democracy is dependent upon its individual citizens and operates as an expression of their will; therefore, there is

---

[7] Harl R. Douglass, *Secondary Education, For Life Adjustment of American Youth* (Copyright 1952 The Ronald Press Company), 60.

seldom any real conflict between the welfare of the individual and the welfare of the state. When conflicts do occur, the schools must give top priority to the interests of society. Therefore, this basic premise must be recognized and carefully considered in making educational decisions.

2. Public education must take its structure according to the characteristics of the society in which it exists. This means, of course, that the fundamenal principles of American democracy must permeate the organization, methods, curriculum, and philosophy of the public school. But it also means that teachers and administrators must constantly assess the changing characteristics of the society in order to reduce the degree of lag which always seems to exist between the evolving school system and the evolving society.

### Our Changing Culture

The most significant and all-pervading condition of modern America is change. It is evident in everything from the annual changes in ladies' dresses to the sudden and dramatic impact resulting from a scientific breakthrough, such as the landing of men on the moon. As an individual, much of your energy is necessarily spent in striving to accomplish more or less satisfactory adjustment to the accelerating changes around you. However, as a teacher you have the added responsibility of attempting to chronicle and understand these changes and to translate them into meaningful terms in order to assist your students to make adequate adjustments of their own.

At this point, some of the characteristics of modern culture which have important implications for adolescents and the secondary school should be noted as a base upon which to build subsequent discussion and study.

*The home.* Today the home is less a real family unit than in previous generations. The family tends to be small, and divisive forces in society tend to make the home more a convenient headquarters for eating and sleeping than a focal point for work and play. Fathers seldom work at home. The need to commute to the office or factory takes them away from very early to very late each day. A large number of occupations (traveling salesman, construction worker, night-shift worker) make it difficult for fathers to participate in the day-to-day activities of the family. Mothers are increasingly finding activities which draw them away from the home. Many seek jobs to augment the family income in the face of the rising cost of living; others are drawn into social and service organizations which claim a portion of their time and energies. Teen-agers, partcipating in the peer group culture, look outside the family unit for social and recreational satisfactions.

Broken homes and increased family mobility further complicate the problem.

*Work.*    Developments in industry and business have fostered complexity and specialization. The very breadth of choice in possible future occupations presents a confusing problem of vocational exploration and selection to youth. In addition, new technological advances may dramatically alter, almost overnight, the occupational structure by creating the need for a number of new and highly specialized skills and, at the same time, making other specialized skills obsolete.

The present trends toward a shorter work week and compulsory retirement seem destined to continue. These present problems in finding desirable use of increased leisure time and adjusting from work-oriented living to some kind of satisfying post-retirement living.

*Anxiety and fear.*    Anxiety is present in every generation, but today the power struggle among nations and groups, the threat of war, the continuing armament race, the drafting of young men into the military services, intergroup conflict, and inflation are conditions of modern living which constantly induce tensions and fears. In addition, these tensions are heightened for most people through (1) lack of real understanding of these conditions and (2) the feeling that they have are caught up in the whirlpool of great forces over which they have no control. Teachers can make a signal contribution at the secondary school level by helping students to gain insight into the anxiety-producing conditions and demonstrating to them that they do have some control over their own destinies.

At present, youth must work within the framework of society as it exists to find or make their own opportunities and work out their problems for, geographically at least, there is no real frontier. However, as space exploration is accelerated and the first attempts at space travel initiated, there may soon open up great frontiers, such as we have never known, to be explored and developed.

*Standards of personal living.*    In a changing world, it is certain that there will be changes in how we live. The continuing move to urban living has placed priority on the need to develop skills contributing to social harmony and interaction. It also has produced more emphasis upon the use of manufactured recreation (movies, television, amusement parks). The problems of securing an adequate degree of privacy and satisfying the need for occasional solitude and reflection have emerged. It seems that reflection has gone the way of digestion in modern America. In the growing suburbs, tall fences and hedges are evidence of an attempt to insulate against the noise and scrutiny of neighbors. The development of tolerance and understanding is essential to the members of tightly-knit communities.

Since World War II, the trend toward self-indulgence and the concomitant emphasis on a higher standard of living seems to have increased. The shift in values during wartime, abetted by stepped-up advertising and installment buying, has encouraged youth to prize material things as the symbols of success. The good life tends to be perceived as consisting of the mink coat, the flashy sports car, and the bulging wallet.

The automobile provides adolescents with the mobility to pursue social recreational interests over a broad arena; however, it also brings with it a tremendous personal responsibility for standards of moral conduct. In a matter of minutes boys and girls can achieve ethnocentric anonymity—they can be miles away from the inhibiting effect of family influences and community mores. Their behavior then depends less upon what other people might think than upon personal codes of moral and ethical values.

In a climate of increasing conflict between generations, relatively small though highly conspicuous groups within our society have adopted long hair, beards, bizarre dress, "mind-expanding drugs," and unconventional social habits and behavior. Some young militants and anarchists have deliberately sought to attract attention through their dress and actions.

Students need a great deal of assistance in gaining perspective of changing standards of personal living. High school teachers are in a position to help them examine their emerging value patterns as compared with those of their parents and the socially desirable behavior expectations in our culture.

## Tasks of the School

The public school takes its form as the wishes and needs of the public are identified by the school board, administrators, and teachers and are translated into changes in the school organization and services. Over the years, school people have attempted to determine the desires of society and have formulated lists of goals or tasks of the school according to their perceptions. These lists vary considerably in specific details, but show considerable agreement in general thought.

Society seems to be looking to the public secondary school to fulfill the following tasks.

*Transmit the cultural heritage.*    Historically, the school has been looked upon by adults as the custodian of much of our cultural heritage and one of the principal agents for the transmission of that heritage to maturing boys and girls. This means that public school teachers must themselves be students of our culture and must help youth become acquainted with their heritage. This inheritance, of course, consists of the organized and distilled knowledge which has been passed down over generations, as well as such essential information as the structure and aims of our society, the laws (written and unwritten) of our communities, and the privileges and duties of each person as an individual and a member of social groups.

*Interpret the cultural heritage.*    Merely to pass down the accumulated body of knowledge and descriptions of the nature of modern American society is not enough. The school must make these truly meaningful by assisting students to integrate isolated facts into meaningful units, to perceive applications of processes and concepts, to develop perspective in viewing society as it exists today in the light of its historical anteced-ents and possible future, to explore the meaning and significance of the values which are prized in our culture, and to grasp the principles of democracy and the importance of intelligent civic participation to the individual and the nation.

*Help the student know himself.*    Adolescents need the assistance of the school in their continuing efforts to realistically assess their own abilities, capacities, interests, and limitations as these develop. This assistance involves the use of a variety of evaluative tests and procedures as well as the opportunity to sample a wide range of interests and activi-ties. The high school may provide opportunities for students to test them-selves in a variety of situations vicariously and directly. For example, work experience programs allow boys and girls to sample certain voca-tions, and books provide vicarious experience in many different life situations.

*Guide youth.*    The school is expected to provide guidance along a number of lines. Youth need guidance toward wholesome social relation-ships, worthwhile leisure time activities, maximum personal adjustment, desirable intellectual pursuits, and vocational decisions consistent with aptitudes and interests. The public school is probably best qualified of all the educative agencies to perform this task. A corps of trained personnel is able to utilize significant test data and pertinent information about students to help them make decisions in an atmosphere of objectivity.

*Unify the peoples of America.* Our American democracy depends for its continuing existence upon a group of citizens unified by common understandings, the acceptance of similar values and social aims, and the recognition of common civic and social responsibilities. Social unification must be achieved if the voters are to participate intelligently in the making of wise social decisions.

The public high school, which enrolls the vast majority of youth, provides the setting wherein boys and girls from the various ethnic and socio-economic groups may get experience in living and working together. For example, in some of the large suburban developments surrounding many major cities, thousands of people may live in a housing tract, the most expensive house of which is worth only $2,000 more than the least expensive. This selective factor effectively produces a group of homeowners which is homogeneous in respect to socio-economic level. The size of the tract justifies the establishment of its own elementary schools. Thus, the children in this development live, work, and play, for the most part, with members of this narrowly selected socio-economic group from birth through elementary school. The large central high school is the first real opportunity for most of them to associate with others of different socio-economic levels. Secondary school teachers have the responsibility to plan meaningful situations (cooperative work situations in class, club, and social activities in the extra-class program) where students may develop common understandings and a common body of experiences which will tend to unify them.

*Provide for differentiation.* Modern America needs to prize individual differences, within certain limits, because our highly developed culture has a multiplicity of jobs to be done. Thus, the individual differences in interests, aptitudes, and abilities in youth need to be encouraged and developed.

As a result of exploratory experiences and guidance, the adolescent comes to know his own particular interests and capacities; beyond this the secondary school needs to provide for the satisfaction and development of these interests along socially desirable lines.

*Help youth develop essential skills.* Society has come to look upon the school as the principal agency which provides for the development of essential skills of living. Although parents usually initially interpret this to mean the 3-R's, in further discussion they almost invariably expand it to include a broad range of fundamental abilities. Youth need help in developing skills related to effective communication, quantitative processes, social relationships, civic participation, intelligent problem solving, efficient study, and prevocational competencies.

These tasks of the school generally describe the charge that society gives to the public secondary school as the educator perceives it. These tasks are many and varied; most are complex and difficult to perform. It may be that as a result of a host of developing pressures on the schools (i.e., overwhelming enrollments, severe shortage of classroom space, little money, attacks on education), a crucial issue in secondary education is emerging. This issue will require a re-examination of the role of the school in the total education of youth, and it will give impetus to developing a more realistic set of aims with the public. Thus, there may come a real partner relationship with the other educative agencies in the culture.

## NEEDS OF THE COMMUNITY

The public school of today is no ivory tower preoccupying itself solely with abstract bodies of knowledge. As you prepare to take your place in the high school classroom, you must concern yourself with the environmental forces surrounding the school, which have definite and pervasive influences upon the curriculum. You need to recognize the interplay of relationships between the school and community. In addition, you should have some understanding of the processes by which you may study the community itself in order to better understand your students and their parents and identify significant interests and concerns of the community which may be used in your teaching.

### The Community

Each high school is established within the specific and immediate context of a community. Community, as it has meaning to the school, refers primarily to the area from which the school's support and students come. Thus, the descriptive definitions of communities vary greatly. For example, the rural school may perceive its community to be within a radius determined by the distance its school buses travel; a large city school may look to a certain section of the metropolitan area as its community.

*The changing nature of the community.*    In the past, the communities tended to be small and, often, fairly homogeneous. However, the population movement toward the cities, increased family mobility, and the unification and centralization of schools have had much to do with changing the nature of the community with which the high school teacher must deal.

New residents of large cities commonly feel less allegiance to the neighborhood than to the larger city itself. Families often are not acquainted with other families in the area and little real unity within the community is likely to develop. In the large suburban developments surrounding the major cities, families are brought together suddenly and possess little in common except proximity, a similar socio-economic level, and a desire to move to a little better area in the event that the family's financial fortunes improve. In areas of high population growth, school facilities quickly become overcrowded and new buildings are constructed. This growth results in periodic shifting of school boundaries and sudden changes in the community. Unification of high schools in rural areas has resulted in much larger communities geographically and less homogeneity of the district the school must serve.

Thus, the community with which the high school is concerned is continually changing; at present, the changes seem to be in the direction of heterogeneity, instability, and disunity.

## School and Community Relationships

Teachers must recognize the relationships existing between school and community. The forces of influence operate clearly in two directions.

The community affects the school most obviously through the principle of local control. Although the authority for education is a state function, most states have delegated the major share of control to locally elected school boards or trustees. This is in line with the fact that most of the support for the school comes from local taxes, even though, in recent years, state support monies have been made available in an attempt to equalize educational opportunities. Commonly, local pressure groups operate through the school board, as the elected representatives of the people, and directly upon the administration and faculty to influence the school program. In addition, local mores and customs may affect the living habits of teachers and raise or lower their morale.

The school is likely to affect the community in a number of ways. Over the years the curriculum of the school and the staff members with long tenure have had considerable influence upon the community. A winning or losing athletic team, cultural contributions of the school (plays, operettas, band concerts, adult education courses), and the work of teachers and administrators on community committees and projects have various and pervasive effects upon the community.

Recent efforts by enlightened school boards and administrators have sought to strengthen and make more positive and constructive the lines of relationship between school and community. In many cases parents and community leaders participate in studying school problems, making school policy, and planning school programs. Schools offer their resources to assist in the solution of community problems. The goal is to make the school a vital part of the community it serves.

*Community Problems*

Every community faces problems which affect all its citizens. Many of these problems may be dealt with in the secondary school. In this way, the community itself forms a real-life learning laboratory for students as they analyze and attempt to solve problems in the setting in which they occur, rather than from the abstract setting of the textbook.

Some of these community concerns include: (1) health of the community, (2) safety in the community, (3) crime and juvenile delinquency, (4) provisions for recreation and leisure time activities, (5) community government, (6) human relations, (7) community beautification, (8) housing, (9) citizenship aid to the foreign-born, and (10) conservation of natural and human resources.

*Studying Community Needs*

In accepting a contract to teach in a high school, you are committing yourself to work within the community which surrounds the school. Each community is unique and different from any other and constantly in the process of change. Therefore, you must set out immediately to study its characteristics and needs as an aid in selecting and organizing content. For this purpose you will need to utilize a variety of procedures and sources.

The beginning teacher will initially need to seek data which describe the status of the community in general. A knowledge of such details as socio-economic levels, ethnic composition, occupational patterns, geographical factors, and historical development will assist you in gaining an understanding of the community and the school in which you will work. Subsequently, as you continue your study to fill in specific details, you will begin to identify community problems and concerns which may be suitable for classroom study.

*The community survey.*    Because of the comprehensive nature of the community survey, it is often an all-school effort or is co-sponsored by the P.T.A. or a local service club. However, highly significant surveys may be made under the guidance of an individual teacher or a small group of teachers involving students in the planning, execution, summary, and interpretation of the study. The work may be divided among different classes and/or spread out over several semesters. Various procedures may be utilized, such as study of state and local records, questionnaire or interview techniques used with a representative sample of the population, correspondence with authorities, inspection tours of the community, survey of local newspapers, and discussion with civic officials and leading business and professional people. Of course, sound survey methods should be used to insure valid data. Sampling procedures, questionnaire construction, interviewing techniques, selective observations, and summary forms are some of the important problems which require study and careful preparation.

Information secured will likely group itself into at least two categories: (1) the physical data—such information as climate, topography, size, soil composition, and natural resources; (2) the human data—such facts as population, sex composition, age distribution, educational and occupational status, ethnic groups represented, history, mores and customs, health status, and social agencies. On the basis of these data, teacher and students may discover important relationships, trends, and implications; for example, population shifts, job market, business trends, labor supply.

*Informal procedures.*    The interested teacher has available many other means for gaining insight into the nature of the community and its needs.

In the classroom, the community concerns and problems are often reflected in class discussions and assigned papers. Persons possessing pertinent backgrounds of experience may be invited to speak to the class to inform the students and the teacher regarding certain community aspects. Personal conferences with students from various ethnic groups, socio-economic levels, and geographical areas will give the teacher a deepening understanding of the community in which he works. Discussions with the principal and teachers who have considerable tenure in the school will produce further pertinent information. As an individual, the teacher needs to be attentive when talking with parents, neighbors, and businessmen; religiously scan the local paper for pertinent items; take periodic tours through the community; secure brochures and reports from the chamber of commerce and other agencies; attend speeches or forums by authorities on local conditions; and, when possible, talk with police, fire, and other city officials.

If you pursue such activities, you are likely to come to a greater understanding of the problems and concerns of the community in which you work and to accumulate a list of resources which you can use in your teaching. Certainly, communities vary greatly, and data obtained in one locality may be completely invalid for another locality. As characteristics of communities change, earlier surveys may be so outdated as to be useless. Thus, your community study efforts must be focused upon your specific community and carried on continuously if they are to be of maximum value.

## THE SUBJECT MATTER

The fourth basis for the selection and organization of learning experiences is the subject matter itself. It is clear that the knowledge explosion has presented us with pressing problems of management and organization of enormous amounts of information. Scholars have become increasingly concerned with means for controlling, storing, and retrieving this knowledge. Thus, it is understandable that much attention has been given to the structure of the various disciplines and the place that the subject matter should occupy in teaching and learning.

Traditional curricular ideas are based on the assumption that knowledge is static and that most subject-matter areas in the high school are fixed bodies of essential academic information. However, as the accumulated knowledge of mankind grows, teachers and scholars must develop the kind of perspective necessary to make intelligent decisions in selecting what should be taught. Moreover, the state of our knowledge is changing; exciting breakthroughs in the natural, physical and behavioral sciences emerge and make whole bodies of material obsolete—what is known as truth today may not be truth tomorrow. Thus the teacher must keep up to date with changing developments in his subject area. Some scholars are able to take refuge in small, highly specialized aspects of their discipline; however, the secondary school educator cannot escape the problems of developing and maintaining a broad perspective of his subject matter and the perennial task of selecting content which is essential to his students in line with the role of the school and its aims.

### Levels of Content

Taba[8] has suggested that subjects can be viewed as consisting of knowledge at four different levels: (a) specific facts and processes, (b) basic ideas, (c) concepts, and (d) thought systems.

*Facts.*    Certainly, one basic part of a subject-matter area includes a body of specific facts and skills. Names of presidents, dates of battles,

---

[8] Taba, *op.cit.*, 175–181.

rules of punctuation, arithmetic processes, and names of various bones in the body are examples. Of course, the learning of certain facts is essential, although agreement on exactly which ones is sometimes difficult to achieve. Moreover, the lifespan of specific facts may be extremely short as today's events alter those of yesterday. Fundamentally, the specific facts may best serve to lead to useful generalizations or to help solve problems and make decisions.

*Basic ideas.* Some "ideas and generalizations constitute what currently is referred to as the 'structure'[9] of the subject: ideas which describe facts of generality, facts that, once understood, will explain many specific phenomena."[10] They provide the learner with a means of control over clusters of specific information and facilitate understanding. For example, the student who learns the basic relationship between natural environment and the nature of the development of human culture is prepared to interpret many aspects of geography and civilization. The idea that the human organism seeks a state of homeostasis wherein conditions are in some sort of balance serves to explain a variety of responses and behavior. These kinds of basic ideas are, in reality, the fundamental content of a subject area.

*Concepts.* More complex and abstract concepts represent another level of knowledge. The term as used in this context refers to higher-level generalizations which depend on a number of different curricular experiences at different levels. For example, the concept of interdependence may be dealt with in the primary grades in relation to family members, later in regard to groups within our nation, and in senior high school in relation to nations in the world. This serves to develop the overall, complex, abstract concept of interdependence itself. Such concepts are seldom the product of a single unit or course, but are made a part of the larger curriculum as recurring themes or emphases.

*Thought systems.* An important part of each academic subject area is its characteristic thought system. This refers to the overall structure through which the body of information and principles is organized and controlled and the accepted methods of inquiry through which new knowledge is sought. Teachers need to explore ways in which they can help their students gain a degree of competence in relation to this dimension of content.

---

[9] See also Jerome Bruner, *The Process of Education* (Cambridge: Harvard University Press, 1960).
[10] Taba, *op. cit.*, 176.

When one becomes a teacher, he must re-examine content so that he may present it in forms which will be most useful and comprehensible to his students.

## REVIEW

In this chapter you have explored the bases for the selection and organization of content. You may wish to check the following items to see if you are ready to proceed to the next topic.

1. Thinking through what you have learned from other courses and the discussion in this book in the light of your own background of experience as a teen-ager, do you have a better understanding of the characteristics of the modern high school learner? Have the lists of needs formulated by adult observers and adolescents made possible concerns more specific and definable? Do you have a clear idea of what you can do as a teacher to increase your sensitivity to students' interests and problems?

2. Do you see the relationship between the public secondary school as one of the many educative agencies in the constantly changing culture and modern American society? Do you know the seven tasks which society expects the school to fulfill?

3. Do you understand the nature of the community within which the school operates? When you accept a position will you have an idea of how you can secure the data you need to help you in planning for your teaching?

4. In relation to the subject matter itself, do you recognize the differences among the various levels of content? Is the nature of the problem of selecting elements of content for teaching and learning clear to you?

# Selected References

*The Current Values and Changing Needs of Youth.* Meriden, Conn.: Connecticut Secondary School Youth Project, 1966.

Doll, R. C. and Fleming, R. S., eds. *Children Under Pressure.* Columbus, Ohio: Charles E. Merrill Books, Inc., 1966.

Dumas, W. and Beckner, W. *Introduction to Secondary Education: A Foundations Approach.* Scranton, Pa.: International Textbook Co., 1968; Ch.

3 "Foundations in Social Dynamics" and Ch. 4 "Foundations in Adolescent Growth and Development."

Ford, G. W. and Dugno, L. *The Structure of Knowledge and the Curriculum.* Chicago: Rand McNally & Company, 1964.

*Life Skills in School and Society,* 1969 Yearbook. Washington, D.C.: Association for Supervision and Curriculum Development, N.E.A., 1969; Ch. 3 "The Changing Society and its Schools."

Mallery, David. *High School Students Speak Out.* New York: Harper & Row, Publishers, 1967.

Selakovich, Daniel. *The Schools and American Society.* Waltham, Mass.: Blaisdell Publishing Company, 1967.

*To Nurture Humaneness: Commitment for the '70's,* 1970 Yearbook. Washington, D.C.: Association for Supervision and Curriculum Development, N.E.A., 1970.

Webster, S. T., ed. *The Disadvantaged Learner.* San Francisco: Chandler Publishing Company, 1966.

*Youth Education: Problems/Perspectives/Promises,* 1968 Yearbook. Washington, D.C.: Association for Supervision and Curriculum Development, N.E.A., 1968.

# three

## Practices in Selecting and Organizing Content

Classroom teachers are involved continuously in the selection and organization of content; recently, the modern curriculum worker has come to recognize the important role teachers perform in curriculum revision. As beginning teachers assess the nature of their functions in this important educational process, they initially tend to ask questions relating to common curricular concepts and terminology, typical practices in the selection and organization of content, forces which affect curricular planning, and the role of the classroom teacher in curriculum development.

Your professional training should help you attain important understanding of each of the following areas of concern.

1. In order to discuss practices in the selection and organization of content intelligently, you must become acquainted with a number of curricular terms and related concepts. This terminology, approached at this point largely as vocabulary building, facilitates communication and serves as an introduction to the formulation of curriculum.

2. The process of selecting and organizing content is continually going on in the secondary schools across America. Some of the practices are good and some of them are less well conceived. Therefore, it is important that you gain some understanding of typical practices as background for making decisions of your own.

3. Teachers do not operate in a vacuum. They must know and take into consideration the kinds of forces and agencies which act to influence curriculum planning. These are part of the realities of the situation.

4. In the process of curriculum development, the teacher occupies a strategic role. You need to develop insight into this role to understand the ways in which you will need to work.

## CURRICULAR CONCEPTS AND TERMINOLOGY

All professional workers engaged in a specialized field of endeavor develop a set of specialized concepts and, for communicative purposes, employ certain descriptive terms which are understood by the personnel involved. This is the case in the field of education.

A frequent and sometimes valid criticism of the teaching profession is that this "educational jargon" has too often been used with lay groups, and this has resulted in lack of communication and misunderstanding. However, in preparing yourself to enter the profession, you need to know these terms and the concepts they represent.

The following are a number of the more common curricular concepts and terminology about which beginning teachers initially tend to need knowledge and understanding. These serve as a base upon which to build a professional vocabulary.

### Curriculum

The term curriculum in recent years has come to mean all the planned activities and experiences which are available to students under the direction of the school. The curriculum embraces the academic activities, the organized courses which carry credit toward graduation, as well as the extra-class activities of the school, which include school clubs, interscholastic athletics, intra-mural athletics, and dramatic presentations. This term is sometimes used in a more restricted sense to mean a specific pattern of courses organized for the benefit of various groups of students (for example, the university preparatory curriculum or the vocational curriculum).

This basic curricular concept differs sharply from the older conception of curriculum as the organized courses for which credit is given toward graduation. The newer idea embraces a wide spectrum of experiences which youth have in connection with the school. It clearly suggests that curriculum is the consciously planned business of education.

### Curriculum Components

The overall secondary school curriculum is made up of four identifiable components: (1) common learnings or general education, (2) special interest or prevocational education, (3) remedial education, and (4) extra-class activities.

The first component refers to that portion of the junior and senior high school program of studies which all students must take regardless of their academic potential, future educational plans, vocational aspirations, and personal preferences. Such courses are considered to be essential to all youth; thus, they are required.

The second component refers to the courses which are elected by students because of their special interests and future plans. The selection usually is the result of conferences with their counselors and advice from parents. Frequently, the decision may require a choice from among curricular patterns (such as business education, college preparatory, vocational agriculture, industrial arts, and the like) which then have "required electives" within the chosen pattern. In addition, there usually is some opportunity for "free electives."

The remedial component includes the courses or special assistance sessions which are specially planned for students who are performing below their capacity or grade-level expectations. These normally are provided in a few basic skill areas such as remedial reading, composition, and mathematics.

Extra-class activities are those activities under the direction of the school for which no credit is given and which are not usually a part of the regularly organized instructional program of the school. Such experiences range from interscholastic athletics to the school-related social and subject-matter clubs.

In the junior high school grades, the common learnings make up the great proportion of the total in-class program. In the seventh and eighth grades, it is usual for students to have all required courses with the possible exception of one elective. As one moves upward, the special interest component assumes a larger and larger share of the students' schedule, until in grade twelve it may make up the entire program. Remedial courses typically are few in number and are more likely to be offered in the lower junior high school grades. Extra-class activities vary tremendously from student to student although participation normally increases considerably in the junior and, especially, the senior year.

### Program of Studies

The program of studies is simply a compilation of all the courses of instruction available in a specific secondary school. It is normally organized by grade levels without reference to curricular patterns, although sometimes it may be developed to show college preparatory, business, general, and other curricular sequences.

### Scope and Sequence

These terms have meaning to the classroom teacher in the way they relate to the course he teachers. Scope refers to the breadth of subject matter encompassed by the course. Thus, an enumeration of the activities and experiences commonly included in a course indicates its scope. The order in which course content is presented suggests the sequence of the course. For example, a course in American history may be taught with sequence determined by the chronology of historical events.

*Subject Matter or Content*

Course content or subject matter means, to the teacher, those materials and activities presented in the course and, to the pupil, those experiences which he has in the course. For both, this involves the materials of study, methods of instruction, and processes or ways of working. Thus, the content may include not only the facts written in books and the concepts discussed by the teacher, but also the processes involved in formulating, attacking, and solving problems.

*Course of Study*

Many schools have developed courses of study which delineate scope and sequence of the content of particular courses for a semester or a year. These often are written by groups of teachers in an attempt to offer some guidance to the classroom teacher in planning the learning experiences of the course. In most cases they are less detailed than the resource unit, teaching unit, and daily lesson plan[1] in order to provide a high degree of flexibility.

## PRACTICES IN SELECTING AND ORGANIZING CONTENT

You have probably attended only one or, at most, two or three high schools in the course of your secondary school education. Therefore, it is essential that you gain some perspective in regard to typical or commonly observed practices and approaches across the United States, because these describe the kind of situation in which you will likely find yourself.

*Characteristics*

At present, the secondary schools in the United States are in a period of curricular ferment. Much innovation is being attempted in curriculum

---

[1] The resource unit, teaching unit, and daily lesson plan are discussed in detail in Chapter 5.

itself as well as in scheduling, staff utilization, school facilities, and instructional media which have signal implications for curriculum revision. However, large-scale changes among great numbers of school districts come slowly. Many of the smaller junior and senior high schools, especially in rural areas, have essentially the same instructional programs as they had twenty years ago. The typical characteristics found by Romine[2] are still present today.

1.  The typical secondary school curriculum is oriented largely to the past.

2.  The typical secondary school curriculum lacks a cooperatively developed, well understood, and actively coordinating philosophy of education.

3.  The typical secondary school curriculum places emphasis upon academic information and skills as educational objectives.

4.  The typical secondary school curriculum is organized largely in terms of subject-centered courses.

5.  The typical secondary school curriculum is based largely upon adopted textbooks.

6.  The typical secondary school curriculum is developed largely by individual teachers.

The past is very much a part of curriculum. The overall curriculum framework is changing very slowly even in the innovative schools. A listing of credits submitted by a student for college entrance today typically will differ only slightly from that of his father a generation ago. In addition, the activities and experiences seldom are oriented to the present and future; for example, the typical U.S. History course often does not extend beyond World War I. In the minds of modern youth, this gap between today's concerns and that rather "ancient" conflict is large indeed.

Many teacher decisions tend to be made on the basis of expediency rather than as a result of a meaningful set of guiding principles or guiding philosophy. Thus, curricular practices within a particular school tend to be inconsistent and illogical.

Teachers, by and large, emphasize academic information and skills in their teaching. Pupils quickly sense that the ability to recite facts and perform certain skills is prized and those who desire success in school take appropriate steps to insure this success. Interests, attitudes, values, and habits, which are the relatively more permanent outcomes of the

---

[2] Stephen A. Romine, *Building the High School Curriculum* (Copyright 1954 The Ronald Press Company), 20–25.

learning situation, generally are neglected—probably because many class-room teachers are not certain how they may be achieved and find it difficult to evaluate pupil progress toward them.

Even a cursory examination of most programs of study indicates courses set up to correspond to generally accepted fields of study. Courses are grouped into fields of English, social science, mathematics, science, foreign languages, music, industrial arts, physical education, and fine arts. As a result, the faculty is organized by departments, and this often leads to the development of blocs of teachers interested solely in their own subject matter. The curriculum becomes compartmentalized; little attempt is made to help students integrate subject matter from different fields into a meaningful whole. Each department assumes exclusive responsibility for the objectives in its field.

In many cases, the real source of the curriculum is found to be the single adopted textbook. At the present time, the common conditions of overcrowding in the schools, inadequate libraries, and insufficient supplementary materials are used by many teachers to rationalize their attempt to evade the responsibility for planning. The presumed expertness of the textbook author serves as the basis of scope and sequence in the course. Often, the real goal of the teacher and class is to "get through the book."

The role of the individual teacher clearly is crucial to the curricular experiences which students have in the classroom. Even though the courses may be set up on the basis of tradition and the adopted textbook may largely establish scope and sequence, the teacher makes final decisions in the day-to-day class procedures. In addition, the teacher's personality has much to do with the quality of experiences which accrue in the teaching-learning situation.

## Trends

In spite of the assertion that significant curriculum change normally takes place at "glacial speed," there are clear trends in the nature and direction of such change today. These trends, if they continue, provide clues to the probable curriculum of the future. The following are a few of the more important trends.

*Academic excellence.* American secondary schools have become increasingly preoccupied with the quest for academic excellence. This is paralleled by a similar shift in values in our society. Especially in suburban areas, there is a general acceptance of the desirability of "solid" academic courses, homework, and the recognition of academic achievement. Students themselves show a marked inclination to approve academic effort, even in a few schools where this was not "the thing to do" in the past.

*Downward shift in content.*   Curriculum revision in a number of districts has resulted in some subject matter being shifted downward. For example, many junior high schools have replaced general science in the eighth grade with the course in biology previously taught in the ninth grade. College subjects are being offered to selected students through advanced placement courses in the senior high school. It should be noted that this has been done without solid evidence regarding student readiness.

*Teaching for discovery and inquiry.*   Many of the instructional programs in math, science, and social studies developed in recent years have stressed the discovery or inquiry approach. Science laboratory experiences, for example, have become a search for answers rather than a sterile repetition of an experiment demonstrated by the teacher and fully described in the text.

*Individual differences.*   A significant trend in curriculum is toward a resurgence of concern for the individual learner. For a number of years, the schools have directed much attention toward making provisions for the gifted student; more recently has come an attempt to attack the problem of the disadvantaged youth. Many of the administrative innovations, such as independent study and non-grading, have sought more productive means for handling differences.

*Controversial issues.*   The "new breed" of teacher increasingly has come to recognize the presence of controversial issues of content in all subject areas and has asserted the need to deal with these issues in the classroom. In spite of counterpressures in some communities, teachers have examined current social issues, utilized controversial literary selections, dealt with competing ideologies, and the like. To do less, they feel, is to sacrifice their integrity as teachers.

## Approaches

The way in which teachers approach the selection and organization of content has considerable effect on the results obtained. It is very important, therefore, to think carefully through the approach you wish to use. Actually, most approaches fall into one of two basic categories or some combination of both. Content tends to be organized either (a) according to the logic of the subject, or (b) according to the logic of the learner. ———> *Approach to selection & organization of content*

*Logic of the subject.* The traditional approach to the selection and organization of content is subject centered. The same logic by which a particular field of learning is organized determines the organization of content of the course. Over the years scholars have, by necessity, organized the great bodies of knowledge in various ways which allow them to control it. For example, in history the usual method employed is to arrange the data chronologically, spotlighting the important events as they happened. Literature tends to be organized according to literary types; the literary pieces are selected and read as examples of the short story, novel, poetry, drama, and essay; the content of the selection is secondary. Literature also may be organized by authors or even chronologically, as in American literature commonly taught at the eleventh grade level. The assumption is made that the organization found to be most convenient and valuable by the scholars in handling these bodies of knowledge is the best curricular pattern for teaching and learning.

An approach based mainly on the logic of the subject tends to lead to a number of conditions. First, the content or subject matter of the course includes academic information and skills which are to be memorized or mastered. Quantity of subject matter takes on especial significance; the book must be covered and students are evaluated according to the amount of academic information they are able to retain.

Second, this organization makes it possible for the teacher to organize the content and even construct the examinations before the course has begun.

Third, if the subject matter may thus be determined in advance, it tends to follow that minimum standards may be set up to indicate the amount of content which must be achieved by all pupils. Thus, the bright student as well as the dull student is held to a common standard.

Fourth, content viewed in this way is almost certain to be abstract and far from the basic, real-life concerns and problems of students. Current problems in the community, state, and nation are also secondary to the events and achievements of the past.

*Logic of the learner.* Teachers who use this student-oriented approach have come to believe that the organization utilized by scholars to control vast bodies of knowledge is not necessarily the best way to teach the material. As the name implies, this approach places the learner and the way he perceives things at the center of the teaching-learning process. It is the student who must learn; therefore, his problems, concerns, needs, interests, attitudes, and values are of vital importance to the teacher. Pupils are seen as real, living personalities possessing singular differences which make them unique individuals. This invalidates the concept of teaching as a process of dispensing a predetermined amount of academic information to all the students enrolled in the course. Instead, growth of the learners is the aim—growth in meaningful knowledge, growth in skills, growth in understanding, growth toward desirable attitudes, interests, and values.

The student-oriented approach implies a number of conditions. First, course content can only be tentatively planned until the teacher meets and becomes aquainted with the group of students who will do the learning. Therefore, the classroom teacher must study his pupils in order to know their abilities, interests, and backgrounds. He must know them as they differ from one another as well. This knowledge of youth is just as important as knowledge of the academic information in the area.

Second, because the logic of the learner is central to this approach, subsequent planning will involve both teacher and pupils. The teacher, due to his maturity, experience, and knowledge, acts as the guide to learning and works cooperatively with students to select activities and materials which will be meaningful to them. He is continually interested in how they look at things, how they react to classroom experiences, and how they feel about the emerging curriculum in his class.

Third, flexibility and variety in teaching activities and materials are necessary. A wide range of individual differences exists in every group of students; thus, a single, standard approach seldom will work equally well for all.

Fourth, the experiences which pupils have in the classroom determine the growth which takes place. The perceptive teacher realizes that the meaningless memorization of abstract facts represents an experience to boys and girls; however, he also realizes that this experience is likely to lead to the growth of undesirable attitudes toward the subject, the teacher, and the school. The aim of good teaching is to provide experiences which will lead to desirable pupil growth.

Finally, the problems and concerns of the present and the predictable future are the foci of the subject matter. The distilled inheritance of knowledge of the past is used in gaining understanding of the present and future and in attempting solutions to the problems in modern America.

As implied above, the two approaches are not mutually exclusive, and many teachers use some combination of both. However, in the light of the bases for selecting and organizing content and the principles of learning,[3] the more satisfying approach is found to be according to the logic of the learner.

## FORCES WHICH AFFECT CURRICULAR PLANNING

Many forces are at work shaping and influencing the program of the school. Some of these are internal and part of your background of experience; most are external and may come from a variety of sources inside and outside the school-community situation. As you prepare to build content for your classes, you must identify and take into consideration the following important forces and agencies which impinge upon the curriculum.

### State and County Influences

Legally, the locus of authority in public education resides in the state. However, in most cases the state has delegated much of this responsibility to the local school board. What authority is retained tends to be exercised through the state legislature and the state department of education.

*State legislature.*    Most states have passed legislation which affects the high school curriculum. In some cases this legislation requires certain courses to be taught. Commonly required are driver training, civics, state history, American history and government, health, and physical education. Sometimes requirements are more specifically stated, such as the effects of alcohol or the evils of narcotics. Often the laws prohibit the teaching of evolution, religion, and other similar topics. In this way the state legislators seek to insure that certain things will or will not be included in the curriculum.

*State department of education.*    The state department of education works to implement the laws of the state pertaining to education. In recent years this body has gained much potential influence over the schools through the establishment and control of the distribution of state support funds. Thus, the schools could be compelled to comply with certain regulations if they are to receive this money. However, in most cases the state departments of education have chosen to act in leadership

---

[3] The principles of learning and their implications for teaching are discussed in Chapter 4.

and consultantship capacities, with only the minimum of inspection and coercion.

State departments often organize and coordinate the selection of textbooks in order to establish a state adopted list. The procedures used in selecting the textbooks are extremely important and should involve the active participation of teachers who will use them. Outstanding classroom teachers are brought together on state selection committees. They review the available texts and make recommendations to the state department of education. In addition, many states are providing for multiple adoptions (two or three approved for each subject) which further improves the process.

*County superintendent of schools.*     In some states the county unit has developed as an intermediate agency between the state department and the local school district. Some states, notably California, have provided funds for the establishment of strong professional personnel and services in the county superintendent's office. These make available coordinative, supervisory, and consultative assistance, especially to the smaller schools in the county. For example, the county staff might include school psychologists, consultants in secondary school curriculum, secondary school coordinators, specialists in various teaching fields, special education consultants, librarian, and audio-visual experts.

*National and Regional Influences*

A number of powerful influences on curriculum decisions come from sources which are somewhat removed from the local school district. Many of these action groups have no legal authority to make curricular changes and are not in a position where they may be held responsible for the results; yet often they have had considerable influence in decisions in the schools.

*Federal government.*     Beginning with the Smith-Hughes Act of 1917, the federal government has made some effort to affect curriculum. However, in 1958 the National Defense Education Act and in 1959 the National Science Foundation marked the point where the federal government moved from its long-standing emphasis on vocational education to deal with curriculum building in such academic areas as science, mathematics, foreign language, English, social studies, and humanities. One illustration of this influence is the federal support of institutes in the new math which sent out teachers imbued with "missionary" zeal and affected the math programs in even some of the most isolated schools.

*National spokesmen.*    Powerful and persuasive national spokesmen such as James Conant have offered suggestions and recommendations in regard to the programs in the secondary schools. Many of these persons sincerely seek to make constructive criticisms of the schools in the interest of better education for all boys and girls. However, others are openly destructive as they pick at the foundations of public education with their dirty fingernails.

*Foundations.*    The private philanthropic foundations also have influenced curriculum. The Ford Foundation's Fund for the Advancement of Education and the Carnegie Foundation are two notable examples of the literally thousands of various foundations in the United States. Some foundations have changed, at least temporarily, whole school districts by means of large sums of money given to implement proposals which were written to their satisfaction.

*Academic curriculum groups.*    Prior to the mid-1950's there was little organized interest among academic scholars in the curriculum of the public schools. However, since that time a great number and variety of curriculum projects have emerged. The "new math" and the "new science" are early examples[4] of the work of academicians which resulted in new course descriptions, textbooks and teaching materials, and teacher guides.

*Professional associations.*    The persons engaged directly in the work of education have sought to influence curriculum. From the influential report by the Committee of Ten on Secondary School Studies of the National Education Association in 1892 to the current efforts by the National Council of Teachers of English, The National Council of Teachers of Mathematics, the Association for Supervision and Curriculum Development and many others, the professional associations have addressed themselves to the problems of curriculum, and through the use of national publicity and national communications channels have attempted to induce change.

*Accrediting agencies.*    Voluntary regional accrediting agencies have emerged in the United States. These groups, such as the North Central Association of Colleges and Secondary Schools, directly affect educational programs through their self-imposed standards.

---

[4] See John I. Goodlad, *The Changing School Curriculum* (New York: The Fund for the Advancement of Education, August 1966) for an overview of the early developments by academic curriculum groups.

*Institutions of Higher Learning*

Colleges and universities have considerable influence on the curriculum of the high school. This influence stems mainly from their entrance requirements, teacher training functions, and the professional activities of the college staff.

*College entrance requirements.* Most institutions of higher learning currently require that a certain pattern of subjects be completed by students in high school before they may be admitted. These requirements have been retained in the face of a number of research studies[5] which indicate that college success has little or no relationship to the typical required course pattern.

A college president[6] wrote, "Clearly the assumption that college success depends on pursuing any prescribed sujects in high school cannot longer be accepted by thinking people." Nevertheless, the secondary school curriculum is tremendously influenced by the courses required for entrance to the state university or prestige institutions nearby. Despite the fact that many high schools in the United States are too small to offer a full program of studies and are unable to meet the special needs and interests of the whole range of students enrolled, they universally attempt first to offer an acceptable university preparatory pattern for the boys and girls who will go on to higher education. This means that the many pupils who need and want courses in line with their probable job expectancies (for example shop, shorthand, bookkeeping, commercial mathematics, homemaking) must enroll in the traditional university preparatory subjects.

Examinations commonly used for entrance or placement in classes after admittance also affect curriculum. The tendency is for some high school teachers, especially in the senior year, to spend much of the class time and effort getting the students prepared to take the exams. In this respect the examinations themselves tend to displace even the textbook as the single basis for the curriculum.

*Teacher training.* The total effect of the teacher training institution goes with the beginning teacher as he begins selecting and organizing content on the job. The teacher is the product of the entire institution

---

[5] See for example Winifred M. Aikin, *The Story of the Eight-Year Study* (New York: Harper & Brothers, 1942).

[6] J. Paul Leonard, "Can We Face the Evidence on College-Entrance Requirements?" *School Review,* 53:332, June 1945.

from which he graduates, not just the school or department of education. His experiences in general education courses, major and minor areas, and professional courses all contribute to the way he looks at the task of the public school and the part he sees himself performing. The methods experienced in college classes often influence the methods he will use in his own high school teaching. Obviously, this preservice and later in-service coursework is vitally important to the teacher and the curriculum for which he is responsible in the classroom.

*Professional activities.* In varying degrees college professors from various departments accept the responsibility to work actively with classroom teachers in the field. The great demand for curriculum consultants in the various subject fields and advisors in methods of teaching suggests the need for the professional assistance of college personnel who are willing to do less "telling" and more working *with* teachers in the local situation on problems the teachers feel important. In addition, contributions are made through participating in conferences and writing articles in professional journals and textbooks. When the resources and process skills of college professors are offered along these lines, the constructive influence of the higher institutions of learning is enhanced.

### Community Influences

As the immediate context within which the school operates, the community affects the curriculum in a number of ways. Some of these influences are likely to be salutary while others are less beneficial to the school.

*Local board of education.* As a non-professional body, the elected school board usually acts as a policy-making group and leaves curricular planning to the school staff. However, in representing the people the board attempts to remain sensitive to the wishes of the community and may investigate the content of any subject and rule upon whether it should be included or not. As a result of the leadership of some school administrators, a number of school boards have adopted statements of policy regarding the teaching of controversial content in order to protect both teachers and students.

*Pressure groups.* Almost every community contains certain groups which attempt to influence what is taught in the secondary school. Many of these are moved by the sincere desire to insure the best possible education for youth. However, other groups are motivated by different, less altruistic motives. Organized pressure groups[7] representing industry, labor, patriotic societies, religion, professional associations, and parents actively work to influence curriculum in the light of what they individually feel to be best for the students and/or themselves.

*Community attitudes.* Attitudes vary considerably from community to community and must, of course, be taken into consideration in curriculum making. Community mores, attitudes toward sex, religion, labor and other influences may inhibit the teacher's classroom presentation. Favorable progress has been made in some communities through joint committees of teachers and lay persons working on curriculum problems. As soon as parents come to understand what the school is trying to do and gain confidence in the professional staff, notable freedom in teaching and improved school support is likely.

### Influences Within the School

Beginning teachers quickly become aware of conditions within the school itself which influence the selection and organization of content. These conditions are usually immediate and pressing; thus, they are likely to affect the curriculum disproportionately to their importance.

*Attitudes of the staff.* Occasionally the new teacher will find a relatively large bloc of teachers who resist change and encourage conformity to their traditional approach to curriculum. However, on almost every high school staff there will be found teachers who are interested in new and challenging approaches and willing to share ideas and sources. In any event, the beginning teacher is likely to have more freedom than he wishes to plan and carry out curricular organization. Teachers and administrators tend to be fully involved in their own work, and the new teacher seldom receives all the help he needs and desires.

*School plant.* The nature of the school plant and equipment may make certain curricular experiences difficult, if not impossible. Lack of materials and facilities often restrict the kinds of activities teachers are able to provide in the classroom. As enrollments swell more and more, schools find themselves overloading classrooms, using makeshift housing, and getting along with an impoverished library, insufficient instructional equipment, and inadequate audio-visual aids. In spite of this, a creative

---

[7] *See,* for example, R. P. Curry, "Pressure Group Curriculum," *Educational Leadership,* 26:451–454, February 1969.

teacher may accomplish the impossible through the use of homemade materials and improvised equipment.

*Teacher turnover.* Many schools today experience high teacher and administrative turnover. This makes it difficult to preserve continuity in curriculum improvement from year to year. Some schools in less desirable locations report as high as 50–90 per cent teacher replacement each year. This means that half or more of the teachers are new to the community and/or teaching and must work to become oriented to the school, acquaint themselves with the community, and study the students in their classes in order to plan satisfying classroom experiences. The following year they may leave the district for a more desirable location, a better paying job in industry, or marriage.

## TEACHER ROLE IN CURRICULAR DEVELOPMENT

The school exists for the purpose of providing educative experiences for youth. Thus, the school buildings, facilities, administrators, supervisors, and the classroom teacher may be ultimately justified only in terms of how each contributes to this primary task. Myriad agencies and influences in our culture complicate this function as they seek to affect the selection, organization, and implementation of content. However, no influences are as central and all important as the teacher himself.

At this point you undoubtedly are concerned about the role assigned you by the nature of your position as teacher and interested in gaining insight into the lines along which you may be expected to work.

### The Teacher: A Central Figure

Democratic practices operating in the modern secondary school and recent, clearer understanding of the nature of the teaching-learning process serve to spotlight the teacher as the key figure in curriculum construction. The practice of imposing rigid and detailed courses of study upon teaching faculties is rapidly disappearing. Instead, the teaching staff increasingly is involved in cooperative decision making in regard to curriculum policy, stated aims and objectives of the school, adoption of textbooks, selection of materials, and planning new school plant and facilities. Administrators and curriculum workers now realize that relative permanency of curriculum change results only as teachers themselves change. They encourage the teacher as a creative individual to work along the lines most pertinent to his mastery of the subject area, understanding of boys and girls, knowledge of the community and society within which he works, understanding of the learning process, and point of view relative to the nature and functions of secondary education.

## Ways of Working

Beginning teachers seldom initially recognize the crucial role they play in determining curriculum. The individual classroom teacher is without question the chief determiner of content for his classes. In addition, he is likely to be involved with various teacher groups, inside and outside the school, which work on curriculum problems.

*Teachers work individually.* The most immediate responsibility facing individual teachers is to select and organize the content for their own classes. The courses of study, resource units, teaching units, daily lesson plans, and study guides are preliminary to and subordinate to that which happens in the teaching-learning process.

Beginning teachers often seek to evade the responsibility of selection and organization by following closely the adopted textbook or suggested course of study. However, it is an inescapable and vital part of teaching, and all the teachers should face squarely their curricular obligations. They must plan for and with their students a satisfying pattern of experiences which are in line with the bases for selection and organization of content and the principles of learning. The day-to-day decisions made in the classroom, the materials selected for study, the learning activities and processes utilized, and the classroom climate all affect the curriculum.

The teacher, if he is to achieve the best possible results and is to continue to improve, needs certain facilitating conditions, as follows:

1. The teacher needs freedom to try new things with the support of the administration and faculty. Too often teachers are expected to be right one hundred per cent of the time. They must have the right to experiment with promising new practices, and to fail occasionally.

2. The teacher needs help in curriculum making. Assistance in the form of consultants, materials, professional publications, and supervision will help instructors produce top-level work.

3. The teacher needs time for class preparation. Many school districts are fighting to preserve one planning period a day for each teacher in spite of burgeoning enrollments. Time may also be provided through paid summer workshops or planning sessions for teachers.

4. The teacher needs encouragement. Ideally the school should possess a climate which welcomes new ideas and stimulating differences

in opinion. Teachers need others who are willing to cooperate in planning, share resources and thinking, and act in mutually supportive ways.

These conditions should facilitate the individual teacher's curriculum-making efforts. However, the beginning teacher should take a variety of measures on his own. Such measures as the following may serve to keep the teacher from falling into the trap of complacency.

The habit of professional reading should be initiated from the start. Much of the frontier thinking in curriculum and teaching procedures is found in the educational periodicals. In the high school the individual teacher will often find copies of journals containing articles describing new methods, materials, problems, and concerns in the major subject areas, in curriculum improvement, and in the teaching profession in general. Books of some pertinence to teachers are being published continually, and need to be sampled by the interested faculty member.

Professional associations at national, state, county, and local levels seek to assist teachers in their work. For example, they may organize conferences, sponsor workshops, publish professional journals, engage in significant research, back important legislation, offer placement service, and defend teachers against unjustified attacks. Probably the most interesting and stimulating groups to classroom teachers concerned with curriculum building are the subject-area associations, such as the National Council of Teachers of English, National Council for the Social Studies, and National Science Teacher Association. The beginning teacher should become affiliated with and actively support one or more of the professional associations. He should attend and participate in the national, state, and local meetings of these organizations because these programs are pointed primarily to current teacher concerns and curricular problems. He will hear the leading experts in the field and meet other teachers interested in new and challenging ideas.

Interested teachers will continue to study. As teachers pursue their work, they all tend to find gaps in their training which require filling. Later, as new developments occur in subject fields, they come to feel the need to bring themselves up to date. As they become interested in new techniques and special aspects of the classroom teacher's job, they may decide to learn more about the use of audio-visual materials or to explore the more specialized techniques of counseling and other recent innovations. Probably the best single way to accomplish this is through university extension or summer session courses. Almost all colleges and universities offer an extensive selection of classes in extension centers in the evening and on campus during the summer. If this is impossible, the individual teacher may study professional materials on his own or form a small discussion group in his school.

The beginning teacher should seize any opportunity to visit other teachers. Years ago, teachers seldom if ever were able to observe another person teaching once they had completed student teaching. However, more and more schools are setting up provisions whereby interested teachers are encouraged to visit other teachers in the same school and neighboring schools.

Procedures of self-appraisal need to be initiated and continued if the teacher is to continue to grow in his job. As the students and teacher plan and carry out evaluation of the classwork, the teacher must keep clearly in mind that the process is appraising the curriculum as well as the students. Thus, the teacher continuously tests himself as well as his pupils.

*Teachers work in groups.* Modern administrators and curriculum workers recognize the great potential which may result from groups of interested teachers working together on some problem which is important to the curriculum of the school. For this reason, you are likely to be involved in a variety of groups at several levels; for example:

1. Regular teachers meetings are scheduled largely for administrative purposes. However, an analysis of common agenda items indicates much that relates to the curriculum. Moreover, the discussions often lead to later, more intensive group effort on topics or problems of some concern.

2. Faculty committees commonly work on matters which are of interest to the total faculty. Many schools have a standing Curriculum Committee representing a cross section of the teachers. Other committees may be established on short-term or long-term bases to work on such problems as grading, reporting, promotion, school philosophy, dropouts, and followup.

3. Departmental meetings involve only those teachers who are responsible for courses within a certain subject field. It is within this group that the beginning teacher is likely to find the greatest initial satisfactions. The departmental discussions usually build self-confidence in the new teacher as he discovers that what he is doing in the classroom is not much different from what the other, more experienced teachers are doing. Often, he gets better perspective of the total departmental program. This, also, is how many of the ideas and plans emerge which will lead to curriculum change.

4. District-wide committees often operate in the large school districts. Many of these address themselves to problems which affect elementary, junior high, and senior high school education. They draw together teachers from various levels and from different schools.

5. Local teacher associations, through collective negotiation, have great potential to influence curriculum. Even in the early agreements, it became clear that almost any item might become subject to negotiation. Local association leaders recognize that they represent organized teacher power and seek to effect changes desired by the membership.

6. County and state groups commonly work under the sponsorship of the county superintendent of schools, the state department of education, the governor, and various county and state organizations. Although the beginning teacher seldom is asked to participate in one of these groups, he should follow their work closely. The important job of textbook selection often occurs at these levels as well as other tasks which have broad implications for the education in the state.

Thus, the groups in which teachers work on curriculum and curriculum-related problems range from state to local in scope. However, for teachers new to the profession the small, informal groups which evolve within each school as staff members with similar concerns and interests are drawn together tend to provide the most helpful and stimulating context within which to work.

*Comprehensive curriculum revision.* Although much of the individual teacher's efforts toward curriculum revision will be focused on his own courses, modern curriculum change often develops in a comprehensive, all-school framework. Thus, it is desirable for a beginning teacher to have some perspective of the larger process. Romine[8] recommends seven steps in such a framework, as follows:

1. Taking stock of the existing curriculum.
2. Framing a philosophy of education and stating other guiding principles.
3. Determining life problems and formulating educational objectives.
4. Evaluating the existing curriculum.
5. Planning the revision program.
6. Executing the plan of revision.
7. Evaluating curricular changes and the resulting program.

The individual teacher may not be completely aware of the first step as the administration seeks to *take stock* of the existing curriculum. This involves a quiet, unobtrusive study of every aspect of the program. It is based upon the assumption that the present situation is the only realistic starting point for curriculum change. Teachers, students, and parents may be surveyed regarding their opinions of the curriculum.

---

[8] Romine, *op. cit.,* 464.

Interested teachers may be involved in studies of the present status of dropouts, college success of graduates, achievement levels, study habits, and faculty preparation.

The second step aims to achieve faculty consensus in regard to the *philosophy of the school.* Each teacher participates in the cooperative formulation of the aims or guiding principles of the school. Every teacher is assumed to have some idea of what he is trying to do in the classroom, and why. This step seeks to give expression to the direction in which the total faculty is working or would like to work.

Specific *educational objectives* form a base from which to make a meaningful evaluation and, in addition, to plan subsequent curriculum revision. Each teacher cooperates in the task of making explicit the ways in which his own courses contribute to the overall aims of the school. He must identify the specific educational objectives (skills, understandings, habits, interests, and attitudes) which he seeks to develop in his teaching. These are probably best stated in terms of behavioral objectives—ways of behaving which are essential to exploring and solving life problems.

All teachers assist in the comprehensive *evaluation of the curriculum.* Using the first three steps as bases, this evaluation attempts to assess present practices in the light of what is desirable. One process[9] which is often used involves self-evaluation by the school and subsequent appraisal by a visiting committee. A variety of procedures are utilized in the comprehensive evaluation of the school, such as: standardized tests, teacher-constructed tests, opinionnaires, interviews, sociometrics, and study of student cumulative records. All possible resources need to be explored to appraise the present program.

The fifth step entails *planning the revision* of the curriculum. This must be done by a group which has a real perspective of the overall process. Of course, as individual teachers work together in the previous steps, many uncoordinated changes develop, but the comprehensive revisions which demand cooperative effort over a period of time require careful planning. Long-range plans and short-range plans are formulated and discussed with the faculty. Curriculum workers realize that the revision will be successful only if the individual teachers participate in and accept responsibility for these plans.

---

[9] Gordon Cawelti, *High School Evaluation Guide* (Experimental Edition) Chicago: North Central Association of Colleges and Secondary Schools, April 1966); *Junior High School/Middle School Evaluation Criteria* (Arlington, Va.: National Study of School Evaluation, 1970) or *Evaluation Criteria for the Evaluation of Secondary Schools* (4th Ed.) (Washington, D.C.: National Study of Secondary School Evaluation, 1969) and current editions of these documents.

The *execution of the revision* comes next. This step often involves a movement toward change on a broad front. That is, long- and short-range plans may be initiated simultaneously. It is essential that the revision should proceed slowly and carefully. However, if teachers understand and support the plans, they are likely to move ahead with enthusiasm and vigor.

The final step includes the *evaluation of the changes*. Actually, the individual teacher continuously appraises the changes as they occur. Clearly, the need is to determine whether the planned revision is desirable or not, and this step seeks evidence of all kinds to establish the worth of the changes and the resulting curriculum itself. Again, a variety of procedures, both formal and informal, are used in this appraisal.

Comprehensive curriculum revision is a difficult job for all concerned. It invariably entails extra work, time, and effort beyond the normal teaching load expectancies. However, the rewards may be considerable. In addition to the important curriculum changes, the individual teacher is certain to grow professionally as a result of his participation.


## REVIEW

Chapter 3 seeks to introduce the preservice teacher to the area of teacher practices in curriculum development. The following questions will help you pinpoint the desired outcomes of this section.

1. Do you feel you understand the curricular terms and concepts as a beginning professional vocabulary?

2. After studying the commonly observed practices and approaches, do you have a better idea of what to expect in the "typical" high school?

3. Are the nature and variety of forces and agencies which affect curriculum clear to you?

4. Do you recognize the importance of the classroom teacher's position in curriculum making, and do you have a good idea of the variety of ways in which you may need to work?

# Selected References

Anderson, V. E. *Principles and Procedures of Curriculum Improvement,* 2nd ed. N. Y.: The Ronald Press Company, 1965.

Bent, R. K. and Unruh, A. *Secondary School Curriculum.* Lexington, Mass.: D. C. Heath and Company, 1969.

Clark, L. H., Klein, R. L., and Burke, J. B. *The American Secondary School Curriculum.* New York: The Macmillan Company, 1965.

"Curriculum for the 70's," *Phi Delta Kappan,* 51:(entire issue), March 1970.

Davis, E. D. *Focus on Secondary Education: An Introduction to Principles and Practices.* Glenview, Ill.: Scott, Foresman and Company, 1966; Part 2 "A Study of the Secondary School Curriculum."

Doll, R. C. *Curriculum Improvement,* 2nd ed. Boston: Allyn and Bacon, Inc., 1970.

Douglass, H. R. *Trends and Issues in Secondary Education.* Washington, D.C.: The Center for Applied Research in Education, Inc., 1962; Ch. 3 "Curriculum Offerings, Organization, and Administration."

Goodlad, J. I. *The Changing School Curriculum.* N.Y.: The Fund for the Advancement of Education, August 1966.

Olivia, P. F. *The Secondary School Today.* Cleveland: The World Publishing Company, 1967; Unit II "The Secondary School Curriculum Today."

"Projects, Packages, Programs," *Educational Leadership,* 27:(entire issue), May 1970.

Trump, J. L. and Miller, D. F. *Secondary School Curriculum Improvement.* Boston: Allyn and Bacon, Inc., 1968.

Wright, J. R., ed. *Secondary School Curriculum.* Columbus, Ohio: Charles E. Merrill Books, Inc., 1963.

# four

# Guiding
# Classroom Experiences

The two vital elements in the teaching-learning situation are teacher and learner. The learner, of course, is the most important single element, but the teacher, as a mature, specially trained individual has certain fundamental responsibilities. He must set the stage for desirable and appropriate learning experiences; he seeks to act in ways which facilitate rather than inhibit significant student learning; he searches for evidence of progress toward educational objectives.

Teachers develop ways of working which are based on theoretical understandings and beliefs and modified or reinforced by the apparent results of these procedures in the classroom. Choice of instructional approach is at least partially dependent upon the classroom teacher's conception of the nature and role of the school in modern America. The school staff comes to feel it is especially well qualified to perform certain essential services in preparing youth for adult life. In a real sense, the schools are established and maintained so that boys and girls will live a wiser, richer life. It is ridiculous to debate the "life-adjustment" role of the school. The only justification that society has for compelling boys and girls to attend school is the assumption that the skills, knowledge, understandings, interests, and attitudes learned inside the classroom will transfer to life outside the classroom and assist them to become better citizens, realize their potentialities, secure a satisfying vocation, and attain other goals. The school is a basic institution supported by the society so that youth may be prepared to take their places as productive participants in that society. If teachers come to strong beliefs such as these, the way in which they work with boys and girls is bound to be affected.

As beginning teachers, you ought to reflect upon several basic questions with which this chapter will deal.

1. There are several different ways of categorizing method. Even though it is sometimes difficult to place a teacher clearly in one or another of the categories, what are some of the "name" methods of teaching and what are important implications of each?

2. A satisfactory method depends to a great extent upon understanding of the nature and conditions of learning. What are important elements of learning which instructional procedures must take into account?

3. Each teacher must work to clarify his own thinking and come to a personal decision regarding teaching method. What are important considerations in this decision?

## A TEACHER WORKS WITH STUDENTS

Good teaching is something other than a mechanical process. It goes far beyond the teaching machine of today. It involves a sensitive, well-prepared, highly trained teacher operating in the complex interpersonal relationships of the classroom. Methodology is best seen in view of its effects upon the learner.

*Classroom Description*

A university professor was engaged in making a curriculum survey of a medium-sized high school. In the process, he began to interview a pretty, sophomore coed. Responding to his questions she began to tell of some of her teachers.

> Take Mr. Bee, for example. I have had him two years for social studies now, so I know him pretty well. I like him, even though most of my friends don't, because I know he means well.
>
> I know what kind of tests he will give and I know just how to study for them. He tells us that we must know the material and before long all students realize that he means just that. We must remember the dates, names, and events in history because he asks for these on the tests.
>
> Every day is almost the same in his class. We all are supposed to have read the assigned chapters in the book. As soon as he takes roll he begins at the first of his roll book and calls on a student and asks him one question from those at the end of the chapters. If a person doesn't know the answer, Mr. Bee asks the next student in order to try it. My last name begins with a "W" so he doesn't get down to me very often, except once in awhile when he starts at the bottom of the list and works up.
>
> Mr. Bee never smiles or cracks jokes as some teachers do; he seems almost afraid to. Instead he is very serious and tries very hard to use illustrations and examples which help us understand the material. He says that we must understand history, and this will make us good citizens.

Every semester we have to write a paper. We must choose a topic from a list which he puts on the board. Judy, my girlfriend, asked him if she could write on something else and Mr. Bee said that he was the teacher and it was his job to do the planning for the class.

His class is not the most interesting one I have; as a matter of fact, I don't like social studies as well as I used to. But at least I know how to study for his tests and I can get good grades.

## *Implications*

As the student described her version of the procedures of one of her teachers, several obvious implications became apparent.

1. Mr. Bee obviously sees the end of the educative process as consisting mainly of the mastery of academic information. He tells his pupils that he wants them to know the material, and his tests are constructed to check this kind of learning. Most students rather quickly come to understand this and adjust study habits to produce the desired results. They study and memorize the names and dates in order to get good grades. Thus, the nature of the teacher's goals influences the students' approach to learning.

This is an important and pervasive aspect of the teaching-learning situation. The students' concept of the subject matter of any course is bound to be greatly influenced by the goals of learning held by the teacher. For students, history tends to become simply a quantity of names and dates, and the goal is to remember a sufficient number of these at least long enough to pass the examination, if the teacher has this orientation.

This method is similar to that used by the physical education instructor who taught health and safety by first requiring students to locate and memorize the names of all the major bones and muscles in the body. By the time students struggled through this task, the pattern for the rest of the course was set. They simply memorized certain facts which they felt the instructor might ask on the exam, without really relating the material to their lives. They never applied what the text revealed about good health and safety to themselves. Learning was nothing more than an abstract exercise of memorization of facts.

2. The major justification for studying social studies, according to Mr. Bee, is that it will make students good citizens. Therefore, the effort involved in learning historical facts is defended because it is assumed that this is a means through which the ultimate goal of good citizenship may be accomplished. Actually then, the classroom practices of the teacher focus upon the means. The mastery of academic information becomes the end of education in this social studies classroom. It may

be assumed that, because the goal of good citizenship is somewhat vague, hard to define, and difficult to evaluate, the means activity (learning dates, names, and other specific facts) naturally is emphasized. Unfortunately this means becomes the goal of learning for students and teacher.

3. This social studies teacher emphasizes communication. Most of his effort in planning goes into trying to find ways to transfer the academic information from the textbook to the minds of his pupils. In his eyes, the task of the teacher is to establish this communication and then to check to see how well it was accomplished. He is preoccupied with vocabulary difficulties in the material, reading level of the textbook, illustrations, and examples which all assist the communicative process.

4. The textbook largely structures the scope and sequence of the course. Mr. Bee follows the text, starting with the first chapter, and works toward the back. Thus, the textbook writers really have planned his course. He uses the questions at the end of the chapters to bring out important points and to check on the students' reading. He has accepted uncritically the work of the experts, without modification for his classes. The text content is the fixed element, and he seeks to facilitate student mastery of it.

5. Mr. Bee has a certain conception of the teacher role in the classroom. He sees the teacher as the person responsible for learning; that is he told Judy that he was the teacher and it was his job to do the planning for the class. He obviously feels that the teacher, with the help of the textbook, plays the role of the "know everything" and the pupil is the "know nothing." It is the teacher's task to teach, and it is the pupil's job to learn. He will accept no suggestions or tolerate interference from his students. This teacher is really a sort of benevolent dictator in the classroom.

6. From the girl's description of Mr. Bee, it is clear that for him learning is a very serious, dour process. The classroom is not a proper setting for lightness or frivolity. He may take the attitude that for learning to be good it must be disagreeable. As a result, the atmosphere of his classroom is serious and at least mildly disagreeable. The girl's confession that she does not like social studies as well as she used to is partial evidence of the effect of this atmosphere on the students.

Mr. Bee, as seen through the eyes of his student, is not at all atypical of what an observer would find in many classrooms in many high schools across the country. He illustrates a type of traditional teaching which violates much of what is known about the nature of the process of learning and which rests upon a number of the following beliefs, which are at least partly fallacious.

*False Assumptions Regarding Teaching*

Nathaniel Cantor has pointed up nine assumptions which are implicit in the traditional practices still to be seen in the United States today. These fallacious assumptions underlie the classroom procedures of a rather large number of teachers, and must be replaced or modified if the instructional practices are to be improved significantly.

1. "It is assumed that the teacher's responsibility is to set out what is to be learned and that the student's job is to learn it."[1] This assumption necessarily implies that the teaching-learning process is one way— it alway moves from teacher to pupil. The teacher becomes some sort of all-wise person who knows exactly what every boy and girl must learn. Students are consistently placed in the role of docile recipients of these essential learnings.

2. "It is assumed that knowledge taken on authority is educative in itself."[2] This view sees the task of education as furnishing the mind with appropriate academic information. The teacher and the textbook represent the authority, and students must memorize the information presented. Examinations, which test whether or not the material has been memorized and retained, verify the learning. If the knowledge is simply accepted on faith, the question may be asked whether or not it will ever make a difference in the students' behavior. The pupil is seldom allowed to look critically at authoritative statements or even encouraged to check what he hears with his own past experience.

3. "It is assumed that education can be obtained through disconnected subjects."[3] Typically, the secondary school consists of a variety of disconnected subjects scheduled in some chance fashion. Students proceed to English class and then, at the sound of the bell like Pavlov's dog, they click off English, rush down the hall to biology and, at the sound of the next bell, click on biology. They become proficient at compartmentalizing subject material. It may be assumed that the individual somehow, sometime, puts the subjects together. However, subjects learned separately are seldom automatically integrated. The integrative process takes special conditions and special help.

4. "It is assumed that the subject matter is the same to the learner as to the teacher."[4] Some teachers innocently believe that a fact is a fact, and that it means the same thing to every student as it means to

---

[1] Nathaniel Cantor, *The Teaching-Learning Process* (New York: Holt, Rinehart and Winston, Inc., 1953), 59.

[2] *Ibid.,* 59.

[3] *Ibid.,* 61.

the teacher. Two important factors prevent this from being so: (a) the teacher possesses a considerably different level of maturity and set of values from those of his students and (b) the teacher views a certain datum from a different frame of reference than his pupils. The instructor presumably has a considerable background in the subject, far beyond the material normally dealt with in the usual high school classroom. This condition alone is likely to invalidate the assumption.

5. "It is assumed that education prepares the student for later life rather than that it is a living experience."[5] Teachers cannot deal constantly in deferred goals. All students, especially the immature, are concerned with present, immediate goals, for they are living now. They recognize a vague, dimly lit future ahead, but today, this week, or next month are more real to them. The learning experiences which affect boys and girls now, of course, have effects upon their future lives, yet the teacher must teach out of context of the present if maximum learning is to occur.

6. "It is assumed that the teacher is responsible for the pupils' acquiring of knowledge."[6] This belief ignores the essential relationship between student and teacher. Each pupil must do his own learning; no one can do it for him. The right and proper role of the teacher is as a "facilitator" in the classroom. He guides and assists the learner. He must stand by and watch the learner accept or reject this help. He must realize that the students' questions are more important than the teacher's questions, and the students' problems are more significant to learning than the teacher's problems.

7. "It is assumed that pupils must be coerced into working on some tasks."[7] This same sort of logic has led parents to force their children to eat spinach and oyster stew "because it is good for you." Many teachers have learned that the mental discipline or "mind muscle theory" is invalid, and they no longer justify the taking of disagreeable subjects on this basis. However, teachers commonly force students into certain academic experiences because of the fond hope that later they may grow to enjoy the subject. Cantor pointedly describes the probable results when he says,

> Forcing disagreeable tasks on pupils–demanding, for example, certain reports on readings which hold no inherent interest for the pupil–creates distaste and habits of slovenly workmanship, of getting by with the least

---

[4] *Ibid.*, 64.
[5] *Ibid.*, 65.
[6] *Ibid.*, 67.
[7] *Ibid.*, 68.

effort, and, often, of dishonesty and cheating. . . . Love of literature or mathematics, like love for a human being, cannot be forced upon anyone.[8]

8. "It is assumed that knowledge is more important than learning."[9] Certainly the modern American culture is fact oriented—witness the sales appeal of all sorts of books of facts and the popularity of many types of quiz shows and quiz games. It has come to be a sign of the educated man if one has a sizable quantity of facts at his command ready to be brought forth to impress people. To this limited degree, these facts have some utility. However, information has real meaning only when it is related to the learner's background of experience and integrated into his ongoing flow of experience. Facts which are learned in an abstract academic vacuum are not meaningful, are not applicable to the problems and difficulties of living. This sort of knowledge is useful only to pass examinations, not to enrich the pupils' lives.

9. "It is assumed that education is primarily an intellectual process."[10] Recent critics of the public schools have demanded that more attention be focused upon "intellectual excellence." However, students bring their arms and legs and all the rest of their physical equipment with them when they come to class. The emphasis on excellence must affect the entire personality. Humans are illogical and inconsistent by nature, and this makes working with them one of the most interesting tasks imaginable. Humans, we know, respond more effectively to feelings than facts, yet teachers overlook the emotions present in the classroom. They neglect the relatively more permanent affective learnings (attitudes, interests, values) and mistakenly spend the bulk of their time on purely intellectual content.

These false assumptions have led teachers to many of the traditional teaching practices. Modern research in learning and teaching has provided insights into the invalidity of these assumptions and has encouraged teacher scrutiny and experimentation.

## METHODS OF TEACHING

Teachers are observed working in different ways with students in the classroom. However, many teachers tend to follow a pattern of procedures which often may be characterized as a method. The following section describes a number of those commonly accepted methods of

---

[8] *Ibid.,* 69.
[9] *Ibid.,* 70.
[10] *Ibid.,* 71.

teaching. In many cases, these represent consistency in approach rather than, strictly speaking, separate methods.

*Lecture Method*

The lecture as a consistent, day-after-day procedure is commonly found at the college level and is enjoying a resurgence in popularity in the high school as some secondary school teachers, in the quest for intellectual excellence, follow the methods of their recent instructors.

The lecture is seen to have some very real and positive advantages.
1. It is valuable in introducing new material to the entire class.
2. It allows the teacher to go beyond the material in the textbook.
3. It provides a means for the teacher to adapt the content to the characteristics of his pupils.
4. It allows the teacher to place increased emphasis on items which he considers vital.
5. It is economical in relation to the time needed to cover a body of material.
6. It is adaptable to student questions and misunderstandings.
7. A gifted lecturer may stimulate added interest and enthusiasm in his students.

However, the lecture has some limitations when used with immature learners. Junior and senior high school students may not profit from consistent use of the lecture because of some of the following reasons.
1. The average high school student may not have suffpicent attention span to attend closely to a full fifty-minute lecture.
2. High school pupils seldom have been taught how to listen for central ideas and to take clear and well-organized notes.
3. The lecture is found to be more efficient in covering ground but less efficient in learning.
4. The student is placed in a passive role as recipient of the material.
5. The pace of the lecturer may not be adjusted to the majority of the students.

When seen in perspective, the lecture, especially the formal lecture, is generally ineffective when used as a method of teaching. However, all teachers utilize lectures, formal and informal, to introduce material, to explain complicated concepts, to refer students to pertinent readings, to illustrate principles, and to summarize.

*Assign-Study-Recite Method*

This method follows a regular sequence. Usually the teacher assigns some reading in the textbook, the students are expected to read the material and prepare answers to questions which appear at the end of each chapter or are presented by the instructor. The teacher then checks on this study by a subsequent recitation session in the classroom. This approach is aimed at the coverage of a predetermined portion of subject matter. Student progress is regulated by the assignments.

This approach obviously places great emphasis upon the textbook. The organization of the text, with slight modification, if any, determines the organization of the course with teacher and students typically tied to the single adopted text. Logical organization of the subject matter is followed. Student reading ability is very important because the text is assigned a chapter or two at a time. Classroom activity usually involves recitation and assignment for the next day. Occasionally the teacher may lecture on an obscure point, students may be drilled to master specific material, and tests are given at appropriate points in the grading period.

This procedure is a popular but often criticized method of teaching; its main advantages lie in the reliance upon the textbook. Many new teachers seek the security afforded by the textbook as the curricular decisions are already largely made by the author. The task becomes mainly to get as far through the book as the time allows. The disadvantages clearly are many. The central goal is simply the communication of information from text to student. The learner is prevented from gaining any experience planning his own learning activity. Individual differences among students are ignored. Differences between classes are ignored when standard, uniform assignments are made to all.

*Discussion Method*

Some teachers characteristically use a procedure which depends upon student discussion. If the method is worthy of its name it must go beyond sheer recitation, teacher-dominated, question-and-answer sessions. Usually the teacher identifies an area of discussion and then operates largely as a process person as discussion leader. In order to facilitate student discussion the leader must act to assist the orderly flow of the discussion, screen out the obviously non-pertinent comments, stimulate further discussion when the process begins to bog down, encourage wide participation, reflect back the feelings and concerns of the group, help integrate and relate ideas, and summarize the final points. These are important and difficult skills, and obviously not all teachers are equally competent in their ability to operate as discussion leaders.

The discussion method has important values in its provision for the involvement of students and the possible practice given in assessing, relating, summarizing, and applying ideas. Stovall[11] compared the lecture method with the discussion method and concluded that the latter promises advantages in stimulating critical thinking, promoting deeper understanding of the material learned, affecting attitudes and interests, and developing desirable relationships in class.

Probably the most serious error made by teachers who employ this method is revealed by the charge that too often the class discussion is a "sharing of ignorance." Of course, students must possess a pertinent background of experience and knowledge if the discussion is to be productive at all. Thus, the preparatory activity before the discussion begins is crucial. Students must read, do research, consult authorities, introspect upon pertinent, past experiences, and other like activities in order to prepare for the discussion.

*Project Method*

The project method, as seen in the modern classroom, involves student formulation of individual or group goals, the supervised planning of activities which are likely to achieve the goals, the execution of these plans, and the evaluation of the process.

Shop teachers have long used the project method as they guide students in planning and building cedar chests, coffee tables, and cabinets. In other classes, projects may range from the making of a scrapbook to the writing of a history of the community. For example, a United States history teacher might use the project method in the organization and study of this subject. A variety of important issues facing our society today are identified. Students, singly or in small groups, choose the issue which they wish to explore and later make a report to the class. With able guidance by the teacher, the student list of issues is comprehensive and the sum total of the resulting projects adequately covers the subject.

Obviously, certain advantages may accrue: individual differences may be taken into consideration, student interests and purposes are incorporated into the planning of learning activities, student creativity and expression are emphasized, and meaningful learning is more likely to result as students are involved in stating goals, planning activities, and evaluating projects. Disadvantages include: difficulty in preplanning the curriculum, possibility of gaps in coverage of subject matter, problems in finding teachers adequately prepared to handle this method, and need to be sure the project is pertinent, worthwhile, and practicable.

---

[11] Thomas F. Stovall, "Lecture vs. Discussion," *Phi Delta Kappan,* 39:255–258, March 1958.

*Problem-Solving Method*

Some educators have recognized the purposive nature of learning and have come to a conception of the problem-solving method. Much of our learning in life is an attempt to solve problems and overcome difficulties. Therefore, it seems logical for teachers to focus deliberately on the problem-solving process in the classroom and teach pupils the skills essential to improved problem solving. This method implies a curriculum which is made up of problems that may come from a variety of sources. Teachers may directly propose problems for study or provide classroom experiences which point up problems, and students may suggest problems which come out of their immediate experiences. Ideally, the student activity tends to follow a problem-solving process which includes certain elements, as follows:

1. Recognition and formulation of a problem which is of some concern to the person,

2. Search for data which are pertinent to the situation and the difficulty to be resolved.

3. Proposal of hypotheses about possible solutions to the stated problem.

4. Testing of the selected hypothesis and verification of the results as to whether or not the problem is solved.

This method tends to place emphasis upon the process skills of problem attack and solution, as well as upon the academic information necessary to solve the problems. In addition, the factual knowledge is placed in a functional context as it contributes to the understanding of the problem rather than being taught in the abstract.

Major difficulties in this method center around problem selection and clarification. Teachers must know a great deal about the concerns and needs of their students. They must be able to guide boys and girls toward problems which are pertinent to the subject and real to the students themselves. They must be helpful in encouraging pupils to examine and assess their goals. In addition, the teachers must develop great skill in assisting students to progress through the process of problem solution.

*Unit Method*

In recent years the unit method has gained considerable support, and currently is being used in a great many classrooms across the country. This method also breaks away from the textbook domination of the curriculum. Instead of one long, uninterrupted (except for periodic examinations) sequence, the course is organized into units of work. The classroom teacher seeks to identify units or recognizable portions of subject matter which have some cohesion. In literature, rather than assigning the selections simply as they are found in the anthology according to chronology or authors, the literary pieces may be grouped according to literary types (e.g., short story, poetry, essay, biography), and are read as they illustrate the various types. The selections may also be organized into units focused on important ideas or themes such as courage, survival, or friendship

Units may be divided into two types, the subject-matter unit and the experience unit. The main difference lies in emphasis. The former utilizes mainly the logic of the subject, and the latter utilizes the logic of the learner in the identification and organization of the unit. This is not an either/or situation. Both kinds of units are desirable and useful.

Significantly, the growth of the unit method has developed through some very real advantages. The unit approach tends to minimize piecemeal teaching, because the organization emphasizes unity of material which is related to a central idea or concept. Continuity between lessons is thus enhanced, because the individual lessons are not taught in isolation but as they relate to and contribute to the understanding of the unit theme or core. Good unit teaching is based on sound principles of learning, takes into consideration individual differences, focuses learning upon student needs, encourages student participation in planning and evaluation, provides for cooperative student effort and makes possible a variety of learning activities.

Unit teaching requires considerable time and effort in planning. It often calls for a range of materials far beyond the single, adopted textbook. It demands a high degree of flexibility and process skill on the part of the teacher. Many beginning teachers have little confidence in themselves, seem to require the security provided by reliance upon the single, adopted textbook, and thus are reluctant to use the unit approach.

## Method in Perspective

After an examination of actual classroom practices, an obvious conclusion for one to make would be that few teachers adhere strictly to one method to the exclusion of other approaches. Most teachers are eclectic in that they pick and choose among the possible approaches those elements which seem to be best suited to their personalities, the subjects being taught, the nature of their students, and the desired learning outcomes. The procedures are tested in practice and are modified, retained, or rejected. Various techniques are utilized when they seem desirable. Selection of teaching approach also is affected by the teacher's knowledge and understanding of the principles of learning, past educational experiences, and the resulting conclusions regarding the nature of the teaching-learning process.

To a great degree, the way in which the average teacher works with students is a point of view, rather than a systematic, rigorous, conceptual framework about method. A teacher is observed doing many different things, often modifying techniques in mid-lesson, in order to produce the desired learning. However, such factors as the way in which the instructor looks at the nature of his subject matter, the relative degree of focus on content or students, and the conception of teacher role tend to determine his consistent approach to teaching.

## LEARNING AND TEACHING

Even though there is no comprehensive, unified theory of learning which is generally accepted at present, a number of principles of learning are solidly grounded and form the current bases for methodological thinking and research. All teachers should possess certain insights into the nature and conditions of learning which will help them choose sound teaching approaches and modify and improve them. The more important of these are listed below.

### Learning Is Individual

In the public schools, pupils are formed into groups as they learn, yet the individual either learns or does not learn. Regardless of the group context, it is the individual student who must do the learning—no one can do it for him. Learning is personal and individual.

Actually, the learner has few rights in the average classroom. For example, he seldom has the right to reject the opinions of the teacher. He seldom has the right to reject or significantly change the assignment given him. Nevertheless, one irrevocable option which he does possess is the power to make the decision as to how he will use the time in school. Whether he will learn or not is his personal responsibility. Of course, this is a frustrating insight for teachers. The student may be encouraged, guided, coerced, or ignored by the teacher and still, by the very nature of the learning process, may retain this option. Further, each student learns in his own particular way, and there may be many different pupils learning in many different ways in the same class.

### The Student Learns what He Needs to Learn

In the classroom, as in life outside, the individual learns only what he needs to learn. When present responses are adequate for satisfying active needs, the person has no interest or need to acquire new responses. When students learn lists of names and dates in history class, they typically have little desire to accomplish this learning. However, they may need to learn these to pass the examination and to receive a passing grade in history, they may be impelled to compete with classmates, or some other pressing motive may be present. Learning the list of names and dates is merely a means by which other needs are realized.

Learning is purposive. It proceeds in relation to learner purposes and seeks to satisfy active needs. If all pupil needs were satisfied, he would not learn. Therefore, teachers are rightly concerned with problems of encouraging students to formulate goals which are pertinent to the subject and of showing pupils that the course content is relevant and valuable in accomplishing their purposes and meeting their needs.

*Learning Involves Effort*

Learning is essentially an active process. The learner is impelled to action, and through listening, speaking, writing, reading, thinking, and acting he learns. The really passive student is a spectator, a non-participant in the learning process.

If learning is active, it involves effort. That is, an individual must be impelled to act. In the classroom students are observed doing a variety of things, but why do they put forth effort? The great majority of boys and girls will do most of the things asked of them—even some fairly ridiculous things. High school students sometimes spend hours searching through magazines, clipping out pictures, carefully preparing labels, and pasting them in a scrapbook to be handed in at the teacher's request. Others commit great amounts of time and effort to constructing model volcanoes, duplicating classic experiments, or collecting and classifying moths so that their school will have entrants in the local science fair. Students dutifully, if not cheerfully, memorize long lists of words, paraphrase essays, make Roman togas, trace maps, and do a variety of other tasks, many of which are repetitive, sterile, and uninteresting. A rewarding and enlightening activity for beginning teachers is to investigate the reasons why students are moved to put forth this effort.

Obviously, boys and girls are stimulated in a number of ways to expend effort in school-related tasks. The observed motivation may be classified into two categories, extrinsic and intrinsic motivation. Unfortunately, the greatest number of influences which impel student effort are extrinsic to the learning. That is, they are really outside the learning activity itself. When students work for grades, prestige, diplomas, teacher praise, and approval, or when spurred on by classroom competition, teacher sarcasm, and ridicule, the motivation is essentially external to the learning. It is something which comes *after* the learning effort. The learning is simply a means to achieve the external reward. Intrinsic motivation comes out of the learning itself. If the learning activity helps the student to know himself better, provides answers to his questions, reinforces previous interests, enables the pupil to establish satisfying relationships with others, and assists in solving his problems the reward comes *with* the learning. In the former the focus is upon the external reward, and in the latter the focus is upon the learning activity itself.

## *Learning Activity Is Modified by Consequences*

Student behavior is modified by the consequences of this behavior. In every area, all humans constantly are engaged in experiencing and evaluating or interpreting these experiences. Responses to learning situations set up by the school are retained, rejected, or modified according to the learner's interpretation of the consequences.

Some purpose or need, strong enough or imperative enough to move the individual to action, must be operating. The chosen response presumably has some chance of achieving the goal. The important factor is the learner's judgment of the consequences of the response. Satisfaction or annoyance in the learning situation depends upon the learner's interpretation of the success or failure of the activity to accomplish his goal. Thus, the actual nature of the student's purpose and his particular definition of success or failure of the activity are often two unknown variables in the learning context as far as the teacher is concerned. Because of immaturity, peer group pressure, parental influence, and the like, the student's purposes and interpretation of the consequences of learning activity may be considerably different from that of the teacher.

Obviously, the teacher must help the student gain knowledge of his progress. The learner makes better achievement when he knows what the teacher expects, possesses information about his progress as compared to his past achievement and as compared to the group, understands the nature of his mistakes, and is encouraged to set up realistic and challenging standards for himself.

## *The Student Learns from His Background of Experience*

Any learning situation will have real meaning only in terms of the learner's background of experience. Understanding is built upon pertinent experiences. Thus, the new is made meaningful by joining it with the old. New learning builds upon past learning.

Some students gain a certain amount of facility in the manipulation of abstract words and concepts, but it is more like the arrangement and rearrangement of nonsense syllables than real learning. Before genuine understanding and personal involvement can occur, the content dealt with in class must have some relevance to the backgrounds of experience of the students. For example, a social studies teacher was dealing with the U.S. Constitution. He had the class read the appropriate chapters in the text and discuss the apparent meaning. He sensed that somehow they were thinking of the Constitution as something far removed and not particularly important except as miscellaneous information about their country and its history. In desperation he asked the boys and girls to bring into class copies of the constitutions of their social and service clubs. They proceeded to analyze these and to discover the ways in which they affected the rights and privileges of the members. Some students, never having read them before, discovered things they wanted changed and things which might be added. From this activity, real and close to the students, the instructor was able to move back to the U.S. Constitution and assist his pupils in securing insight into the importance and real meaning of this document to all American citizens.

Teachers must be concerned with the experiential backgrounds of their students. These backgrounds establish limits within which the teaching-learning process may operate.

### The Pupil Learns what He Is Ready to Learn

Every teacher comes to recognize the factor of readiness. English teachers, for example, often report that a poem about death simply doesn't communicate much to most junior high school boys and girls. They haven't lived long enough, and are concerned about almost anything except death. So it is in other subjects that the bulk of the youngsters are most ready because of physical, mental, and emotional readiness and appropriate experiences, to learn a particular thing at a certain time. At present, with the pressure to push curricular content downward into a lower grade than it has customarily been located, this problem of readiness is becoming even more crucial.

Teachers often attempt to deal with this problem in three ways: (a) wait until a significant number of the class has reached minimal readiness for a particular activity before initiating it, (b) adapt instruction to the level of readiness possessed by the learners, or (c) set up classroom activities to aid in developing readiness.

Readiness is a real and insistent problem. It involves the misplacement of content as well as the observed fact that individuals possess varying degrees of readiness. The problem has been the subject of far more attention in the early grades than in high school. For example, educators have excellent tools for assessing readiness for beginning reading, yet we still admit children into the first grade according to the criterion of chronological age. Thus, we must carefully group students within the classroom according to degree of readiness for reading if optimum learning is to occur. In the future, similar concern regarding the best time to introduce algebra, grammatical concepts, health education, and other subjects may be expected.

## Learning Is Multiple

When a person learns, his physical, intellectual, and emotional makeup becomes a part of the process. No matter what the teacher's lesson plan lists as objectives, the learning outcomes in any learning situation are multiple.

Some teachers envision the role of teacher and school as dealing simply in the realm of intellectual learning. Inevitably, the student is affected by the classroom experiences in many different dimensions. The pupil may memorize a poem and prove it to the teacher's satisfaction by reproducing it on paper or reciting it aloud. However, at the same time he is building attitudes toward the subject, teacher, and school, he is developing interests or aversions, and accomplishing a great variety of other learning.

The learner may respond to many different aspects of the entire classroom situation. The climate within which learning takes place includes the methods and materials of instruction, the pattern of social interaction existing among the students and teacher, and the physical conditions of the environment such as temperature, humidity, ventilation, lighting, and attractiveness of the room. Varied learnings result as boys and girls respond to certain aspects or combinations of conditions which exist in the classroom. Students may react to the information presented in class and certain learning will result; however, at the same time the teacher's method itself may produce certain outcomes. There is considerable evidence, for example, which indicates that the autocratic teacher is likely to produce aggressive and hostile behavior in his students, while a teacher using a more permissive, democratic method is likely to encourage more creativity, spontaneity, and task-oriented activity.

Teachers must recognize that learning in their classrooms will be multiple and varied, take into consideration the many possible outcomes, and attempt to evaluate the total effect of their teaching.

*Learning Seeks Answers*

Learning involves the search for answers and solutions to questions and problems which are important to boys and girls. Two critical teaching errors are made in this regard. One, teachers consistently make the mistake of giving students the answers too soon; and two, the teacher involves the student in working on problems and questions which are really the teacher's problems and questions.

Actually, at the same time an individual learns the solution to a problem he is inhibited in discovering any other solution to the same problem. As long as the first solution adequately solves the problem, even though it may not be the best possible solution, the learner is not impelled to seek another, different approach. Creativity, which depends upon innovation, is hampered when answers and solutions are immediately given. Mathematics, for example, almost invariably gives students the procedure for solving a particular kind of problem and then requires the students to practice this procedure by solving a series of closely similar problems. It is little wonder that students seldom discover other ways of solution.

In most courses, pupils spend most of their time dealing with questions which are raised by the teacher or the textbook. Boys and girls complain that not only are these questions of little apparent significance to them, but also how seldom they are engaged in answering questions which do not have nicely phrased answers already written down somewhere. In other words, they want to work on questions which are clearly relevant and important to them. Part of the art of teaching is to plan so that the learner will seek answers to questions which are pertinent to the subject matter, yet challenging and real to the student.

A teacher works with students in order that he may change their responses. He comes to define learning as change in behavior and evaluates his teaching in light of the evidence of behavior change. Certain basic insights into the nature and conditions of learning are essential to the successful teacher. These provide guidance in selecting and adapting effective methods and materials of instruction. Whatever instructional procedure you decide to use must at least not be in conflict with such conditions of learning.

*Your Method*

Every teacher comes to evolve a certain characteristic approach to instruction. This is likely to be a product of your past experiences as a student in various schools, your teacher training program, and your experimentation as you work at teaching. It is affected by your conception of the nature of your subject matter, the role and aims of the secondary school, and the relationship of teacher and pupil in the learning situation. It is for you to decide which approach to use.

One almost universal motive which beginning teachers carry with them into teaching is the desire to serve youth, the desire to help boys and girls become better citizens and wiser and happier persons. In other words, men and women who go into teaching tend to place the welfare of their students as top priority. Many people choose teaching as a profession because it allows them to work in the academic context, to deal with people and ideas without the pressures of outselling a competitor or speeding up the production line. In addition, you are likely impelled by the desire to become not simply an adequate teacher, but an excellent teacher, to improve constantly your skill in teaching and your mastery of the subject. Thus, teachers strive to find an instructional approach which will be most beneficial to the boys and girls in their charge, which will be satisfying and challenging to themselves, and which will be judged by other professional workers, in the light of its results, as successful. This decision is for you to consider and resolve in your own way.

## Developments

Much of the innovation and experimentation in the schools has taken three general directions: (a) a search for a technological breakthrough which would reduce the need for highly trained teachers, (b) an attempt to find better ways to use staff talents and energies, and (c) an exploration of means to further individualize the teaching. As a result, a number of significant developments have emerged opening up new instructional possibilities. All classroom teachers need to keep themselves well informed regarding these developments and to explore the possibilities inherent in them in order to use them to best advantage.

*Educational television.* Even though educational television has not lived up to its early promise of great economy in education, many schools feel strongly that ETV is an exceptionally valuable resource. Trends appear to indicate that television use is moving away from straight broadcast to closed circuit TV and video taping. The great advantage possible here is for a single, gifted teacher to instruct a large number of students. The development of relatively inexpensive video tape recording equipment has made it possible to record the production, store it indefinitely, use it, and re-use it upon demand. Educational television channels offer a steadily increasing quantity of useful material.

However, as school districts come to use the resource of television, teachers often must make certain necessary methodological adjustments.

During the television presentation, the classroom teacher must accept the fact that he is no longer the pivotal figure in the learning situation. In fact, he may actually become largely a disciplinarian charged with keeping order while the class views the screen. Following the lesson, he may need to perform a supplementary function by helping the students understand the televised material. The roles thus may be completely reversed; instead of the machine aiding the classroom teacher's presentation, the teacher now must act to supplement the machine. Curricular decisions regarding sequence and rate of speed within the series of televised lessons are often beyond the teacher's control. Thus, to some degree, teacher responsibility for curricular planning may be infringed upon. On the other hand, certain real advantages are found to accrue when television and film lessons are intelligently used. Teachers may be released from the necessity of making repeated, lengthy explanations of largely factual nature—the sort of instruction most easily presented via lecture—and they may be able to devote more time and effort to the subtle and demanding tasks of working in discussion situations with students and dealing individually with their problems and needs. In this way the energies of teachers are used in situations where the sensitivity, creativity, and skills of the professional teacher are most needed.

*Programmed instruction.* An enormous amount of energy has been expended in the development of instructional programs by commercial firms and school districts. These have most often taken the form of teaching machines, programmed textbooks, and computer-based arrangements. They tend to represent attempts to provide a teacher surrogate, at least for short periods of time. All depend upon a well-developed instructional program. The most popular of these is the linear approach in which the material is programmed in progressive, minute steps. Each person works at the program to which he is assigned. He may move at his own rate according to his ability and motivation. He progresses by tiny, logical steps which reduce the possibility of error. At each step in the sequence, the learner is rewarded immediately by knowledge of his success or discovers immediately his error. Where all students must move through the identical sequence in a linear program, the branching approach provides a variety of paths depending upon the student's responses. For example, if the student selects an incorrect or inadequate response he may be referred to a review of the material which seeks to reteach. He is then retested on the concept. Bright students are able to move rapidly through the program. Obviously, the branching technique is far more complicated to develop and to organize than the linear programs.

Programmed texts present the material and ask for a response before directing the pupil to turn to another page to find the answer. The teaching machine is often set up with a non-reversing tape which secures a response and then is moved on to reveal whether or not the response was correct. The computer-based teaching machine in its more advanced form includes a computer, a master console for the teacher or director, and a series of terminals for individual students. The individuals, independent of each other, interact with the computer in moving through the program. Material may be presented to the student by visual, audio, and typed means and the student communicates back to the computer through a standard typewriter keyboard, some special buttons, and possibly a "light-pen" to make responses on the television screen. Given an appropriate program, the computer has the capacity to tailor-make a program of instruction to fit each individual. Few schools at present have the money to utilize the computer-based machine although many districts have explored the use of teaching machines and programmed textbooks.

Obviously, certain learning material is more amenable to the sort of programming necessary for teaching machines. Content which is made up largely of specific facts and information is more likely to be successfully mechanized. In English, for example, the teaching of grammar, spelling, and vocabulary is more suited to this approach than literature and composition. Therefore, teaching machines are not viewed as substitutes for the teacher except in certain narrow content areas. Teachers are not likely, in the near future, to become obsolete and, like academic fossils, no longer needed in the learning process. Nevertheless, teachers must use the teaching machine to best advantage. Routine, repetitive, factual learning may be mechanized and the time and energies of the skilled teacher saved for more demanding instructional situations.

*Continuous progress units.* A number of junior and senior high schools have explored the use of specially prepared materials which individual pupils may use in learning. Each "learning activity packet," as they are sometimes called, is addressed to the student. It tells him the objectives of the unit, the rationale behind the plan, and presents a pre-test to help the pupil know his present status. It leads him into the learning activities via a carefully designed study guide. Some of the activities are required, some are optional, others are for enrichment, and some are for recycling certain pupils back through some of the important content. The plan includes evaluation instruments, the satisfactory completion of which signals the student to proceed to another section or to another packet. This device is aimed at allowing the student more control of his own learning and, at the same time, freeing the teacher to become more nearly a guide to learning. It is a modern development stemming from the early workbooks and clearly embodying the basic principles of the unit approach to teaching.

*Schedule modification.*    Many school principals have worked to make administrative provisions calculated to remove some of the obstacles to improved teaching. A relatively large number of schools have employed the modular schedule. Instead of the standard 45- or 50-minute period length, the school divides the school day into 15-, 20-, 25-, or 30-minute modules. Thus, the usual six-period day is now divided up into twelve to twenty-four periods or modules. This provides a good deal of potential flexibility, for theoretically a class may be assigned any combination of modules each day. Some subjects may be scheduled a larger or smaller number of modules per week than others. For example, "personal typing" may receive six 25-minute "mods" per week while English has sixteen modules. These are scheduled when possible according to the teachers' preferences. An art instructor may well prefer fewer class meetings per week if he can have the students for a longer session each time because of the time lost for setting up the art material at the beginning and the cleanup at the end. In most cases, once the new modular schedule is set it becomes as rigid as the conventional schedule.

A few schools have tried a genuinely flexible schedule. Individual teachers plan three days ahead what block of time, if any, they want scheduled with their different classes and what location (classroom, laboratory, resource center, etc.) they need. Conflicts are resolved and a master schedule is prepared which tells teachers and pupils when and where they are scheduled. This is done day by day with the teachers always planning three days ahead.

A few high school principals have developed what is called "college-type scheduling." This means that the administrator sets out to reduce the scheduled contact between students and teacher by forty to fifty per cent. Time which is now freed is used by students for independent study, conferences with teachers who are available in their offices at designated times, work on projects, reading in the library, and the like. In addition, a variety of other schedule alterations have been attempted; for example, rotating periods on different days, rotating days, rotating several special schedules, block scheduling each teaching team and its assigned students and allowing the team to determine the actual use of the

alloted time. All of these attempt to open up new patterns and opportunities for teachers to improve teaching and learning.

*Non-graded schools.* The conventional high school is organized into
grades; the student must complete seventh-grade English before moving
to eighth-grade English. The whole graded structure is set up and students are fitted into it. In reaction to the inherent restrictions, some
schools have developed various approaches to non-grading.

Ideally, a fully non-graded school would allow an individual to pursue any subject in which he was interested and could achieve without
concern for grade level or course sequence. In practice, a number of
secondary schools have replanned curriculum within departments, developing a variety of eight-week courses designed to be appealing and
appropriate for students of different talents. For example, the senior high
English program may be set up this way with a large list of possible
short courses. Each student may elect any course he wishes as long as
he is continuously enrolled in some English course. Possibilities may
range from "Greek Drama" to "Job Applications." Another approach
is to develop a cycle for required courses. Rather than planning U. S.
history, world history and contemporary problems, for example, for a
specific grade level, one of these is offered to all students each year.
Everyone in the high school would take the same course but would be
assigned to a level which is appropriate to his ability and achievement.
While none of these yet approaches the ideal, it seems certain that
further innovative effort will continue along these lines.

*Team teaching.* Another educational development has resulted from
attempts to explore staff patterns which would make more effective use
of the special competencies and skills of school personnel. This has
most often taken the form of teaching teams. It breaks with the traditional concept of assigning a single teacher to a series of classes each
of which contains thirty to thirty-five students. Instead, a team of
persons is assigned a large group of students. For example, a team, made
up of one highly experienced master teacher, one inexperienced teacher,
and one non-certificated teaching assistant or clerk might be given a
class of ninety to one hundred students. Team planning, use of special
abilities of members of the team, and instruction in a variety of settings
(large group, small group and individual) characterize the methodological approach. As you go out into teaching it is possible that you will
have the opportunity to participate in such a pattern.

The team approach allows an inexperienced teacher to work and
plan under the guidance of a master teacher instead of jumping directly

into complete charge of classes. It makes it possible for teachers to take
the lead in instructing in subject areas of their greatest strength. It allows
the use of non-certificated teacher aides to take over routine, non-teaching duties such as taking roll, passing out and collecting materials,
checking out textbooks or supplementary materials, maintaining order in
the halls, scoring objective tests, and the like. It provides an opportunity
for students in teacher training to get experience in the schools before
student teaching. At the same time, the team approach often is seriously
handicapped because of present school buildings and equipment. The
plan requires the administrator to look upon each of his departments as
a total resource and to employ teachers with complementary strengths
and competencies. It forces him to tackle the knotty problem of assigning
personnel who can work together successfully in the intimate, cooperative way required by team planning and teaching.

*Independent study.*    Increasing interest among teachers has developed
in relation to the possibilities of independent study. Such study tends to
be learning activity undertaken by an individual which reflects his
interests and aims and which involves the teacher mainly as a resource.
Independent study may be related to a course in which the student is
enrolled or it may be quite independent of an existing class or, in some
cases, a whole course may be taken as independent study.

In theory, all students should be given the opportunity for participation in independent study activities. However, the better, highly
motivated pupils are more likely to receive these advantages. Although
the conventional high school may make provisions for increased independent study, the modern secondary school with schedule modifications which open up blocks of time, with team teaching arrangements
and with appropriate facilities, such as resource centers, instructional
materials centers, and study spaces, obviously is better suited for full
implementation of the independent study concept.

*Simulation or gaming.*    A variety of devices are being developed
through which the students may be placed in a simulated situation in
which they act out decision-making roles. These range from the driving
simulator, in which the pupils practice meeting traffic problems before
getting into the actual automobile, to rather complicated strategic games
which call upon students to play the parts of key groups involved in
social or world siuations. For example, one of the latter now available
sets up a simplified world situation of nations and international organizations and provides the participants with the experience of decision
making in the complex international world of today. Early experience

with simulation devices points to high-level student interest and unique opportunities for teaching certain outcomes. However, the expense and the time required are limiting factors.

*Performance contracting.*   Following early experiences in Texarkana,[12] the concept of guaranteed achievement or performance contracting has spread to a number of school districts. Under this system certain teachers in the district or an outside commercial agency agree to produce specified learning results. Payment is geared to actual pupil achievement. Early efforts were focussed on students considered to be potential dropouts who were lagging in achievement in basic skill areas. Special materials, individualized and often programmed, and extrinsic rewards, such as portable television sets, transistor radios and special privileges, were used. Teachers or Rapid Learning Center managers received bonuses if their students achieved exceptional growth. Great interest has been displayed in this development by school board members across the nation and future emphasis upon the principle of accountability seems assured.

## The Teacher As Guide

The modern teacher tends to approach his decision regarding method with a somewhat different orientation from that of the traditional teacher. The lack of a single, unified, comprehensive theory of learning which is agreed upon by the majority of educational psychologists and the element of change present in such experimentation as is being done with teaching devices and staff patterns make him more open-minded toward new developments and possible future changes in secondary education. He tends to be firmly eclectic, picking and choosing among possible approaches according to the goals of instruction, rather than seeking a single, rigid conception of method which would be *the method* for all to use.

The high school teacher accepts the realities of mass education and the changed nature of the secondary school as an upward extension of the common school. He recognizes that the multiple objectives of such a school go beyond the mere transmission of knowledge. The instructor has come to realize that the real content of education is human experience, and he must prepare himself to deal helpfully and constructively with the experiences of his students.

---

[12] Stanley Elam, "The Age of Accountability Dawns in Texarkana," *Phi Delta Kappan,* 51:509–514, June 1970.

The fundamental relationship between teacher and pupil is realized as each assumes his position in the school situation. The student himself must learn; therefore, his needs, interests, problems, and questions are of focal importance. The teacher organizes the environment, sets in motion certain processes, provides appropriate resources, and generally facilitates desirable pupil learning. The teacher is the mature, professionally trained participant in the teaching-learning process. As a participant and as the adult present in the classroom, he does not leave learning to chance or to the whims of the learner. Inevitably, the modern teacher comes to recognize his right and proper function as that of a guide to learning. Through his knowledge, training, and skill he seeks to guide youth toward the learning objectives of the school.

## REVIEW

The classroom teacher is one of the two elemental parts of the teaching-learning process. The other, of course, is the student. Because of his maturity, training, and position, the instructor must accept certain basic responsibilities in dealing with his pupils. He must make important decisions in regard to how he will work with boys and girls in the classroom. After reading this chapter and pondering about method, you ought now to be able to answer the following questions.

1. Among a number of recognized methods of teaching, which seem to be less subject to fallacious assumptions than others?

2. What are basic conditions of teaching and learning which a desirable method must provide?

# Selected References

Anderson, R. H. *Teaching in a World of Change*. New York: Harcourt, Brace and World, Inc., 1966.

Beggs, D. W., III and Buffie, E. G., eds. *Independent Study*. Bloomington, Indiana: Indiana University Press, 1965.

————, *Nongraded Schools in Action*. Bloomington, Indiana: Indiana University Press, 1967.

————, ed. *Team Teaching—Bold New Venture*. Bloomington, Indiana: Indiana University Press, 1965.

Douglas, L. M. *The Secondary Teacher at Work.* Boston: D.C. Heath and Company, 1967; Ch. 12 "Methods of Teaching."

Fallon, B., ed. *Educational Innovation in the United States.* Bloomington, Indiana: Phi Delta Kappa, 1966.

Gage, N. L., ed. Handbook of Research on Teaching. Chicago: Rand McNally & Company, 1963.

Hamm, R. L. "Methods of Teaching and Learning in the Junior High School." *NASSP Bulletin,* 47:59–66, October 1963.

Hoover, K. H. *Learning and Teaching in the Secondary School.* 2nd ed. Boston: Allyn and Bacon, Inc., 1968: Unit 2 "Effective Group Methods" and Unit 3 "Some Emergent Instructional Patterns."

"How High Schools Innovate." *Nation's Schools,* 79 (most of issue), April 1967.

*Life Skills in School and Society, 1969 Yearbook.* Washington, D.C.: Association for Supervision and Curriculum Development, N.E.A., 1969.

Lumsdaine, A. A. and Glaser, R., eds. *Teaching Machines and Programmed Learning.* Washington, D.C.: Department of Audio-Visual Instruction, N.E.A., 1960.

Risk, T. M. *Principles and Practices of Teaching in Secondary Schools.* 4th ed. New York: American Book Co., 1968; Ch. 15 "Teaching Creative Problem Solving."

Shumsky, A. *In Search of Teaching Style.* New York: Appleton-Century-Crofts, 1968.

Swenson, G. and Keys, D. *Providing for Flexibility in Scheduling and Instruction.* Englewood Cliffs, N.J.: Prentice-Hall, Inc., 1966.

Trump, J. L. and Miller, D. F. *Secondary School Curriculum Improvement.* Boston: Allyn and Bacon, Inc., 1968; Ch. 18–24.

Unruh, G. G. and Alexander, W. M. *Innovations in Secondary Education.* New York: Holt, Rinehart and Winston, Inc., 1970.

Walton, J. *Toward Better Teaching in the Secondary Schools.* Boston: Allyn and Bacon, Inc., 1966; Ch. 4 "The Methodology of Teaching," Ch. 6 and Ch. 7 "Methods of Teaching."

# five

# Planning
# Classroom Experiences

The continuous and vital job of planning for teaching places heavy demands upon the classroom teacher. Many dimensions of the teacher's background, training, and experience are called into play during this process. Significant knowledge and perspective of the subject to be taught, perceptive understanding of high school youngsters in general and of the teacher's own students in particular, some sort of satisfying decision regarding instructional method, and a set of developing skills in organizing and evaluating teaching-learning activity are required.

Teachers seek to provide situations in the classroom wherein optimum learning will occur. Appropriate materials and processes must be used to produce desired learning experiences. As you read about and consider this vital task you will observe that this chapter is oriented around the following aspects of planning.

1. Teachers must engage in long-range planning. In order to develop and maintain perspective, this planning must be concerned with the overall conception of the course. The teacher is most likely to need skills in developing resource and teaching units which provide content organization within the course.

2. Short-range planning must be flexible and adaptive, and must focus on the day-by-day teaching-learning activities in the classroom.

3. As the lesson or unit develops, the learner should be given opportunities to contribute significantly to its planning. Beginning teachers need to recognize the ways in which students and teacher may plan together to enrich the possibilities for achieving learning objectives.

## A TEACHER PLANS FOR TEACHING

Planning is, as the word implies, something which is done largely in advance. Successful lessons are usually pre-planned. In addition to this need to pre-plan or pre-think, to organize lessons in advance, teachers sometimes find it necessary to revise, augment, and supplement plans, and to build new ones as the teaching progresses. As an example, read the following description, noting any implications for planning which it may contain.

*Description*

    A young English teacher was winding up a drill session on English grammar. The class had been working on practice exercises which had to do with the recognition and use of the predicate nominative. Suddenly one of the students raised his hand.

    "Miss King," he asked, "why do we have to study this old stuff?" The response of the whole ninth-grade class attested to the general concern.

    After a moment the teacher replied, "Tommy, that is a perfectly legitimate question. I see that the majority of the students is also interested in it. Let's try to find an answer. What do you think we would have to do to answer the question and eliminate Tommy's concern? Would you like to devote some class time to this?"

    The students responded enthusiastically to the suggestion. Then the teacher said, "All right, let's think of what this question involves and of what we will have to do to answer it. Jot down your ideas on scratch paper."

    As Miss King waited for her pupils to think about the task at hand, she looked into the file drawer of her desk. In a few moments she removed a folder marked "Selling English, A Resource Unit for High School Students." She leafed through it while the students quietly worked.

    "All right, boys and girls," she said later, "what do you think we will have to find out to answer the question, 'What good is English?' "

    Then she began to write the student suggestions on the board. A partial listing read as follows:

Find out why four years of English are required in high school.
Find out how useful English is in college.
Find out what employers think of the importance of good English in getting a job.
Find out how important good English is in becoming a success in various occupations.
Find out what teachers of other subjects think about the value of good English skills in getting good grades.

Survey opinions of adults regarding the value of different parts of the English program.

A few minutes before the bell rang Miss King stopped the student contributions in order to make this assignment: "For the next twenty-three hours I want all of you to keep a communications diary. Divide a sheet of paper into four columns, one for each of the four communication skills—reading, writing, speaking, and listening. Each person is to tabulate as accurately as possible the amount of time spent in his daily life doing each of these. For example, if you spend fifteen minutes walking home with some friends, estimate how much of this time you listened to them talk and how much you talked. If you listened approximately ten minutes and talked about five minutes out of the fifteen, then write 'conversation—ten minutes' under the column titled 'Listening'; write 'conversation—five minutes' under the Speaking column. Do the same sort of thing for listening to the radio, reading the sports page, writing your homework assignments, and talking on the telephone. In this way we will be able to get a picture of the communication demands placed on the average high school student for at least the next twenty-three hours. Is this clear? Are there any questions?"

Thus a new unit of work began for Miss King's ninth-grade English class. Subsequent activities included construction and administration of a questionnaire to all non-English teachers in the high school. The questionnaire was designed to obtain teacher judgments regarding the value of English skills in relation to success in other courses. In another activity, students divided the world of work into various levels: unskilled, semi-skilled, skilled, and professional. Smaller groups each selected a particular category, interviewed workers within the category as to their opinions of the worth of studying English, and reported the findings to the class. Another group wrote letters to college officials for their statements in regard to the value of good English habits as related to college success. Other research was gathered to discover whether such English skills as diagramming sentences and identifying parts of speech were remembered in adult life. For this experiment, an examination modeled after certain exercises in the textbook was written. It was then duplicated and administered to a sizeable group of adults in filling stations, drug stores, cleaners, supermarkets, and any other place where an adult would consent to the test. After completing the test, each adult was asked for an opinion of his past training in English. Then all of these data were summarized and analyzed in class. Finally, the personnel manager of a nearby plant was invited to speak to the class about those English skills he looked for in interviewing young people for a job.

After this, the teacher and students re-examined their original question, along with a list of sub-questions, and went on to use the information gathered to come to logical, defensible answers.

*Implications*

This partial description of an actual teaching situation in a West Coast high school contains several interesting implications.

1. It is clear that Miss King seized upon obvious student interest to initiate a unit of study. Tommy's question by itself probably would not have been enough to start such a study. But the teacher observed that class feeling concurred with Tommy's concern; therefore, she decided to proceed in a direction which was obviously not the intended one.

2. The teacher possessed a definite plan. She had a prepared plan close at hand for organizing the teaching-learning activity. She knew where she was going. This was not an attempt to "play it by ear."

3. The teacher and pupils, once committed to solving the question, planned the learning activities together. The teacher allowed her students freedom to contribute to the organization and direction of these activities.

4. The overall question was real and immediate to the students. By encouraging student suggestions, the teacher helped to insure that the sub-questions would also be real and pertinent to the lives of the pupils.

5. Specific processes of problem-solving were utilized. Although it is not directly stated in the above description, Miss King guided the class through at least the basic steps of problem-solving. She and the class started out with a problem that was identified as being of significant and personal concern to all. Jointly, they explored the problem, divided it into sub-questions, formulated hypotheses, set out to secure data, and then sought to use that data to come to logical, defensible answers.

6. A variety of resources and research activities were utilized to answer the questions. Of course the overall problem lent itself well to such methods of solution, yet a less imaginative teacher or a teacher who had no definite plan available might have attempted to answer Tommy's question by herself and then have moved on to something else. In this case, however, exploration of the basic question resulted in sub-questions, each of which suggested pertinent sources of data.

7. Students formed groups to do research, secure data, and report to the class. Presumably, student preference had some part to play in the grouping; that is, students were encouraged to indicate which of the sub-questions they would prefer to explore.

8. Miss King was receptive and democratic in her treatment of the students. She accepted the original question as a "legitimate" one. In fact, probably the most important single symptom that a healthy teacher-student relationship existed lies in the fact that a student had sufficient confidence in his teacher to ask what might be considered a ludicrous question. Nor was Miss King threatened by the question. She possessed enough confidence, both in the worth of her subject and in the ability of her students to make logical decisions, to allow the students virtually to motivate themselves to new effort, and thus, to new learning.

9. The teacher made sure that the aims and outcomes of the unit were consistent with the desired aims and outcomes of the course. Many important language skills were utilized and developed in solving the problem. Moreover, the real and personal nature of the problem placed these language skills in a desirable relationship to the student's own objectives. Pupils were careful in constructing the questionnaire, to use language that would insure against "loaded" questions. They studied and practiced interviewing skills in order to achieve worthwhile results. They carefully proofread the letters to college officials, and they spent much time in developing their test for adults. Miss King realized also that if the answers to the questions were secured by the students themselves, student attitude and effort in English would be much more favorably affected than if the answers were supplied by her.

The description, and some of its obvious implications, then, point up many of the advantages of planning, both before and during the learning activity. This teacher made use of the real and obvious concern of her students, to move into a new learning activity. The unit had been planned in advance, yet the students were encouraged to contribute to the planning activity. The learning had direction, orientation, and focus because of the problem-solving, question-answering nature of the activities involved. Because of wise planning, the entire activity possessed unity—a real beginning and a satisfying conclusion.

## LONG-RANGE PLANNING

Many kinds of long-range plans are likely to be made by school personnel. Sometimes statewide groups of teachers are formed to develop state curriculum guides. Often committees of teachers within a school system work together to write system-wide curriculum outlines. Individual schools build courses of study which indicate the scope and suggested sequence of various courses in general terms. All of these plans usually involve a number of teachers and so are normally beyond the control of any one teacher.

The classroom teacher, however, is responsible for the actual planning of course content. He works within the generally understood meaning of the course title. Often, a previously outlined course of study provides suggested limits and some guidance for this planning. The teacher also observes or asks what other teachers do in this regard. The administrator, supervisors, and department head may offer him some assistance and suggestions. However, within these loosely defined limits each teacher must find his own ways of organizing learning experiences. This is often a lonely job because he himself must combine materials, method, students, and teacher into a productive learning process. The individual teacher must formulate his own plans and then assess the worth of these plans.

Experienced teachers recognize that much of the really important work is done *before* a lesson is initiated. The instructor plans tentatively what he will do and what he hopes will result. He prepares his students so that they are ready to engage in the learning. This often means stimulating interest, reactivating recall of pertinent experiences, assigning preliminary research or background study, and other such preparatory activity. The things which are done prior to a lesson are crucial in determining the success of the lesson.

Beginning teachers find that careful planning is indispensable to self-confidence and satisfaction in teaching. Of course, some experienced teachers have taught the same subject for many years and may not feel any further need for written plans. Nevertheless, principals, supervisors, and consultants almost unanimously agree that planning is not only desirable but necessary for the beginning teacher.

Long-range planning involves the crucial problem of perspective. Many beginning teachers have taken a great number of courses in their general teaching area yet have never developed real perspective of the subject. Teachers must be able to see the organized body of knowledge with which they deal in the large view. So many seem to be preoccupied with minute, specific details that they neglect some of the really important and more permanent aspects. For example, as you think over the courses you expect to teach, what do you consider the vitally important concepts which boys and girls ought to learn in your classroom? Long-range planning will require that you take these into consideration.

As teachers seek practicable and satisfying plans for the school year, they tend to look for clusters of subject matter which possess some unity. They think through the overall content seeking to identify certain themes, ideas, concepts, or generalizations which are important to focus upon. A great many teachers have come to accept some variation of the unit approach. That is, they divide the semester's work into separate units rather than maintaining one long, uninterrupted series of lessons. They have accepted the unit concept of long-range planning.

*The Unit Concept*

The unit plan is the basic means by which the classroom teacher replaces either a blind acceptance of the textbook as the basis for curricular organization or a day-to-day planning largely based on expediency with a series of more meaningful, internally unified learning experiences. The total content of the course is divided into a number of comprehensible wholes instead of being taught as one mass which is parceled out in tiny, separate, unrelated bits, and which is too large and comprehensive to be understood by the students.

   The unit concept obviously possesses advantages which have led to its acceptance. Studies of retention and forgetting have shown that information learned in relation to some broad unifying principle tends to be retained far better than the same information learned separately. Learning is enhanced because the material simply is more meaningful. Units help the teacher focus attention on the desired outcomes of the learning activity rather than upon the subject matter alone. The long-range goals of instruction provide orientation and direction for the planning. The students' interests and readiness for learning are likely to be more seriously considered.

   One problem which often puzzles beginning teachers has to do with the scope of the course. Our present storehouse of knowledge has reached such a magnitude that most courses in high school can but sample the individual learning areas. Consider biology, for example. What would be a wise choice of experiences to provide in this sample— for it is quite obvious that the whole field cannot be covered? Likewise, the world history teacher can select at best only a minute fraction of the total sweep of the world's known history. So it is in most subject areas. The unit concept helps to solve this problem by seeking out the most important ideas in an area and using these as organizing centers for the planning of units.

   Teachers and students both report that learning activity is more satisfying when the year's work is divided into meaningful segments, each of which has a beginning and an end. It is more desirable to plan units of work which are structured according to desired student outcomes and which contain carefully considered ways of introducing new work with enthusiasm and orientation and then to bring each of these units to a satisfying close, than to present the entire course as a sequence of lessons which stretches on and on, seemingly without end, until the final examination comes along to bring some sort of closure. The unit concept of planning is consistent with learning principles and has been validated through many years of classroom use. Teachers plan both teaching units and resource units.

### Resource Unit

A resource unit, as the term implies, is designed to be a resource to the teacher. It is simply a collation of ideas and suggestions which may be useful in planning the actual teaching. As a unit it has cohesiveness in that the suggestions and resources are organized around a central theme, a broad idea, an important problem, or a significant generalization. Thus, the resource unit is a unified collection of ideas which serves as a reservoir for the teacher to use in constructing the instructional plans for a particular class.

A well-made resource unit may be expected to provide (1) an organizing center which may be useful for curriculum planning within a particular course, (2) a suggested list of possible learning purposes, (3) a wide variety of possible instructional activities which are likely to contribute to one or more of these purposes and which are consistent with the unit theme, (4) a list of useful resources of varying difficulty and interest levels, (5) a number of suggestions for evaluating the learning, and (6) some references which may be helpful to the teacher who would like to explore the area further.

Teachers often work together in planning and drawing up resource units, for several experienced people working together may be expected to contribute a wider range of valuable suggestions. However, hundreds of excellent units have been constructed by individual teachers. Many school systems have established central-office, resource-unit libraries for the use of teachers in the system. Some high schools have an instructional resource file which contains a valuable collection of units.

Resource units are found to be organized according to (a) the logic of the learner and (b) the logic of the subject matter. Both kinds of units are useful. Some teachers find themselves typically oriented one way or the other and so tend to use a preponderance of one kind of unit. A series of units on literary types (i.e., The Short Story, Poetry, The Essay, The Novel) would be structured according to the logic of the subject. Units titled Democracy in the School, Courage, Family Relations, Selling English are likely to be structured according to the logic of the learner.

*Parts of the resource unit.* Although units found in different school systems display some divergence in form, certain basic elements are always present. The resource unit ought to include the following parts.

1. Title
2. Overview
3. Content Outline
4. Objectives
5. Learning Activities
   a. Introductory Activities
   b. Sustaining Activities
   c. Culminating Activities
6. Evaluation
7. Bibliography

The title of the unit, of course, should be descriptive of the organizing center which provides unity and focus to the learning. It should state in plain terms the idea, concept, or theme around which the activities and materials are organized.

The overview is an introductory statement to the unit and its possible uses. As such, the overview should explain the philosophy behind the unit, its justification, and how it fits into the school's program. The overview should also briefly state why the unit was prepared, show how and where it might be used, and give further information about what it includes.

The content outline is simply a listing of the subject matter to be dealt with in the unit. It may take the form of an enumeration of topics and subtopics, questions to be answered, projects to be completed, or issues to be discussed.

The statement of objectives[1] is vital to the success of the unit. The ultimate justification of the classroom activity depends upon the worth of the objectives of instruction. The activities are selected because they promise to contribute to the objectives, and the evaluative procedures must assess student progress toward the objectives. Therefore, the list of objectives performs a pivotal role in the construction of the resource unit. In this section the teacher indicates the learning which he expects the unit to promote. The desired outcomes are best stated in behavioral components—how the students will behave as a result of the learning. For example, as a result of the unit students may be expected to secure certain information, display important insights, remember vital concepts, develop pertinent interests, modify or attain certain attitudes, fix appropriate skills, and arrive at other important learning. These statements of desired behavior changes make up the list of objectives.

The body of the unit contains a great many suggestions in regard to possible learning activities and the materials which would be appropriate

---

[1] See Chapter 7 for a more detailed discussion of objectives and their evaluation.

to them. This section is usually divided into three parts. The first part is devoted to a description of activities which are calculated to introduce the unit to the class. These activities should move the students into the actual unit of work with substantial interest, enthusiasm, and involvement. The second part includes a description of instructional procedures and materials which will achieve the educational objectives of the unit. Normally, a variety of activities is suggested so that classes with varying levels of ability may be accommodated.These sustaining activities embody the major work of the unit. The third part is made up of suggested ways for winding up the work. These activities are devised to summarize, draw together, and integrate the unit, and to provide perspective of the learning experiences. This part often will suggest possible transitional steps to the next unit. In every case, this large and indispensable section on learning activities includes more suggestions than any teacher is able to use with one specific class; thus, the teacher may pick and choose among the activities which are best suited for the particular student group for which he is planning.

Evaluative procedures are suggested which will appraise student progress toward the objectives of the unit and which can assess the degree of success of the unit in itself. The major task of the instructor obviously is to secure evidence which will help him to decide whether the activities used accomplished the instructional goals. Every anticipated objective must be evaluated in some way. Examinations constructed by the teacher, standardized tests, student self-evaluation, teacher observation, group discussion, and individual conferences are a few of the many evaluative procedures which may be useful in this task.

*Writing a Resource Unit.* The structure and organization of a resource unit may be illustrated through the process of preparing one. Three junior high school teachers set out to plan a skeleton unit, at least, which would deal with improving study habits. The unit was to focus on an area of concern of a large number of students and would have potential use in a wide variety of instructional situations.

1. The teachers took up the problem of the *title* first. This could very well have been postponed until later, but "How to Study" received tentative agreement as something simple and descriptive.

2. The *overview* statement resulted from a pooling of ideas. It started out as follows:

*Overview.* All students must face the problem of developing effective study habits and skills. Many students achieve less than their potential because they simply don't know how to study. Of course, each individual must develop his own unique pattern of study habits. However, there are some general principles which can be helpful to all.

This unit assumes that the participants are interested in improving their academic performance. It should prove especially useful to entering junior high school students. . . .

3. The *content outline* in this case was simply a listing of the major topics or areas to be included in the unit plan.

*Content Outline.* This unit will deal with the following major topics:

    a. Attitude toward studying
    b. Effective use of study time
    c. Study conditions
    d. Note taking
    e. Textbook usage
    f. Examinations

4. The *objectives* of the unit as conceived by each of the teachers were thrown into a pool and first examined for form, duplication, and overlap. Then a list was developed which represented the instructional aims that the whole group found acceptable. It was recognized that, somewhere in the suggested learning activities, something would be done consciously and deliberately to promote each of the objectives (of course, some activities might contribute to more than one at the same time), and that each objective would be evaluated in some way. This section began as follows:

*Objectives.* As a result of this unit the students will:

    a. Be able to make out a time budget to fit their own needs.
    b. Be able to outline textbook content in relation to important ideas.
    c. Display mature attitudes toward study activities.
    d. Be able to take lecture and discussion notes which will be comprehensive and helpful when they are "cold."
    e. Be able to improve their home study conditions and explain how and why this was accomplished. . . .

5. The *introductory activities* were planned to stimulate student interest or, at least, to capitalize upon present student interests and concerns and lead into the work of the unit. Two of these were the following:

*Introductory Activities.*

    a. The class may be organized to survey high school students in relation to their attitudes toward studying and the actual study procedures which they utilize. Interview techniques should be studied and questions carefully developed so that the results will be meaningful. This activity should reveal student concerns and spotlight actual practices which some students feel are especially valuable to them.

b. Each individual might make a study of his own use of time. Everyone has 168 hours a week. Some of this time is taken up by "must" activities (e.g., classes, eating, bathing, sleeping, dressing, church, going to and from school, and the like). However, a rather substantial amount is open to individual decision. Each student may keep a personal diary of how a certain 24-hour or 48-hour time span is used. Individual summaries utilizing various categories and total class summaries will lead to meaningful discussion.

6. *Sustaining activities* were planned to contribute to the stated objectives. The following represents a very small sampling of the wide variety of possible activities included.

*Sustaining Activities.*

a. Getting started is often a problem. Some persons have pre-study rituals which may serve in a few cases to prepare the individual for work but in most cases actually serve to postpone the unpleasant task. For example, sharpening all the pencils, laying out an ample supply of paper and erasers, preparing a snack, putting the hair up in rollers, etc., are likely to fall into the latter category. Each student may examine and evaluate his own pre-study rituals. The results may be reported in a brief paper.

b. Study conditions are considered to be important. Small groups of students might evaluate each other's study habits. Each group might personally observe, write up a case study, make recommendations, and present a report to the class dealing with a student who volunteers. Analysis of a number of case studies and discussion based on this personal observation might lead to a set of guidelines for improving study conditions.

c. Each person should develop a time budget which fits his own needs, test it out, and make appropriate revisions. A standard form should be discussed in class and each individual should prepare his own budget for the following week in consultation with the teacher. This will be tried out and, the subsequent Monday, discussed in class. Revisions and modifications will follow.

7. *Culminating activities* were carefully selected by the small planning group of teachers to provide closure to the unit. One of these was as follows:

*Culminating Activities.*

a. The class may prepare a guidebook "Suggestions to Incoming Junior High School Students." Student committees may take different topics from the content outline and summarize the material learned into a set of suggestions which they feel would be helpful to new junior high students. The results might be developed into a guidebook to be passed out at the orientation meetings with new students.

8. The *evaluation* section was developed in order to appraise student progress toward the objectives. To accomplish this a variety of evaluative techniques was suggested. One section included ideas for evaluating the unit itself. A few of these were:

*Evaluation of the Learning.* The stated objectives provide the bases of the evaluation of learning outcomes. Clues to changed behavior may be secured through the following procedures.

a. The time budgets for each student will be examined. Personal consultation with individuals will be revealing.
b. Observation of student comments and behavior in class discussions. Changed perspective, increased insight into the problems and attitude changes, are often revealed by the things students say and do in class.
c. Performance tests consisting of the class and teacher taking notes to a taped lecture will reveal growth in this skill.

*Evaluation of the Unit.*

a. The reactions of the students to the unit itself may be secured through a brief questionnaire or a simple open-ended evaluation sheet which asks: (1) What did you like most? (2) What did you like least about this unit? and (3) What are your suggestions?
b. A final discussion of the unit may be held.
c. The degree to which the unit objectives have been achieved is a partial evaluation of the worth of the planning.

The bibliography is not included, but this section normally presents suggested materials for students and interested teachers.

This incomplete plan for a unit is not necessarily an exemplary unit, but is included because it rather clearly illustrates the essential components of a unit.

*Using the resource unit.*    Teachers look to the resource unit for ideas and assistance in planning their teaching. This unit is a resource for it contains more suggestions than any teacher could use with any specific class. As the sample unit illustrates, there are serveral ways of introducing the unit suggested. The teacher looks over these and picks the one activity which seems most likely to open the unit well. Similar choice is made among the many sustaining activities and possible culminative activities. The teacher properly uses the resource unit as a reservoir from which to draw ideas for use in building a teaching unit.

The resource unit is written as a body of suggestions which may be adapted to a variety of classes. However, the teacher reads the resource unit with a particular class in mind and must plan specifically for this group. Only the teacher knows his own group well and can select and modify appropriate learning experiences for this class. Therefore, the teacher prizes the flexibility inherent in the resource unit.

Student participation is utilized in refining the learning procedures. The teacher, wherever appropriate, incorporates suggestions and reactions of his pupils into planning. Thus, the resource unit must be used not as a blueprint for teaching, but simply as a useful storehouse of suggestions for planning.

## Teaching Unit

A unit of work planned specifically for a particular class is a teaching unit. When a teacher selects the objectives he wishes to accomplish, the learning activities he plans to use, and the evaluative procedures which promise to assess student progress toward the objectives, he has the basic ingredients of his teaching unit.

In making up the teaching unit the teacher is concerned with the same elements that are found in the resource unit; namely, (1) title, (2) overview, (3) learning activities, (4) evaluation, and (5) bibliography. However, in every case the contents are chosen for their suitability for a particular group of students. Obviously, a very bright group of pupils would often require substantially different materials of instruction and learning procedures from those of a slow class. Schools which draw students from greatly different socio-economic backgrounds might profitably use different planning.

Basically, the teaching unit attempts to organize processes and materials of learning into larger, unified patterns in place of the piecemeal, atomistic learning of unrelated facts and skills. Newer textbooks are sometimes divided into "units." Yet too often these "units" are simply convenient places to divide up the subject matter rather than being real units of work. A section in the text, a major battle, a certain author, an irregular verb, or a newly discovered planet may not be a unit. Unless all the learning activities are related in some meaningful way to a central idea, principle, theme, or problem, the plan really has no unity and cohesiveness.

This pinpoints one of the most subtle and difficult problems which the teacher comes up against. How long should a unit be? How many activities and how much material should be included? How large a block of subject matter? What should the scope of the unit be? This requires perspective of the subject. It involves sensing, recognizing, a unit of material. As you analyze your course, certain blocks of content will begin to stand out. You will find important themes, ideas, problems, or generalizations which appear suitable for use as organizing centers for teaching and learning. As you teach, certain activities tend to be naturally related and groups of these may tend to display unity and pattern. Students often perceive units of work. Boys and girls sometimes react to content differently from the teacher. Their perceptions of unity and wholeness do offer clues to planning. Thus, you may use two approaches to discover units. First, you may logically analyze the subject, search for major principles, concepts, and generalizations as possible unit bases. Second, by being alert as you teach, you may empirically come to recognize possible units of work. Of course, you should study every pertinent resource unit, course of study, course outline, and curriculum guide that you can get your hands on for further assistance in your long-range planning.

Actually, there is a definite and important relationship which exists among various levels of teacher planning. The resource unit is broader, more inclusive than the teaching unit. The suggestions which the resource unit contains are drawn in the construction of the teaching unit which is prepared for use with a particular class. The teaching unit forms the basis for the specific, daily lesson plan.

## SHORT-RANGE PLANNING

Certainly teachers must engage in long-range planning, for in this way the learning is likely to have direction, orientation, and focus. Long-range plans provide for continuity in the work of the course. However, the day-to-day, short-range planning is fundamental to teacher success. It is the guide to daily operation.

### The Daily Lesson Plan

Every teacher must decide what the class will do on the first, second, third, etc., day of school. He must plan specifically which learning experiences he wants to set up, which materials he will use, the goals of his instruction, and how he will fit these into the realities of the rigid time limits of the daily period, of the nature of the students in his class, of the competing interests in the life of the school and the press of daily routine.

The daily lesson plan is essential to the self-confidence of the beginning teacher. The degree of detail depends upon the need of the person teaching. This is an individual thing; some beginning teachers can do a good job of teaching with a bare outline of the lesson before them. Others feel the need for a careful, detailed, specific description of exactly what is to be done. Actually, a tremendous amount of assurance is derived from knowing exactly what you are going to do each period.

The form of the daily lesson plan should be very simple. The elements listed below would seem to be essential.

1. The goals of the lesson. The teacher sets down very simply and plainly what he is trying to accomplish in this lesson. It would seem reasonable to expect teachers to know what they are trying to do. A long and involved list of objectives is not desirable. Instead, the teacher seeks to indicate the really important, essential goals of instruction for this lesson. These are important for they provide justification and the bases for evaluation of the lesson itself.

2. Learning activities. Here the instructor puts down for himself what he plans to do today in this particular class. He tells himself to have his students read certain materials, write a certain paper, discuss suggested topics, listen to a tape recording, and the like. This section includes step-by-step descriptions of things he has planned to do. It not only provides insurance against forgetting, but it helps the beginning teacher think through his planning. It avoids the expedient, off-the-top-of-the-head teaching which is justifiably and roundly criticized.

The activities here are calculated to accomplish the goals of the lesson. They include detailed information on page numbers, materials to be passed out, papers to be collected, announcements to be made and assignments to be given. Key facts, concepts, questions to be used as discussion stimulators, and other important content items may also be found here.

The beginning teacher is urged to overplan. That is, he should put down more activities than he feels capable of doing in a single period. This will give him a feeling of security for he will never be caught with his lesson plan used up and ten or fifteen minutes left in the period. Few beginning teachers are prepared to ad-lib constructively. Many experienced teachers prepare a file of alternative activities to take up the slack, just in case the planned activities do not go well.

3. The group. In this part of the lesson plan the instructor lists reminders to himself about individuals or groups in the class that are important to the lesson's success. He might remind himself to start the discussion with Terry who just came back from a trip to Europe. He might want to be sure that the person who gave the report last time makes a summary which will act as a starting point for today's lesson. It might be important to place Tommy and Fred on different committees. These sorts of comments can contribute to the success of the lesson.

4. Special materials. Normally the materials used in the lesson will be included in the description and explanation of the learning activities. However, when special materials or equipment are necessary to the lesson, it is helpful to note these in a special section of the lesson plan. Special supplementary readers, thirty-five copies of the *Atlantic Monthly,* tape recorder, slide projector and screen, colored chalk, lectern, extra chairs and table are examples of such special materials and equipment.

5. Time estimate. The quickest way for a beginning teacher to begin to build an instructional time sense is for him to make daily estimates of the amount of time which will be needed for various parts of the lesson. Of course, he must be flexible; often he will be unable to stay even reasonably close to his schedule. However, the problems of building a time sense and insuring better timing during the lesson sequence suggest that this element in the lesson plan is quite important. Your time estimate might look something like the following:

8:30-8:35  Take roll.
8:35-8:40  Read announcements; collect parent questionnaires due today.
8:40-8:55  Pass out assignment sheets for in-class theme. Discuss the assignment. Answer questions. Review the use of *to, two* and *too* which they are to pay special attention to in this written work.
8:55-9:25  Students work on themes at their seats. Teacher moves about the room to supervise the writing. (Check to see that Rex is using quotation marks correctly.)
9:25-9:30  Collect the papers. (Ask Sandra to stop by the room after school to talk about the class newspaper.) Remind the class that the unit examination will be given Friday.

6. Comments. At the bottom of each daily lesson plan you should leave a blank space for your comments. Following the lesson you may want to use this space to write your comments as to how the lesson seemed to go, why you think it went well or poorly, what the students' reactions were, and your feeling about the various activities and ma-

terials. You should ponder the question: How might I do it better next time?

This part is your assessment of the lesson and some comments as to its possible improvement. Actually a teacher who employs this self-evaluation regularly is laying a sound foundation for continued self-improvement.

Of course, the construction of sound daily lesson plans tends to involve a substantial amount of time and effort at first. However, as soon as you discover the amount of detail necessary to your self-confidence, the plans are likely to take far less time in preparation. Nevertheless, the pre-thinking through of the lessons, the planning for teaching, is an essential and ever-present task. It is something which cannot be done as the class progresses, during a five-minute break between classes, or even during a half-hour lunch period. Planning is something which cannot be left to chance. It must be done carefully and thoughtfully.

Lesson plans are always considered tentative and subject to change. They are outlines to guide daily action. Thus, even if a teacher has planned ahead for a week, he should feel free to continue what seems an especially productive class discussion for one more day or to cut short an activity which is obviously not likely to accomplish its purposes. He may even substitute one activity for another or stop to drill at a point of error before going back to the planned work of the lesson. The skilled teacher is sensitive to the students and their reactions to the learning activities, and, using this feedback, makes adjustments in the plans. The teacher must be flexible in his use of the daily lesson plan.

With experience, most teachers try to seek ways to launch each lesson with interest and impetus to learning and to close each period satisfactorily. Students appreciate leaving the room knowing that the work of the day has been summarized, that they have really learned something, and that a transition has been made to the next lesson, rather than having the desperate shout of "Read pages 395 to 451 in your text and answer the questions!" ringing in their ears as they debouch from the room.

## Assignments

The assignment is always a part of the daily lesson plan, yet it is such an important form of short-range planning that it deserves special attention.

Direction and set for learning is provided by the assignment. Transition from one lesson to another may be facilitated. Student attitude toward learning obviously is affected. Thus, the assignment itself and the way in which it is made need careful thought.

Teachers ought to consider the following principles in making assignments.

1. The assignment is part of teaching, not external to or introductory to learning. The careful formulation of assignments is an indispensable part of planning and the evaluation of the assignment rests upon the nature and quality of the learning which results.

2. Assignments are related to purposes. They are made and justified because they presumably contribute to the desired learning outcomes. Assignments must not be simply busywork, calculated only to keep pupils occupied. Instead they must be pertinent to the goals of instruction; the teacher should help students understand the learning objectives and recognize the relationship of assignments to these objectives.

3. The assignment provides orientation to the work. It should tell the student what is to be done. Sometimes the assignment is like a sort of miniature intelligence test; the student finds that the hardest part of the whole thing is to figure out what he is supposed to do. Students are likely to do the wrong things and strive for the wrong outcomes unless the assignment orients them to the task.

4. Assignments should be designed to motivate pupil effort. The teacher knows his students and relates the assigned work to their present interests when possible or seeks to stimulate related interests. Students need good reasons for doing things. They need to see the pertinence of the assigned work to their concerns, problems, and needs.

5. The assignment sometimes requires special preparation of the pupils for the learning task. This preparation is an attempt to insure the success of the lesson. The teacher works to activate memory traces of appropriate past experiences. For example, a Colorado English teacher led a discussion on student experiences in the Rocky Mountains, including the students' feelings about these experiences, as preparation for an assignment to read a literary selection dealing with the challenge of nature. The teacher may need to supply background information or to help students learn skills needed for the completion of the task. The instructor often anticipates errors which might be made in the work and thus makes it more likely that the pupils will learn correctly from the start.

6. Good assignments challenge, not threaten. It is obvious that assignments may be given by the teacher and received by the students as punishment. Many of you have heard your high school instructor say, "If the class continues to be noisy today I'll assign you twenty-five problems instead of ten!" This is hardly calculated to challenge boys and girls to work enthusiastically, or even to develop a favorable at-

titude toward the subject. The classwork comes to be thought of by pupils as punishment and the assignments as threats. On the other hand assignments can be challenging if they are meaningful and promote student involvement.

7. Assignments may provide for individual differences. Because students vary so greatly in interests, aptitudes, and abilities, and because the assigned work ought to be at least practicable in view of the various students' capacities, some provision for individual differences is desirable. A single assignment for all pupils to complete often is too difficult for some and too easy for others. Therefore, teachers often divide the class into sub-groups and provide appropriate assignments for the different groups. Frequently, committees are formed to work on projects, and the instructor attempts to see that the project chosen is adapted to the committee. Differentiated assignments are sometimes made; here the quantity and quality of work expected for various grades are indicated and the student is allowed to choose and work toward the grade he wishes.

8. Assignments should be cooperatively made. Both teacher and students ought to be actively involved. The student ultimately is doing the work, not for the teacher's benefit, but for his own. Thus, he should have an opportunity to contribute to the sort of assignment made.

9. The assignment should be clear. The students need to understand what they are to do and when it is to be submitted. Teachers can increase clarity by using well-selected examples and illustrations so that pupils will know exactly what is expected. Many teachers have assignments duplicated to pass out in order that each student has his own copy. This prevents misunderstanding or mistakes when pupils copy down an oral assignment. It also leaves no doubt later about what exactly was assigned.

10. Assignments deal with work that is important. Students quickly sense work that is not real, and that is made up to keep them busy. The assigned task ought to be important and worthwhile.

Assignments are not to be lightly tossed off as the final bell sounds; they are a vital part of teaching and require serious consideration and thoughtful planning. They can enhance or seriously inhibit learning.

## TEACHER-PUPIL PLANNING

The teaching-learning process directly involves both teacher and students. It would seem logical, then, that both teacher and students be involved in the planning for learning.

Obviously, the teacher is the mature, specially trained, professional person in the situation and has certain vital responsibilities for planning.

Yet it is the student who must learn. Thus, it is very important that the student accept the work planned, and of course, one of the best ways to foster acceptance of the task and to develop a feeling of responsibility for its completion is to allow students a part in its planning.

Teacher-pupil planning does not imply the abdication of responsibility by the teacher. He does not turn over curricular choice and organization to his pupils. In practice it simply means that the teacher offers opportunities for choice and self-determination within certain well-defined limits. As Miss King did, in the situation described in this chapter, the teacher may accept a student concern or question, or he may pose a question or problem himself and then invite students to explore the problem and suggest ways of solving it. Miss King clearly made the decision as to whether or not the whole topic was a pertinent and worthwhile concern in her class; this was revealed by her statement, "Tommy, that is a perfectly legitimate question. . . ." She then allowed her students to help plan ways of answering this question. She offered an area of planning within which students and teacher cooperatively made decisions which were important to learning.

Seldom are students given opportunities to operate democratically, to experience democracy, in the typical classroom. The teacher, even though he may be a benevolent dictator, is still a dictator. Students seem always to be laboring on teacher-planned tasks, to be doing imposed classwork, to be working toward teacher aims, to be trying to answer questions which are more important to the teacher than to themselves. Teacher-pupil planning can provide opportunities for democratic choice within definite limits. Students gradually may be given a wider area of self-determination as they demonstrate that they are willing and able to accept the responsibility. However, they must be given the opportunity to experience some modicum of democracy and to develop democratic skills before they are given wide freedom.

In teacher-pupil planning, the teacher may secure student assistance at various points in the learning sequence. Students may contribute to the objectives and goals of learning. They may make important decisions relating to questions and problems for study; they may suggest learning activities; they may discover materials and resources which are helpful in answering questions and solving problems. Finally, they may make important contributions to the evaluation of teaching and learning.

Cooperative planning with students is likely to contribute to learning in a great many ways; for example:

1. It will help students and teacher to understand each other better.

2. It will provide alignment of assignments and classwork with student goals and purposes.

3. It is likely to foster better adaptation to individual differences.

4. It will develop greater student involvement in curricular determination.

5. It will encourage students to accept more responsibility for learning.

6. It will provide a better classroom climate for learning.

7. It will open the way for more opportunity for cooperative student work.

8. It will place more emphasis upon question answering and problem solving.

9. It is bound to result in greater learning satisfaction to the learner.

Teacher-pupil planning may be of inestimable importance to learning, but teachers who would use it must recognize their own degree of skill or lack of skill in group processes. They also need to assess and take into consideration the nature of the students involved. Attention should focus on student level of maturity, past experience in cooperative planning, and the willingness and ability of students to accept the responsibility required. The advantages of cooperative planning, then, are many, but the teacher needs to carefully define the nature of his role in the teaching-learning situation. He must gradually develop the ability to use the group process, and must come to a thoughtful understanding of the nature and amount of student contribution which is desirable and possible.

## REVIEW

The classroom teacher is greatly occupied with the continuing task of planning classroom experiences. He must organize materials, resources, and processes into class activities which are likely to promote optimum and desirable learning outcomes. Decisions which affect the nature and amount of learning must be made before and during classroom activity.

1. Long-range planning for the individual teacher deals with resource units and teaching units. What is the unit concept of planning and how would you go about constructing a unit for your teaching?

2. Short-range planning provides a guide to daily operation. Do you know how to take a resource unit or teaching unit and break it down into daily lesson plans? Do you understand the characteristics of a good assignment?

3. Students may contribute significantly to the teaching-learning process. At what points in the process and in what ways might teachers encourage teacher-pupil planning?

# Selected References

Alcorn, M. D., Kinder, J. S., and Schunert, J. R. *Better Teaching in Secondary Schools.* 3rd ed. New York: Holt, Rinehart and Winston, Inc., 1970; Part Two "Planning."

Bent, R. K. and Unruh, A. *Secondary School Curriculum.* Lexington, Mass.: D. C. Heath and Company, 1969; Ch. 14 "Planning and Organizing Meaningful Experiences."

Blount, N. S. and Klausmeier, H. J. *Teaching in the Secondary School.* 3rd ed. New York: Harper & Row, Publishers, 1968; Ch. 6 "Unit and Daily Planning" and Ch. 7 "Organizing Meaningful Learning Activities through Unit Teaching."

Douglas, L. M. *The Secondary Teacher at Work.* Boston: D. C. Heath and Company, 1967; Ch. 11 "Planning the Year's Work."

Gwynn, J. M. and Chase, J. B., Jr. *Curriculum Principles and Social Trends.* 4th ed. New York: The Macmillan Company, 1969; Ch. 7 "The Growth of the Unit Plan of Teaching."

Gwynn, J. M. *Theory and Practice of Supervision.* New York: Dodd, Mead & Company, 1964; Ch. 4 "The Unit or Problems Method of Teaching— A New Supervisory Problem" and Ch. 5 "The Teaching Unit."

Harnack, R. S. "Computer Based Resource Units." *Educational Leadership,* 23:239, 241, 243, 245, December 1965.

Hass, G., Wiles, K., and Roberts, A. (eds.). *Readings in Secondary Teaching.* Boston: Allyn and Bacon, Inc., 1970; Ch. 13 "Lesson Planning."

Hoover, K. H. *"Learning and Teaching in the Secondary School.* 2nd ed. Boston: Allyn and Bacon, Inc., 1968; Ch. 4 "The Framework for Instruction: Long and Short-Range Planning."

Oliva, P. F. *The Secondary School Today.* Cleveland: The World Publishing Company, 1967; Ch. 7 "Planning a Learning Unit," Ch. 8 "Planning a Resource Unit," and Ch. 9 "Planning a Lesson."

# six

# Selecting and Using Instructional Materials

Instructional materials are an indispensable part of the teaching-learning process. Broadly conceived, they include a wide range of resources, both material and personnel, which are used in learning activities.

Beginning teachers report that probably their greatest needs in regard to materials of instruction are to (1) look carefully and critically at the use of the textbook, (2) explore the nature and advantages of supplementary materials, (3) learn the proper place of audio-visual aids in teaching, and (4) investigate the community resources which are likely to be useful.

## TEACHERS RELY ON TEXTBOOKS

Traditionally, the textbook is the most commonly used single instructional material. At all levels of education in America, the textbook is found even when other materials are lacking. In the thinking of teachers, administrators, and pupils it tends to come first. In purchasing it receives top priority. In the day-to-day class procedure it is routinely and regularly used.

Read the following description. Analyze it for its implications regarding the learner, the teacher, and its effects on the teaching-learning process.

*Description*

A young high school teacher applied to his principal for a day's leave to visit several experienced teachers in his subject area. The visitation leave was granted, and he arranged to visit the nearby high school from which he had been graduated. After spending the day observing a number of teachers, he sat down to talk with one of the instructors who had taught him when he was a student there. The teacher, now very close to retirement, was explaining his approach to teaching.

I know you young fellows may not agree with me and not all my colleagues agree with me either, but I feel the textbook is the most important single resource to the teacher. I have based my teaching on the textbook for over thirty years now, and I ought to know some of its advantages.

Actually, curriculum planning is not as much a problem as some make it out to be. If you wanted to, you could take the number of school days, subtract the examination days, and then divide the number of pages in the text by this number of teaching days. The result would be the number of pages in the text which must be covered every day. Now, isn't that simple?

Every school I know of has inadequate supplementary materials. The budget just doesn't go that far. Now in recent years, the student body has increased here so rapidly that our library is completely inadequate. Therefore, most teachers have no choice but to try to get a good textbook adopted, and then use it as the main material of study.

The beginning teacher needs the text for support and self-confidence. Teachers feel they can rely on textbooks because they know authors are more expert in their fields and, therefore, are better qualified to plan the materials for specific courses. The authors are national figures; they have a wide grasp of the subject and have tried out the materials before publication. Why not use it then?

Following the textbook is simply easier for the teacher. It cuts down on planning. The text usually has study questions, activities, and exercises included. Most publishers also provide the teacher with test questions for his use. Here you have your course pre-organized and laid out for you.

Use of the single, adopted text is an old, well-known approach to teaching, and my students learn just as much as students in other classes. They do just as well on standardized tests, and the students feel more secure with their own textbook close at hand.

## Implications

As the instructor continued, the young teacher began to reflect upon the readily apparent implications of what had been said.

1. It was clear that for many, many years the textbook had determined the nature and sequence of learning experiences for this teacher.

He had, at least to some real degree, abdicated his responsibility for planning. The textbook *was* his course.

2. The idea of dividing the number of pages in the text by the number of teaching days to determine curriculum reveals the innocent, naive view of planning possessed by the young man's former teacher. At best, it would seem to be a highly arbitrary, mechanical process if one were to use this approach.

3. The rationalization that the supply of supplementary materials and the library are inadequate in the face of today's rapidly growing enrollments is, of course, partly true. However, he seems to be quite satisfied with giving a single learning material to all pupils and making no provision for individual differences. Obviously, any class may contain wide differences in academic aptitude, interests, backgrounds of experience, or goals of learning; therefore, some adjustment for individual differences is necessary.

4. The text authors may be well-known experts in their field and the materials may have been pre-tested, yet the fact is that the textbook was written and published for national distribution. It does not and cannot take into consideration the nature of the local community and the particular group of students with which the teacher works. Some modification of the text seems indicated.

5. Beginning teachers often feel that they need the security of the text, and most of them seek to use it intelligently and with perspective. The danger is that the teacher may allow the text to become a crutch which he is fearful of throwing away.

6. Use of the textbook as described may make teaching easier, and any development which promises to ease the teacher's load is certain to be viewed with great interest. However, economy in the teaching load must be secured without sacrifice to the students' learning. The textbook-determined course is structured by the organization of the book; the point of view in the book becomes the single point of view in the course, and the very goals of learning may be established by the book. The teacher is a servant to the textbook, often to the detriment of learning.

7. Textbook teaching by its very nature is factually oriented and may produce students who do as well as students from other classes on tests which stress the possession of academic information. However, at the same time it is apt to ignore other, highly important instruction.

8. The concept of education implied here is a traditional one. Traditionally, education has come to mean traffic in abstract, verbal symbols. The spoken, written, and printed word has come to be the main medium of education. In a real sense, grades reward the youngster

who possesses high aptitude for manipulating verbal symbols. For years the textbook has been the very essence of this concept of education, although modern texts increasingly offer much excellent graphic material, descriptive experiments, and supplementary activities. It may neglect the pupil who is best helped to learn through other avenues, such as visual images, tactile experiences, and kinesthetic sensations. Modern methods seek to utilize a wide range of materials far beyond a single, printed textbook.

Dependence upon a textbook such as this teacher describes is not unusual or uncommon in the high school. The effects are serious. Of these, probably the most profound influence upon the teacher is in his own conception of his position. He remains the assistant to the textbook. The course is organized and laid out for him, and his task is to follow through. When this dependence exists, the only way to change curriculum is to change textbooks. Such teaching is more nearly in the nature of a technician's job than that of a professional teacher, and such a teacher will welcome the teaching machine, the televised curriculum, and the automated classroom. It is analogous to the technician working with a huge, complicated machine; he knows which buttons to push to start and stop the operation of the machine and where to squirt oil now and then, but he does not know how the machine works— he would be unable to repair it if it broke down, and he does not possess the ability to modify its operations. The technician is a button-pusher and an oil squirter, not the master of the machine.

In spite of the criticism resulting from overdependence upon the textbook, it is a poor medium of instruction only when it is misused. The teacher must use the textbook with perspective and good sense.

### Using Textbooks with Perspective

The textbook is properly viewed as an aid to teaching. It is simply one of many possible materials of learning. Because it is an adjunct to teaching, its use is determined by teacher experience and judgment through its worth in helping the teacher and students achieve the goals of learning. It is used only if it can do a better job than any of the other available materials of instruction.

Teachers find significant advantages in the textbook which are important to learning. It usually summarizes a great quantity of valuable information traditionally associated with a particular course. The text can provide a common resource since a copy is usually in the possession of each pupil. It may prove useful as a resource to the teacher in giving him ideas regarding learning activities, logical organization of content, and possible evaluative procedures. Many good textbooks include pictures, charts, maps, and diagrams which may prove to be valuable in teaching.

Teachers should know their subject so well that they plan the course in advance. They should possess mastery and expertness in their content field so that principles, concepts, generalizations, and important ideas which may be used as organizing centers for unit planning stand out. Goals of learning which are legitimate, worthwhile, and practicable must be clearly apparent. The teacher plans and then searches for suitable instructional materials. The textbook is one among many possibilities. The text may assist in the organization and planning of the course; it must not dominate.

The nature and goals of learning should be conceived of as being far broader than the simple recitation of textbook facts and information. Students need to gain other knowledge in addition to a temporary mastery of the academic information summarized in the book. Completing the material in the textbook is something less than a legitimate course objective. If the aims of instruction are intelligently and broadly conceived and given top priority, the textbook is likely to be used properly.

Sometimes teachers speak of "not being fair to the textbook" implying that one should not jump around in the text, skip some sections or otherwise destroy the organization of the material. Most texts are so written as to be "teachable"; that is, they are planned to teach the course for you. However, if the teacher is competent to be something more than a servant to the text, if he knows his particular student group well, and if he is confident of his ability to plan and to teach, he will be far more concerned with being fair to his pupils and himself. The aims of instruction and his own planning determine how and when the text is used.

There is little doubt that the textbook will continue to be the core of instructional material which is used in the classroom. Moreover, textbooks are constantly improving in organization and format, and they will become more useful and desirable as long as their use is kept in proper perspective.

Many teachers will continue to follow the textbook slavishly, and the great mass of teachers will find it necessary to deal with the text as the main instructional resource. For these reasons, the selection of textbooks is of great importance.

*Selecting Textbooks*

Procedures vary in the selection of textbooks. In some states, a single textbook is adopted for use in a certain course by all high schools in the state. Other states employ multiple adoptions; this means that several texts are chosen and the high school may decide to use any one of them. In other states, the local school district is responsible for selection of a text. In addition, a few states complicate the picture by indicating that preference is to be given to a resident author.

The selection of books by administrative officials is gradually being changed by placing major responsibility with the classroom teachers who must use the textbooks. Committees of teachers are commonly chosen to meet at the state, county, or district level to evaluate all the available textbooks and to recommend adoption to the appropriate agency.

Textbook selection is not to be taken lightly. Once chosen, the book is likely to be used for five or more years. This means that after a selection is made the teachers must use the book for a relatively long period. Therefore, it should be carefully analyzed and thoughtfully selected. A textbook selection committee might well consider the following bases in making its choice.

1. *The list of agreed upon objectives for the course.* Does the textbook promise to contribute to the attainment of the desired learning outcomes? In other words, which textbook under consideration is likely to be the most valuable in attaining the many and varied aims of instruction? Thus, the objectives of the course make up the first and probably most important consideration.

2. *The content of the course.* Teachers first define the subject matter of the course and then evaluate textbooks as to whether or not they contain an accurate, up-to-date, comprehensive treatment of the subject matter. The teachers' conception of the course content should determine the text—the text should not determine the course.

3. *Teaching method and planning procedures.* The descriptions of typically used methods and planning should be considered in evaluating the text. Where a number of different methods are used, the committee must look for adaptability and flexibility in the text.

4. *Nature of the students.* Is the textbook appropriate to the students who must learn through it? Vocabulary level, illustrations, examples, and other features must be suitable and meaningful.

Other considerations include (a) mechanical features (such as type size, format, pictures, binding, and attractiveness), (b) style (is it interesting, thought provoking, stimulating?), (c) author (is the author competent, recognized in his field?), and (4) cost. Of these, the cost is less a factor now, for most texts are fairly similar in price. The most suitable text is not likely to cost any more than a very undesirable one.

The textbook will be selected differently if it is kept in mind how it should be used. The text is an aid to instruction; thus, it must be compatible with the objectives of instruction, the teacher's conception of the content of the course, the methods of the teacher, and the nature of the student group. The text should not dominate instruction. Instead it must facilitate or assist the work of the teacher. Evaluating a textbook from this point of view is profoundly different from choosing a book to determine the course.

## SUPPLEMENTARY MATERIALS

Textbooks are only one of many kinds of instructional materials useful in learning. The text usually is succinctly written, tightly organized and greatly condensed. It is seldom sufficient in itself even for a single very good student. Other materials are used along with the text.

The term supplementary materials is not completely accurate, for it implies that they merely supplement the textbook. The wise teacher chooses material for study because it will do a better job of assisting learning than any other available material. The textbook is most commonly required, and teachers naturally look at it first to see if it is appropriate to the desired learning activity. If not, the teachers search for other materials. In this way, these other materials have come to be called supplementary materials.

Pertinent, worthwhile materials of instruction are everywhere. The teacher and his students should be constantly on the lookout for items in newspapers, magazines, professional journals, brochures, and reports. Materials must be sought wherever they exist. Of course not all will be suitable and practicable for classroom use but the first step is to identify the possibilities. Most teachers build files to which they may refer as the need arises. As students bring in clippings and as the teacher discovers likely reports, pictures, maps and brochures, these are placed in files to assist future planning.

### Choosing Appropriate Material

Locating possible instructional materials is apt to be easier than selecting which ones to use. The material should meet the same general criteria used in choosing a textbook. The material selected for use should (a) contribute to the learning objectives of the lesson, (b) involve significant content planned for study, (c) be compatible with the teaching procedures to be used, and (d) be appropriate to the particular group of pupils who will use this material. In addition, the materials may help relate classroom learning to out-of-school experiences, demonstrate the pertinence of classwork to later needs, stimulate interest in learning, and offer depth and focus to a specialized topic treated only superficially in the textbook.

Many kinds of materials may be identified and selected for use in learning. They are sometimes used singly or in varying combinations with or without the textbook.

*Newspapers and periodicals.*    Available to everyone are a large number of published materials. Newspapers and magazines vary greatly in quality, yet much valuable information is to be found in them. Every school library subscribes to a variety of newspapers and periodicals, and the classroom may be supplied with an adequate number of the local newspapers. In a number of schools, the students are asked to buy a weekly current events publication. Of course, papers and periodicals of all types are likely to be found in the homes of the pupils.

Teachers sometimes organize committees of students to scan publications and clip items which appear pertinent to the classwork. Other teachers simply encourage pupils to bring in clippings as they find them. Probably the most difficult job is to help boys and girls become more critical and mature in their evaluation of such materials. Most junior high students, for example, feel that information must be true if it is printed somewhere. Obviously they need to develop some understanding of the point of view represented, the reader audience to which the publication is directed, the need to look carefully at the writers and to develop a healthy skepticism. Most students find only a very limited sample of publications in their homes; thus, it is desirable that they have the opportunity to read and compare a comprehensive selection from the great range available.

*Pamphlets and bulletins.*    Brief, paperback publications by governmental agencies, public service organizations, and industry are often helpful in teaching. These may contain the most recent, up-to-date information to replace sections of the textbook which have become obsolete. Many of them are free or inexpensive enough that they may be secured and replaced easily.

There is a reason, of course, why pamphlets and brochures are published and made available to the public and the schools at a cost of millions of dollars each year. Industrial firms, governmental agencies, and other groups do so in order to sell products, create a favorable image in the minds of the public, develop consumer demand, or to otherwise change public opinion. Thus, the instructor needs to be careful in evaluating the materials before use in class to be sure that the commercial or advertising message is restrained and unobjectionable, because the teacher may be criticized if he appears to be working as a salesman for a particular brand of beer, automobile, construction equipment, or other merchandise. He needs to be certain in using such materials that the prejudice or bias of the publication is pointed out.

*Books.*    Some teachers are fortunate in having reference books, other textbooks, and library selections which are pertinent to their subject fields. Beginning teachers usually make it a point to survey the library for books of all kinds which may prove useful. Often, fiction as well as non-fiction may be valuable. For example, alert science teachers know and recommend exciting, soundly grounded science fiction titles to their students. These often stimulate general interest in science itself, illustrate applications of science, encourage creative approaches to science, and sometimes effectively show students that not all the important questions are answered nor are all the important discoveries already made.

Reference books are indispensable and usually are found in the classroom library. In addition, secondary references may be shelved in the school library.

Some schools have several sets of textbooks. Because certain texts may present a particular topic especially well, the teacher may wish to use other than the basic text part of the time or make other texts available to those students who want to read beyond the class treatment of the topic.

*Workbooks.*    Considerable disagreement exists between the critics and the advocates of workbooks. The main advantages seem to center in the help this resource can give to the teacher. Workbooks may improve assignments, provide material for study in convenient form, effect economies in time for the teacher and students in copying assignments and exercises, and offer teachers a wider range of possible instructional activities. On the other hand, they may restrict the freedom of the teacher (that is, if the workbook is required, then it must be used); they may overemphasize specific factual, academic information; and they often are not developed to provide for individual differences. Probably the most serious criticism leveled at the workbook is the charge that it promotes "busywork." Pupils spend hours filling in blanks, completing sentences, recognizing the correct or incorrect word, choosing the wrong answer, and other such activities short of thinking and working the whole thing through themselves. The teacher assigns pages in the workbook in order to keep the students occupied while he grades papers, plans the next lesson, or confers with remedial students. Thus, workbooks must be carefully evaluated and their use determined before they are adopted.

*Seeking Assistance from the Librarian*

Experienced classroom teachers have learned to consult the school librarian for help in locating the best possible supplementary materials. More than anyone else in the school, the librarian will know what the resource center presently contains and will have immediate access to and familiarity with the lists and catalogues of possible materials which may be ordered.

Modern junior and senior high schools increasingly include a multimedia resource center, centrally located and placed under the direction of the librarian. Such a center, as the name suggests, contains the whole spectrum of printed and audio-visual resources which the school owns. The librarian-director is likely to have at least skimmed most of the printed materials and is the best source of information about how others are using certain materials and resources as well as how students are reacting to them. This person usually has been a teacher prior to completing the essential training for the librarianship. The librarian-director is in a key position to provide helpful instruction assistance. The beginning teacher should make it a point to get to know her and to draw upon this valuable resource in improving his teaching.

## AUDIO-VISUAL AIDS

The army of audio-visual aids to teaching is like other instructional materials, simply adjunctive to the work of the teacher. They are not some sort of magical substitute for the instructor. They aid the teacher in his efforts to promote learning.

Many beginning teachers think of audio-visual aids as primarily movies, film strips, tape recorders, and recordings. Actually, this category includes many different items. Teachers customarily and routinely use such resources as the chalkboard, bulletin boards, large maps, and models, all of which are audio-visual aids.

Because of the mystery and misunderstanding which surround audio-visual materials, many teachers are uneasy about exploring their use. Machines are often involved, and a large number of teachers are unsure of their ability to operate the machine and particularly to handle an emergency. For example, what would they do if the sound motion picture film snapped? Could they make an emergency splice? What if the tape recorder needed adjustment? Could they turn back and re-run a portion of a tape without erasing the recording? These and similar fears plague the average teacher. Actually, only a minority of teachers feel comfortable using the machines which are necessary for some of the audio-visual aids.

Some school districts offer workshops to assist the teacher in developing skills needed to operate audio-visual machines. Classes are available through the extension services of most colleges and universities. In addition, the audio-visual coordinator in many high schools sponsors an audio-visual club. Interested students are trained as movie projectionists and equipment maintenance men and are available to operate the machines for teachers. This is, of course, a great advantage to the classroom teacher. He can concentrate upon the material and the supervision of the class without being preoccupied with the machine.

*Values of Audio-Visual Aids*

It is difficult to generalize for all audio-visual aids because there are so many types, but they may offer some very special values to the teacher who makes intelligent use of them. They may:

1. *Provide a multiple approach to learning.* Not all boys and girls learn best through the usual media of instruction. The great variety of audio-visual materials offers other channels for communication.

2. *Broaden experience.* Dramatic audio-visual materials provide vicarious experiences which extend and enrich the experimental background of the students. Content, which often is abstract and lifeless as it is found in the text and workbook, comes alive through such resources as the sound motion picture, television, and recordings.

3. *Capture interest.* Audio-visual aids, partly because they differ from the usual classroom procedure and partly because of their very nature, possess the power to catch and hold the attention of boys and girls. They are likely to stimulate a desire to know more.

4. *Increase learning.* Audio-visual procedures are closer to actual experience than the typical, abstract verbalism found in most classroom methods. They involve sharp sensory impressions. They affect student emotions, a dimension of learning largely ignored by most teachers. Because of these and similar factors, learning and retention are enhanced.

5. *Improve the learning climate.* Use of a number of different audio-visual aids will provide variety and freshness to teaching. The entire environment will be improved as pupils enjoy their learning.

In opposition, some teachers cite the apparent disadvantages of audio-visual aids. To many school people they simply are too much trouble. They must be previewed to be sure they are useful. They may be difficult to schedule when needed. Difficulties of room darkening, machine location, seating, and other physical arrangements sometimes appear imposing. Cost of equipment and upkeep may be discouraging. Some of them are inflexible (for example, a movie proceeds at a certain rate which is very difficult to change; a film strip is fixed in regard to sequence). Finally, they may stress entertainment above learning.

There seems to be much room for improvement in the use of audio-visual materials. In most high schools, only a small proportion of the teachers make much use of them. What are some of the kinds of audio-visual aids and their uses?

*Using Audio-Visual Aids*

Audio-visual aids are simply adjuncts to learning. They are learning materials which show great promise for making learning more important and effective for the student. The inventive teacher is likely to use one or more of them at almost any point in the teaching.

Because of their attention-getting qualities, audio-visual aids are often used to introduce a unit or lesson. During the learning sequence, they may provide necessary background for optimum understanding of the lesson. Certain audio-visual resources are rich in pertinent content with which to augment the text. They may be used to summarize and tie up the loose ends. They may help develop relationship and pattern among the parts of the lesson and foster an understanding of how the topic under consideration fits into the whole subject. Some audio-visual aids teach a specific skill, such as use of the dictionary, diagramming or note taking quickly and well. Thus, the interested teacher needs to explore the nature and possible uses of some of the various audio-visual aids.

*The chalkboard.*    Almost every classroom teacher uses the chalkboard daily. The classroom wouldn't appear to be fully equipped without it. Nevertheless, this valuable and standard resource is not always well used.

Teachers need to keep certain things in mind in order to improve their utilization of the chalkboard. A teacher should (a) develop skills of printing or writing clearly, (b) be sure the material on the board is large enough to be seen and read from any seat in the room, (c) use a variety of colors of chalk in order to make important items stand out, (d) use what drawing ability he possesses to illustrate points (for example, stick figures if necessary), (e) keep the items uncomplicated and succinct so that clarity and emphasis are preserved, (f) use the board for its great value in illustrating, emphasizing, organizing, and summarizing points which are made during the ongoing flow of class activity, rather than transmitting long columns of material which should be duplicated and passed out to all students, and (g) strive constantly to improve his use of the board.

Beginning teachers often are observed making meaningless marks on the chalkboard as they lecture. Actually some of these accomplish very little beyond releasing physical tension in the teacher; they often communicate nothing to the students and may actually distract their attention. Fear of making errors in spelling often plagues beginning teachers. One enterprising young teacher covered his insecurity by informing his class that spelling is an important skill and occasionally he would test the class by purposely misspelling a word. His pupils were to see if they could catch him.

*The bulletin board.* Most classrooms possess a very small bulletin board attached in what is often an inconspicuous location. Typically, if the bulletin board contains anything, it is likely to have pinned to it some cartoons, a clipping or two yellowed with age, and the instructions for a fire drill.

Bulletin board space can be a valuable medium. As billboards are erected on the sides of highways, to advertise products to motorists, so the bulletin board may accomplish similar results with students *if* similar techniques of attention getting and interest catching are used. Obviously, displays featuring bikini-clad young ladies might be viewed with something less than enthusiasm by the principal, yet worthwhile, effective bulletin board displays can be constructed to tie in with teaching.

Some English teachers choose a committee to screen new books coming into the library and nominate selections for "Book of the Month" and "Dud of the Month." Book jackets, along with student comments, are displayed. Social studies teachers sometimes select a series of themes which parallel the course work to govern the material placed on the bulletin board. Committees sometimes choose certain themes or topics for which they will be responsible. Occasionally, a teacher may place an enigmatic question or statement on the bulletin board in order to stimulate student interest. These suggest some of the many uses which may be made of this resource. Actually, the greatest weaknesses in bulletin board use seem to be (a) the teacher has no plan for its use, (b) displays are infrequently changed, (c) bulletin board material is not coordinated with the teaching, (d) a mixture of different items is displayed without apparent purpose or theme to give unity and meaning, and (e) students are not involved in planning, organizing, constructing, and evaluating bulletin board displays.

*Projected materials.* Materials of instruction may be projected by using a number of different machines and techniques. The sound motion picture, slides, and filmstrips are most commonly thought of in this regard. However, the opaque projector allows you to display a certain item to the entire class at the same time. A small photograph may be magnified and projected on the screen for all to see. English teachers may project a student paper with the grammatical, language usage, and spelling errors shown. The science teacher may show an illustration from a technical book or periodical without even clipping it out.

Microprojectors make it possible to project the image seen in a microscope for the entire class. It is greatly magnified and thus makes many points clear. Students do not have the problem of adjusting focus and slide individually. All students see the same thing as the teacher points out important features.

Overhead projectors enable the teacher to face the class, project an image on the screen, and even write on the slide while the class observes. Dramatic illustrations of the changes in national boundaries may be made by the geography teacher using overlays on a map background. Using a special pencil, he is able to draw symbols and write key words on the transparency as he talks.

Audio-visual libraries have secured thousands of valuable movies, sets of slides, and filmstrips. Teachers should explore the possibilities of the great resources available in their individual fields. Three serious difficulties, however, face the instructor who would use one or more of these. First, the projected material must carefully and thoughtfully be previewed. Only in this way can the teacher be certain it will fit into his plan. Second, scheduling must be arranged. Sometimes this can be a problem. For example, a few school districts require that teachers place their orders for the entire year at the beginning of school in the fall. Obviously it is quite difficult to know ahead of time that on a certain date you will be on a certain topic which is related to the movie or filmstrip you wish to use. Third, arrangements for the showing must be made. You may need to move your class to another room which may be adequately darkened. The projector and screen must be secured and set up. The material must be efficiently projected.

The values of projected materials are obvious and significant. Their drawbacks are known and important. It seems clear that teachers need to develop skills and understanding which will help them use these materials and techniques with confidence and effect. It may be that as team teaching becomes more common, the projected materials will become even more useful in working effectively with very large groups.

*Recorded materials.*    Recordings on discs or tape provide a measure of flexibility and convenience which encourages their use. English teachers often use recordings of literary selections presented by professional actors or by the authors themselves. Music teachers, of course, find the quality and variety of today's records a great help to them. Tape recorders make it possible for the science instructor to capture an important speech or discussion with an important person in the field. Social studies teachers tape current news items for discussion in class. Students use tape recorders to record interviews, thus preserving the flavor and realism of the original comments. Sometimes students write a play, rehearse it, and tape it for subsequent presentation to the class. Speech teachers use the tape recorder to help students develop a sensitivity to their own patterns of speech, and to identify speech faults needing remedial attention. Some teachers tape their classroom presentation as it occurs and play it back later in order to evaluate their teaching. These and a number of other uses suggest the values of recorded materials.

*Radio and television.*    No one can deny the powerful impact possible through these mass media. In-school use depends upon the vagaries of scheduling. The program desired may be scheduled at a different time from when your class is scheduled. In this case, you may prepare the class for the program and assign it for homework. A few school districts offer programs of great value through educational television channels and school radio stations. These are usually planned so that the maximum classroom use is possible.

Important educational experiences are available through these media. Inauguration ceremonies, the signing of an important document, eyewitness reports from war-torn areas, news conferences, and deliberations of legislative bodies are a few of the events which may come through the on-the-spot coverage of radio and television. These events become living and real, they convey a sense of participation in the concern of today, and they expand the environment of the school to include all the world.

Teachers cannot ignore the offerings of radio and television. The alert teacher knows and uses programs in and out of school which are pertinent to his subject.

*Other aids.*    Charts, maps, globes, models, and still pictures are some of the other audio-visual aids which may be useful in teaching. Charts may facilitate comparisons and contrasts of data. Their visual nature often provides clear and immediate insight which may be difficult and time-consuming to explain verbally. Maps and globes are indispensable to the geography and history teacher to foster spatial concepts necessary in these subjects. Models of all kinds are found in many different classrooms to reduce the level of abstraction of the teaching. Many teachers seek out and mount still pictures for possible instructional use.

The resource center usually will include a variety of programmed materials for teacher and student use. Programmed textbooks and teaching machines, for example, may be placed there for students to check out and use by themselves or with the help of a teacher aide.

The alert, resourceful teacher approaches audio-visual aids as possible means by which his teaching may become more dramatic and more effective. All classroom teachers could profit from a continuing effort to know more about the nature and possible uses of these materials.

## COMMUNITY RESOURCES

One of the most exciting as well as the most accessible resources at hand is the community. The students themselves are resources to learning. Their experiences, opinions, attitudes, and problems are regularly taken into consideration and utilized in learning by some teachers. However, the community within which the school exists may be largely ignored in the preoccupation with academic information, courses of study, and textbooks.

### Values in Community Resources

The community is likely to contribute to learning in three general ways: (a) the students bring their interests and enthusiasms developed toward community events into school with them; (b) the community supplies problems for study and questions to be answered, thus expanding the content of the class; and (c) the community contains a full range of resources in both material and personnel which may be used to enrich learning. Teachers may bring certain aspects of the community into the classroom, and they may take their students out into the community for learning activities.

Actually, the use of community resources has the following important values:

1. Community resources bring the validity of real life to learning in school. Students know that much of their work is hypothetical and not of any real moment. They also believe that most of the real problems of

the everyday world exist in the community. When these are the subject of class attention, students feel that the classwork is meaningful and desirable.

2. When teachers open their classrooms to community concerns, they automatically tap new and rich sources of motivation. As school work contributes to the solution of community problems and answers to questions of concern to the community, the intense interests attached to these out-of-school concerns may be transferred to school tasks.

3. Transfer of training may be enhanced. Learning through community resources tends to be lifelike. Application of classroom skills and knowledge are clear to pupils. Processes of problem solving are seen to have value to the solution of many other problems besides those found in the workbook.

4. Community resources reduce the level of abstraction. Community experiences used to illustrate, apply, and make more meaningful the concepts and ideas discussed in class are close and real to the pupils. The textbook abstractions are related to experiences of neighbors, friends, relatives, and students themselves. Thus, classwork is likely to fit into the background of meaning possessed by each boy or girl.

5. Community problems in the curriculum involve school work functionally. School work then is not done for the teacher or even for a grade, but to solve a problem which is really important to the people involved. Mastery of schoolroom learnings is contributory to the answering of questions and the solving of problems.

6. Attention to the community tends to help boys and girls evaluate the expectations of the adult world. They must take into consideration values, behavior standards, and social relationships of adult life. They may be less preoccupied with the ephemeral demands of the peer group culture, because they have some idea of the expectations which they must meet when they take their places as adult members of society.

7. Use of community resources opens up two-way communication between school and community. The school is sensitive to what is going on in the community and no longer pretends to be isolated from the day-to-day problems of the community and its citizens. The school tends to become a more effective part of and influence upon the community within which it is situated.

## Using Community Resources

Probably the most important characteristic of the teacher who is successful in using the community to help in teaching is the development of sensitivity and interest in both students and community. This teacher seeks to coordinate classroom tasks with real events and concerns in the lives of the pupils and the community in which they live.

Learning activities may bring the community into class or take the students out into the community. A history teacher may seek to develop a time sense in her students by having them interview adults of various ages in the community to secure accounts of the impact of the development of the radio, silent and sound movies, the automobile, the airplane, or television. A homeroom teacher may ask students to talk to parents and grandparents in order to compare dating customs. A journalism teacher might take his class to visit the local newspaper plant. A science teacher could arrange a tour of a nearby industrial complex. An English teacher may send his students out to make a study of vocational possibilities in the community. A social studies teacher and his students might wish to seek old documents, consult town records, talk with pioneers, and write a history of the community. A guidance director may invite representatives of various occupations to speak to students on "occupations day." An art teacher could arrange a showing and critical evaluation of his students' work by the community art group. An agriculture teacher may invite a successful farmer to speak to his class regarding some of his methods. A chemistry instructor might ask a research chemist to answer student questions in regard to vocational possibilities for those who are interested in chemistry. These are but a few of the possible ways in which teachers can make it a practice to use constructively the resources to be found in the community.

Certain procedures sometimes present special problems for teachers. The speaker whom you invite in to address the class must be given a clear idea of what he is to discuss and why. The class then should be made ready for the talk. Learning is improved and the asking of pertinent questions of the speaker encouraged if the students know what to expect in advance. Lay resource persons usually have little understanding of classroom demands, thus they usually welcome suggestions by the teacher.

The field trip is another procedure which requires special preparation. Permission of the administration must be secured. The trip itself should be previewed by the teacher beforehand if at all possible. The class must be made ready for the learning experience. They need to know what the purpose of the trip is, what to look for, and what learning activity will follow the excursion. During the field trip, careful supervision is necessary. Afterward, the experience is discussed and evaluated.

Many schools districts maintain extensive lists of various kinds of possible community resources. Teacher comments and class evaluations are often included in order to help the beginning teacher in his tentative

planning and to give him ideas for other, similar materials and procedures. Community resources are not for entertainment purposes; they
have legitimate and rewarding uses in the teaching-learning process.

## REVIEW

Instructional materials enable teacher and pupils to proceed with learning activities. These materials include a whole spectrum of possibilities.
Any teacher who would strive for increasing and continued success must
develop insight and competency in the use of many of these resources.
As a step toward this goal, you should have answers to these questions.

1. The textbook is at once the instructional material which is most
often found in the classroom and the one which is probably most often
misused. What role should the text play in planning and teaching? How
can textbooks be selected wisely?

2. Supplementary materials are available to the teacher who would
go beyond the textbook. What are some of these and how should they
be used?

3. Audio-visual aids have developed an aura of mystery. What is
their proper relationship to teaching? What are some helpful audio-visual
materials and procedures, and how are they utilized in the classroom?

4. Community resources are extremely valuable in teaching. How
may teachers tap this potential for enriching learning?

# Selected References

Brown, J. W., Lewis, R. B., and Harcleroad, F. F. *AV Instruction: Media
and Methods.* 3rd ed. New York: McGraw-Hill Book Company, 1968.

Clark, L. H. and Starr, I. S. *Secondary School Teaching Methods,* 2nd ed.
New York: The Macmillan Company, 1967; Ch. 13 "Audio-Visual
Materials" and Ch. 14 "Other Materials of Instruction."

de Kieffer, R. and Cochran, L. W. *Manual of Audio-Visual Techniques.*
Englewood Cliffs, N.J.; Prentice-Hall, Inc., 1962.

Erickson, C. W. H. *Fundamentals of Teaching with Audio-Visual Technology.* New York: Tht Macmillan Company, 1964.

Finn, J. D. "Instructional Technology." *NASSP Bulletin*: 47:99–119, May
1963.

Gordon, G. N. *Educational Television*. New York: The Center for Applied Research in Education, Inc., 1965.

Grambs, J. D., Carr, J. C., and Fitch, R. M. *Modern Methods in Secondary Education*. 3rd ed. New York: Holt, Rinehart and Winston, Inc., 1970; Ch. 6 "Medium and Message: Resources for Learning."

Hoover, K. H. *Readings on Learning and Teaching in the Secondary School*. Boston: Allyn and Bacon, Inc., 1968; Ch. 23 "Audio-Visual Materials and Resources."

Kinder, J. A. *Using Audio-Visual Materials In Education*. New York: American Book Company, 1965.

Soghomonian, S. "The Textbook-Tarnished Tool for Teachers." *Phi Delta Kappan*, 48:395–396, April 1967.

# seven

# The Evaluation of
# Teaching and Learning

The processes of evaluation are essential to effective teaching and learning. The teacher attempts to obtain evidence which allows judgments to be made regarding whether or not he and his class are achieving their educational aims. He seeks some gauge to indicate the degree to which students have learned what he hoped they would. The instructor searches for data by which he may appraise the techniques and organization being used to teach the material. In addition, the student is assisted, with the help of his teacher, to interpret, to assess, the experience in which he is participating.

All this and more is implied in the term evaluation. Thus, it is a vital and indispensable part of your teachng. At this point you should consider the following:

1. Evaluation differs in definition from measurement. You should understand the broader concept of evaluation in the classroom and the basic ideas in this process.

2. Teachers find they must make some sort of evaluation. After all, various reports are required, and grades must be given and even occasionally defended. Practices vary considerably according to such factors as the philosophy of the school, the specific course aims and objectives, and the degree to which the teacher understands and uses sound principles of test construction. You should have a keen insight into the process of evaluation. You should know not only what you are looking for, but also what basic steps of evaluation to employ.

3. In the search for a variety of evidence regarding various classroom objectives, many different devices and procedures may be used. You must have a good idea of the possible instruments and techniques of appraisal which are available to help you.

# NATURE OF EVALUATION

Evaluation has special meaning for experienced teachers. Thus, a careful definition is essential to understanding this function.

## Definition

The two terms "measurement" and "evaluation" are often confused in the thinking of beginning teachers. Actually, the former is included within the latter. When one seeks data on the characteristics of a person in an objective, scientific manner, he is said to be measuring. When one utilizes these data in making judgments about a person, he is engaged in evaluation.

Evaluation is usually based on measurement of some kind. However, data of all sorts—some very subjective and intuitive—may be used in (a) ascertaining how well the educational objectives have been achieved, (b) identifying strengths and weaknesses in the individual student so that teaching for him may be improved, and (c) discovering how effective the teaching methods and materials have been. Evaluation is also the basis upon which grades are given and reported to parents and upon which students are promoted.

The teacher's general aim in the teaching-learning process is to change student behavior or to reinforce already existing, desirable behavior. Thus, a very important task for teacher and school is to determine what kinds of behavior are desired. The process of evaluation then focuses upon the need to appraise whether or not the educational activity has resulted in changes in behavior and whether or not these changes are in the desired direction.

## Basic Ideas in Evaluation

Evaluation is neither to be thought of as separate from teaching nor as an adjunct to teaching. It is an integral part of the teaching-learning activity. Certain fundamental ideas are helpful in understanding the nature of evaluation.

*Evaluation begins with goals.*    The process of evaluation is directly concerned with the establishment of educational objectives, for the central task in evaluation involves the appraisal of progress toward these objectives. The work of evaluation does not start after the objectives are formulated and the educational activity completed. Rather it begins with the statement of objectives, for they may be stated in such a way as to facilitate or inhibit their evaluation. One authority concludes, "There is evidence to support the observation that conscientious teachers who practice improved methods of defining their goals *can expect marked improvements in both their methods of teaching and the ways they measure children's progress.*"[1]

Every teacher must make decisions regarding what will be taught. Since these decisions are stated as objectives, it is apparent that the most fruitful formulation is in terms of pupil behavior. If the aim in teaching is to change behavior, then the objectives ought to describe the student behavior sought. This will automatically suggest evaluative procedures to secure evidence and allow judgments regarding student progress toward the objectives.

*Evaluation uses a variety of procedures.*     Classroom teachers are concerned with a multiplicity of learning outcomes. Therefore, many different techniques and instruments must be utilized. This means that paper and pencil examinations are only one dimension of the total process. If the appraisal activity is narrowly restricted to these instruments, some very unfortunate things are likely to happen to the attitude of the learner. Students, after considerable experience with memorizing and recalling items of academic information on schedule, come to operate by vote. In Cantor's words:

> Schools are training people to play parlor guessing games or to participate in commercial quiz programs. Pupils gather information, which they are taught to supply on demand by an expert, or quiz master. The "average" curriculum, on all levels of education, consists almost entirely of some teacher's answers to problems seldom raised by the pupils.[2]

Only as multiple objectives are stated, implemented, and evaluated by the teacher, do the pupils, themselves, begin to accept a variety of goals.

Teachers utilize essay examinations, objective tests, questionnaires, checklists, interviews, anecdotal reports, comments from parents, and personal observation in the total evaluative process. They search for pertinent data which may be either quantitative or descriptive. Thus, a description of student behavior in a certain situation may be far more valuable in ascertaining progress toward an objective than any score on any test.

---

[1] Murray Thomas, *Judging Student Progress* (New York: Longsmans, Green and Co., Inc., 1954), 16.

[2] Nathaniel Cantor, *The Teaching-Learning Process* (New York: Holt, Rinehart and Winston, Inc., 1953), 200.

*Evaluation concerns all aspects of pupil growth.*    The teacher is concerned with what is happening to the total personality of youth. For example, we know that students learn many things in class not found in the list of educational objectives of the unit or lesson. Concomitant learning includes those things which boys and girls learn in the classroom aside from what we have planned for them to learn. The history teacher who requires that his students memorize the names of all the presidents of the United States and the dates of their inauguration *may* secure this learning from his students. However, at the same time, they may be learning very effectively to dislike history, teacher, and school. Evaluation attempts to see into all aspects of pupil growth.

Many high school teachers list objectives which have to do with the development of attitudes, interests, appreciations, and ideals, yet few make a real attempt to assess growth in these areas. This is due, in part, to the difficulty of securing objective evidence on these aspects of student growth. However, some teachers feel that somehow these objectives are less legitimately their concern, for these may involve significant emotional or affective components and are not as clearly intellectual in content as is the possession of academic information and skills. Yet experienced school people know that learning related to attitudes and interests is likely to be far more permanent than academic facts and details. Teachers must not neglect this important consideration in the evaluation of their classes.

*Evaluation occurs continuously.*    Teachers and pupils typically look upon evaluation as a process which takes place periodically—at the end of a unit, midway through the semester, or at the end of the term. However, just as everyone is constantly evaluating each other in ordinary social relationships, so do teachers and students constantly assess the ongoing activities in the schoolroom. If teachers are sensitive, they remain alert for feedback from student reaction to their planning and teaching. They get a feeling about how the classwork is going; they may get a hunch about what they ought to do next. Teachers should try to keep in touch with the shifting interests and enthusiasms of their pupils. The process of evaluation is continuous, a functional part of teaching and learning.

Often, progress charts are kept, especially in remedial subjects, of each individual's growth in certain skills. For example, in remedial reading the tendency is to use growth profiles of reading speed and comprehension. In regular classes, if the evaluative activity is placed at the end of the teaching-learning activity, it is then too late to do anything about the results. If the final exam reveals a gross misunderstanding in the minds of most of the students, the time is past to help them correct this; the semester is over and no remedial teaching is possible. Thus, the evaluative activity should begin with pre-tests and continue throughout the years as an integral part of the classwork.

Recognizing the limitations of the paper and pencil examination, other possible evaluative procedures must be instituted as the work proceeds. A variety of instruments and techniques is used at appropriate points in the teaching and learning.

*Evaluation requires help from pupils and parents.*   Current trends in teaching tend to place more of the responsibility for learning on the learner. Thus student self-evaluation becomes more and more important. Pupils and teachers cooperate in four ways: (1) in the establishment of aims, (2) in the assessment of present levels of competence, (3) in the formation of instructional plans which seem likely to contribute to the aims and, (4) in the evaluation of progress toward the objectives. In this way, the student, with the help of the teacher, learns his strengths and his weaknesses and is assisted in interpreting the learning experiences. He develops the habit of participating in the ongoing work of the schoolroom. He becomes an active participant in the business of securing a meaningful education. His progress and his status are not kept a secret from him until report card time. He is privy to the essential information about his own learning, information which may assist him in improving his progress.

Parents, too, may contribute significantly to the process of evaluation, for they are in a position to see evidences of learning which occur outside the school and thus beyond the knowledge of the teacher. Through teacher-parent conferences they may report on the degree of transfer of such important behavior as desirable language habits, mathematical skills, problem-solving abilities, and critical thinking to out-of-school situations. They have a big stake in the education of their children. Teacher and parent cooperation may enhance the total in-school experience of boys and girls and may extend the range and validity of the evaluative process itself.

*Evaluation operates within realistic limits.*   Such factors as time shortages, energy limitations, and competing demands limit the effort which may be expended in evaluative activity. From the point of view of the teacher, two important restrictions exist. First, most of the evaluative activity is undertaken within the classroom. This, of course, is not the best place to assess progress toward some of the objectives. For example, the typical schoolroom would be a poor place in which to observe behavior which in adult life would be termed as characteristic of citizenship. The teacher must be realistic and recognize the severe limitations this situation represents. Second, every teacher must operate within personal limits. Teachers find they have a certain quantity of energy resources. A certain amount of this may be committed to work without neglecting family or self. The teacher of English knows that the best way for boys and girls to develop facility in writing is for them to write, and write some more. However, if he teaches five English classes a day and asks all his students to write a short paper every day, this might mean that he would read about 175 papers each night, and about 875 papers each week. Nobody's eyes could last long at this rate. Teachers, then, must look at the vital task of evaluation with some perspective and realism.

## THE PROCESS OF EVALUATION

Teachers use varying procedures in relation to their students in the interests of evaluation. Sometimes these procedures have a sound basis and sometimes they are utilized because of tradition, desire for popularity, or for some other non-pertinent reason.

Every teacher makes his decisions regarding appraisal procedures and then must live with the consequences. Consider the following conversation. How does this teacher evaluate his students? How does he view the process of appraisal?

As you project yourself into this description of one teacher's practices and the tentative reactions of one person to them, what questions come to your mind? Think of a course you hope to teach in the light of certain questions which your principal, supervisor, coordinator, or department head might quite legitimately ask. For example, what are you trying to accomplish in this course? How do you know whether or not you are accomplishing these things?

*Description*

Recently a curriculum coordinator sat talking with a young social studies teacher in the teachers' lounge of his school. About halfway through the second cup of coffee the conversation drifted to the problem of evaluation.

"I'm concerned about evaluation in my classes. Frankly, I am not satisfied with what I am doing," the classroom teacher said.

"All right," the coordinator said, "start with what you do, let's say, in U.S. History."

The teacher explained, "In United States History, I insist upon a thorough knowledge of certain important dates, names, and events. History is made up of essentially these sorts of things; therefore, students either know this information or they don't know history. I give a midterm and final examination each semester, both of which stress facts. I used to use objective exams, but many of our graduates who are in college now tell us they need more practice in writing essay examinations, so I presently use essay exams. In the grading I am careful to count off for misspelled words and grammatical errors.

"In addition to this I require a term paper each semester written on one of a list of topics which I make up and pass out to the class. Beyond this I keep a portion of the grade for my rating of the student in citizenship. I feel U.S. History is fundamentally justified on the basis of its contributing to the good citizenship of boys and girls; therefore, I grade them as citizens in the class.

"Actually my total evaluation is broken down approximately into twenty per cent for the midterm exam, forty per cent for the final exam, twenty per cent for the term paper and twenty per cent for citizenship.

"This plan is similar to what many of the other social studies teachers do yet I somehow feel dissatisfied with it. What do you think?"

The curriculum coordinator replied, "Why don't you let me visit your class a few times, look at some of your materials, and then we can have another talk."

*Implications*

When the coordinator had completed the visit, talked to students, and analyzed the gradebook and examinations, he began to see certain possible implications in the evaluative practices of the teacher who had asked for help.

1. It was clear that the way the young social studies teacher looked at the matter of his course affected the sort of evaluative procedures he used. He saw the content of U.S. History as basically consisting of academic information. Events, names and dates *were* history for him; therefore, his teaching and his examinations frankly emphasized this. However, considerable research[3] exists which indicates that principles and broad concepts are likely to be retained, but that tremendous rates of forgetting occur with specific academic facts and information. One challenging question which might have been asked of the teacher is: What are the concepts or generalizations which students should derive from the study of U.S. History? This particular teacher's narrow conception

---

[3] See for example Ralph W. Tyler, "Permanence of Learning," *Journal of Higher Education,* 4:203–4 (1933), or J. M. Sawrey & C. W. Telford, *Educational Psychology* (Boston: Allyn and Bacon, Inc., 1958), 142–43.

of what made up the content of history obviously limited the nature and variety of evaluative instruments used.

2. Other than insisting that his students know the facts which make up history, the teacher felt that good citizenship was a defensible goal of a U.S. History course. Because of this objective, he reserved one-fifth of the total semester grade for a rating of how students behaved as citizens of the class.

The coordinator found from his observation, interviews with students, and scrutiny of the gradebook that actually the items which went into the rating of citizenship were closely related to conforming or nonconforming behavior. Students who handed in their daily homework on time (this was checked off and not graded), who were not discipline problems, who "facilitated" class discussion instead of asking questions which called for lengthy explanations or provoked spirited differences of opinon, who were not often absent or tardy, and who were amenable to the suggestions of the teacher received high grades. Thus the teacher rewarded conformity with one-fifth of the total grade, probably without realizing it.

It became clear that regardless of the teacher's definition of good citizenship, some of his practices in evaluation were promoting submissive, conforming behavior. Even though the general objective of promoting good citizenship may have been highly laudable, the evaluative process was defeating any genuine attainment of the objective. A specific redefinition of what constituted evidence of good citizenship obviously was needed.

The important objectives of the course, then, for this teacher, were good citizenship and a quantity of academic information. This would seem to be an incomplete list of the legitimate and desirable objectives of studying U.S. History.

3. The practice of using the essay form for the examinations seemed to be justified mainly on the basis of opinions from former students now in college. These students felt that they had needed more practice in taking essay type exams before going on to higher education. The teacher adopted this form of test because of the presumed needs of the college-going students (who made up slightly more than one-third of the total student group in the high school), and with little thought as to the special advantages and disadvantages of different kinds of examinations for differing levels of students. His decision was not based on the obvious need to find the evaluative process with the greatest possible validity and reliability for the task at hand.

4. The teacher asserted that he counted off for misspelled words and grammatical errors. What, then, did the grade on the examination mean?

The test grade seemed to represent some judgment regarding a demonstrated knowledge of historical information plus an undetermined degree of skill in spelling and writing. If the examination was viewed as a measure of achievement in history, then the grade was diluted by the amount of weight given to grammar and spelling. If students and teacher interpreted the examination grade as some combination of achievement in factual learning and writing ability, then the practice was justified. The real issue raised at this point was whether or not the teacher really knew what his examination grade meant.

5. The term paper was assigned, not because of some planned objective to be evaluated, but probably just because it was always done in American history courses. The young teacher had never thought through his practice. Certainly term papers in U.S. History can be justified, but he had never faced up to that task.

Because of this and other symptoms, the coordinator concluded that the teacher in question was considerably naive about evaluation; and, as many of his fellow teachers followed similar practices, some of them were probably somewhat unclear in their conception of the nature and aim of evaluation also.

Teachers typically are patent behaviorists. They see the goal of education as changed behavior and are something less than satisfied unless they see evidences of learning revealed by actual behavioral change. However, some of the very important learning acquired by students may never be revealed to the teacher. These changes in behavior may not show themselves until years later—and far away from the classroom situation. This is one of the great frustrations for teachers. Doctors may judge rather quickly the worth of their therapy or medication; the patient gets better or he doesn't. Lawyers win or lose their cases. But teachers must make judgments about their teaching within severe limitations and often with very tenuous data.

### Levels of Evaluation

During wartime the armed services and other agencies[4] have considerable control over the environment of subjects to be evaluated. For instance, to find out if certain survival instruction has influenced student behavior, a group of men in training can be dropped ten miles offshore, each in a one-man life raft containing survival gear, and then be kept under surveillance to see if they are able to survive. Or a group might

---

[4] See for example, *Assessment of Men* (New York: Holt, Rinehart and Winston, Inc., 1948) for a fascinating account of situational testing by the O.S.S.

be placed in a deep jungle area, and then be given maps and a compass. If they are able to find their way back to camp by themselves, they have demonstrated the desired learning. Some branches of the service have developed such "situational" tests which assess the behavior of a soldier as a prisoner of war.

Schools have no such strict or extensive control over the environment of their students. Therefore, they must evaluate them at several levels.

*Behavioral level.*[5]     Evaluation at this level involves direct observation of student behavior. The teacher sets up a spelling test and observes whether or not the students are able to spell correctly. He scrutinizes the term paper and appraises it for neatness. Students type or take shorthand at a certain rate and with an observable degree of accuracy. The music teacher observes a pupil to see whether or not he can read music. Essay examinations are used to observe the thinking of the student—whether or not he can summarize data, outline ideas, and draw logical conclusions. From observing the work of the math student, especially if he is required to show on paper how he arrived at his answers, the teacher can determine whether or not his student understands how to work specific problems. In teacher-set tasks or classroom situations, behavior is judged directly.

*Planning level.*     Since the objective of the school is to change behavior, the behavioral level of evaluation is admittedly the most valid. However, it is obvious that some important outcomes are simply not easily observed or measured directly by the teacher. Thomas[6] uses an illustration in which a group of seventh graders are taught to sterilize water when there is a doubt as to its purity and fitness for drinking. But whether these students will be able to apply this knowledge if the necessity should arise at some future time, is uncertain and is not subject to direct evaluation.

By contrast, if you were a commanding officer in a military unit and wanted to evaluate this ability in your men, you could march them through the hot, dusty desert, and finally, at the end of the day, pitch camp on the bank of a stagnant pool. Then you could take out your record book and evaluate the men's behavior in relation to your objective. Let us hope that you would have a first aid crew nearby to pump the stomachs of those who react negatively!

---

[5] Thomas, *op. cit.,* 27–31. Discusses the behavioral, planning, and understanding levels of evaluation.
[6] *Ibid.,* 27.

Naturally, evaluation of this practical sort would be less than enthusiastically received by parents if used in the public schools.

Teachers must sometimes move a long step away from actual behavior and evaluate their students instead at the planning level. At this level of evaluation, the student may be confronted with a situation described on paper and asked what he would do in such a situation. The pupil reports what he would plan to do.

This, of course, introduces some chance for error in judgment, for people do not always behave as they plan to. Yet we know there is considerable agreement between what people say they will do and what they actually do. Pilots often pre-think emergency situations. They plan what they would do in different emergencies. This is found to facilitate the correct response in a real emergency. At any rate, teachers assume a positive correlation between the planned actions and the actual behavior.

*Understanding level.*    Much of the teaching and learning in high school has to do with factual information and knowledge. The teacher presents the material, explains it, and expects the pupils to remember it. This learning is appraised at the behavioral level. The teacher examines the students' changed behavior—they should now be able to respond to certain items of academic information without hesitation when they couldn't before. If the objective reads "As a result of this unit the students will be able to list the causes of the American revolution," then, of course, the teacher would evaluate on this basis. He would ask the students to list the causes and then see whether or not they were able to do so.

If some objective is difficult or impossible to evaluate at the behavioral level, then another, less valid approach is possible. For example, if the stated objective is "As a result of this instruction on the hazards of cigarette smoking, the students who now smoke will stop and the others will not start," the instructor is faced with a problem. Admittedly, this is a rather ambitious aim but certainly it lies at the very heart of the purpose of such instruction. The only way to attempt direct evaluation would be to spy on the students out of school to see if they were smoking, or one might check the nicotine stains on their fingers. Actually, the teacher would be more likely to test the pupils on their knowledge of the hazards of cigarette smoking. He might ask them to list the reasons for not smoking and to describe the long-range effects on the body. The teacher assumes that, if the students know these facts, they will stop smoking. He is evaluating at the understanding level.

Teachers assume that the comprehension of knowledge will cause appropriate behavior—that pupils will act in ways that are consistent with the facts which they possess. Yet we know that human beings are inconsistent and illogical. Decisions are influenced by emotions and conflicting motives. For example, many adults feel intuitively that the inhalation of noxious tobacco fumes cannot possibly be good for anyone, and medical reports during recent years substantiate this; yet great numbers of men and women continue to smoke, and, because of this added concern, may actually increase their smoking. Or, to take another example, a young man passes the written and driving tests for his driver's license and then gets a ticket on the way home for violating the speed limit. On all sides you can see examples of human behavior which are inconsistent and illogical in relation to the known facts.

Teachers further assume that if a person can remember academic information or can explain a process, he understands it. Tests should be constructed to appraise symptoms of understanding. A student may know that the explosive force of the early atomic bombs was about equal to the explosive force of blocks of TNT piled six feet deep over the area of a football field. But does this mean he really understands these data? A junior high school pupil may be able to recall the capitol, the main cities, the major rivers, the most important imports and exports, the area in square miles, the name of the president, and the general living conditions in Chile. But does this mean he really understands the country?

At this level of evaluation, the teacher moves two steps away from actual behavior via two very uneasy assumptions. Does the paper which "successfully" answers your question justify the belief (a) that the student really understands and (b) will act in accordance with this knowledge?

*Level of beliefs.*    Attitudes, prejudices, interests, and other affective elements are very important volitionally. Only if we can discover what a person feels or believes about certain things, can we predict his probable behavior with some accuracy. For example, the teacher may test a student regarding the characteristics of a certain minority group. But because that test probably will not reveal the student's personal attitude, the teacher cannot always predict the student's behavior toward members of that group. However, if a test is constructed specifically to appraise student attitude, the teacher may be provided with enough insight to be able to predict future student behavior with a reasonable degree of certainty.

Attitudes, interests, and prejudices strongly influence behavior. Affective elements such as these impel people to action. Therefore, it is desirable to seek evidence at this level of evaluation.

Teachers should attempt first to evaluate by judging student behavior directly. If this is very difficult or impossible, they should then seek evidence at other levels of evaluation. Teachers need to know and use techniques which will best appraise the aims and objectives of instruction. Some procedures are more appropriate than others at the various evaluative levels. Whatever specific methods are used, a characteristic sequence of action tends to be employed.

*Basic Steps*

As classroom teachers go about the business of evaluation, they normally follow certain basic steps in the evaluation process. This common pattern includes the following:

*State objectives.* The first step is to carefully formulate the objectives of the unit or lesson. If the principal should visit your class and afterward ask the perfectly legitimate question, "What were you trying to accomplish with your students today?" what would you say? Do you know what your goals are?

This list of objectives ought to include items which you realistically feel you can and will do something about in your teaching. This is no place for aims which are too high-flown to be achieved. Instead, this list must include those aims which you are actually working towards in your class. It doesn't seem unfair to insist that the teacher not list objectives which he intends to do nothing about or has no intention of evaluating.

General objectives might include such items as the following. This unit will help the students (1) learn to think more clearly, (2) develop improved study skills, (3) become more sensitive to the feelings of others, and (4) develop a healthy self-concept.

The teacher lists objectives toward which he believes the content of his course will contribute. The learning activities, instructional materials, and evaluative procedures are keyed to and are justified by the listed objectives.

*Restate in behavioral terms.* Rather than stating objectives in the light of teacher activity, the teacher finds it more desirable to restate the objectives in terms of student behavior. The student is at the center of the learning process; it is his behavior which the teacher hopes to change. Thus the objectives ought to be phrased in specific pupil behavioral components. They must indicate the desired student learning outcomes.

The objectives must attempt to describe the student performance that the teacher is seeking to develop. In restating the general objectives, the best approach is to consider what kind of changed behavior will be displayed by students who have successfully mastered this objective. How will they now behave? What can they now do that they couldn't be expected to do before?

The general objective of "Helping the students learn to think more clearly" could be restated more specifically through a series of descriptions of the student behavior judged to be symptomatic of one who has successfully demonstrated learning in this area. For example, some of the behaviors of the pupil who has learned to think more clearly might include the following: Students will (1) be able to summarize specific facts logically, (2) be able to draw valid implications from a well-described situation, (3) be able to develop valid generalizations from a set of basic data, (4) be able to apply generalizations to other situations, and (5) be able to approach new problems objectively.

Objectives are statements of instructional intent.[7] They should clearly communicate to others what you have in mind. The reader may not accept all the objectives in your plan, but he ought at least to comprehend rather precisely what they include. Broad objectives are often so abstract that few people can argue with them, but few people also can agree on their exact meaning. Some words are open to varied interpretation and, by themselves, make the objective fuzzy and almost meaningless. For example, what does it mean "to understand," "to appreciate," "to grasp the significance of," "to become acquainted with" or "to be exposed to" something? Such phrases often have been used in the past by teachers in the statement of their objectives. They provide little help in planning learning activities calculated to foster these aims, and they are of even less value in suggesting appropriate evaluative procedures. To illustrate, "As a result of this lesson the pupils will be exposed to outstanding examples of modern art" is an objective which leaves a good deal to be desired. The instructor must ponder the question of how does one go about "exposing" students to something—exactly what do you do? And, even more significant, how will you know whether they have been exposed to it? Is the student supposed to catch something? How should someone behave now that he has been exposed?

More common is the use of "understand." But again, how will the student who understands behave? Will he be able to recall pertinent facts, list appropriate concepts, apply certain principles, or correctly

---

[7] See Robert F. Mager, *Preparing Objectives for Programmed Instruction* (San Francisco: Fearon Publishers, Inc., 1962), 3–11.

match battles and dates on an objective exam? What do you mean by "understand the Bill of Rights?" If you actually plan to have the students read the chapter in the text, to present the Bill of Rights and explain it in class, and then to test them to see if they can write the Bill of Rights, then you ought to be accurate and formulate your objective forthrightly as "The students, as a result of this unit, will be able to list the Bill of Rights." The teacher must seek objectives which are written in terms of the changed student behavior which he hopes to promote through the classroom activities and which he will evaluate as evidence of successful learning.

Once the desired behavior is described with some specificity, the description, itself, usually implies the use of certain evaluative procedures. Where the general aim sought is the ability to think more clearly, such specific descriptions of desirable student behavior as "The student will be able to summarize specific facts logically" and "The student will be able to apply generalizations to other situations" immediately suggest practical ways of appraising progress toward the objective. Thus, this second step is vital to the success of the evaluative process.

*Seek evaluative situations.*    Next the teacher must look for possible classroom situations wherein students may display the behavior which he is attempting to develop. At this point, he must make some decisions regarding which objectives he can evaluate at the behavioral level and which must be appraised at other evaluative levels. The teacher must try to set up a situation in which the student is given the opportunity to behave in ways which reveal his growth toward the desired objectives.

Of course, the teacher can merely acquire a *sample* of the student's behavior. In a test situation the student usually realizes that his work is being sampled, and this realization gives rise to special conditions which may not obtain at other times. For example, Anne may spell every word correctly on a spelling test, but does this sample of her spelling skill allow you to assume that she will spell these same words correctly in a letter to a friend? Teachers should not assume that the test or any other form of student observation is always predictive of student behavior in other, more pertinent situations.

Because learning outcomes of many kinds are sought, evaluation utilizes many different procedures. Teachers must analyze the classroom situation for its evaluative possibilities and must understand the various testing instruments and evaluative processes in order to make appropriate choices. These instruments and processes must produce evidence regarding student growth toward the learning objectives.

*Define success.* What level of progress will you accept as satisfactory? The teacher must define "success" or "improvement." To illustrate, in a beginning Spanish class the instructor gave his pupils a vocabulary test of one hundred words. He found the test scores ranged from one hundred per cent correct to sixty-three per cent correct with the other scores distributed rather evenly in between. Now, what could he conclude from this? Obviously he was pleased that all students had learned the meaning of *some* Spanish words, for, as beginning students, they presumably knew few, if any, before the course began. In regard to the behavior sampled, the teacher found that at least one student knew the meaning of all the words and at least one other student knew only sixty-three of them.

Could this teacher set up a minimum standard of acceptability? For example, could he say that everyone who knew less than seventy-five per cent of the words on the test failed? If so, upon what basis could he justify his decision to define success at this particular level?

Actually, many experienced teachers, having developed ample "Jehovah complexes" along the way make this sort of arbitrary decision without noticeable concern. Cantor cautions, however, that

> At the extreme, if individuals are immutably different, if each one learns what he wants to learn, what he can afford to learn, or what he needs to learn, no general criteria can be applied. The performance of a specific pupil cannot be compared and ranked according to the performance of other pupils.[8]

If one student brings with him an IQ of 70, and another, an IQ of 130, can they both be held to a minimum standard? Should they both be expected to attain the same level of success? A minimum standard is unfair to both. The bright youngster is not challenged by it, and the slow youngster finds it impossible to reach with his intellectual equipment. Remember, both these pupils are required to attend school by law. Neither of them had the opportunity to choose his IQ. Yet the minimum standard assumes, in theory at least, that all students are capable of achieving at a certain level, otherwise the existence of such a standard would be completely absurd. Yet under a system of compulsory education it would seem a certain type of ridiculous logic that would consistently force a student to strive for a "standard" beyond his power to attain and then day after day punish him for not being able to attain it.

Sometimes teachers use the performance of the entire class as a criterion. The average score of the class is assumed to be some sort of a bench mark. Teachers can say that a student is achieving above or below

---

[8] Cantor, *op. cit.*, 201.

the average. But does the typical performance of the Spanish class set a standard for all students? In practice, it is as unfair to the bright student as to the slow student to set an "average" goal for all.

Obviously the classroom teacher works within some realistic limits. Some high school teachers teach six classes a day with an average of thirty-five boys and girls in each class. This totals 210 students with whom they must deal each day. Therefore, a completely individualized evaluation program is impossible. Yet a rigid definition of success and failure for all pupils is completely unfair. Teachers must know their students well and, must within limits, make some rough predictions of success or improvement for them. Thus, the Spanish student with an IQ of 70 may be achieving "successfully" if he scores sixty-three per cent correct on the Spanish vocabulary test; while the other student, considering his potential, may be seriously *under-achieving* if he scores eighty per cent. Many experienced teachers strive to know the capabilities of their students and to think of them in clusters. A small handful of students may be slow, so expectations for them ought to reflect a reasonable level of achievement. Another handful may be bright; therefore, their possible achievement is high. The bulk of the class clusters around the average range, and for them a substantial level of achievement, based upon the teacher's past experience with average students, may be expected. In addition, in a heterogeneous group, a youngster may be found who is especially slow or bright, and for whom the teacher needs to think individually about probable achievement. Homogeneous grouping may reduce the range of intellectual aptitude, yet such important factors as motivation, interests, and background of experience remain widely distributed. Here the teacher must still make multiple definitions of success in relation to his knowledge of his pupils.

## DEVICES AND PROCEDURES

The beginning teacher must study the various devices and procedures which are available for use in evaluation. There are a number of these, and each has special advantages and disadvantages. This knowledge enables the instructor to select the most appropriate procedure for his needs.

*Essay Examinations*

The essay exam is not dead! However, past experience has shown it to be notoriously unreliable in one sense; that is, in the grading of the examination. Different teachers reading the same exam paper do not agree on the grade. The same teachers reading the same papers after an interval of time do not agree with the former grade they assigned. Yet the essay examination is especially useful for appraising progress toward certain objectives. In using a varied approach to evaluation, essay questions have a real part to play.

Advantages of this form include the following:

1. The essay examination, if carefully prepared, can place emphasis upon the students' ability to use knowledge rather than merely retain it. The examination questions provide situations wherein students may organize ideas, summarize data, identify the most important facts, apply knowledge to the solution of a problem, creatively combine ideas, and the like. Pupils are required to recall pertinent information and use it in writing their answers.

2. Teachers may secure insight into the thinking of the students, for the answer to a discussion question usually is a record of this thinking. Points at which the material is incorrectly understood, misinterpretations, and gaps in knowledge are examples of the sort of learning problems which are likely to be revealed.

3. The use of essay tests tends to promote a certain type of study habit. The best preparation for discussion questions requires intensive study rather than extensive study. For most objective examinations, the students are likely to skim everything they have on the subject—lecture notes, papers, textbook. Essay exams encourage the making of outlines, summaries, comparisons, contrasts, lists of principles, and the identification of central ideas and concepts. This is really a different approach to studying.

4. The essay examination tends to eliminate guessing.

5. It allows students to display their learning. Many pupils report great frustration when the objective questions sample only superficially an area in which they feel very well prepared.

6. The essay examination is easier to prepare. Any good test question is difficult to formulate and, of course, essay exams require fewer questions than objective tests. The questions do not have to be duplicated, although the practice of writing the questions on the board might place some handicap on students in the back of the room who must squint or possibly come forward to copy them down.

Possible disadvantages might include the following:

1. The essay exam is not usually a comprehensive test of subject matter. The practice in most high schools is to give the essay test in a single class period. This means that the teacher can only narrowly sample the classwork which was covered. Actually, these four to eight questions, unless they are so broad that each would require the bulk of the period to answer, cannot sample the learning, except to a limited degree.

2. Extraneous factors, other than the actual test questions, come into play in grading an essay exam. Spelling, handwriting, grammatical construction, and neatness often enhance the "halo" effect when teachers allow the appearance of the paper to influence the grade. Some authorities have pointed out that the essay examination overrates the importance of knowing how to write well and underrates the importance of having something to say. Ability to distribute time wisely and skill in writing concisely are often very important to success. But, if these kinds of factors weigh too heavily on the examination grade, we are diluting the grade. If the student did not complete the essay exam in biology because he spent his time on the first few questions and simply did not have time to answer the last two, the grade, which presumably communicates something regarding achievement in biology, has been diluted to some degree; it may reflect ineptness in test-taking rather than poor achievement in biology.

3. Essay examinations are subject to subjective grading. The teacher's physical and mental state, his attitudes toward the subject, and his conscious or unconscious feelings toward the student all affect the way he grades. Teachers find, unless special precautions are taken, that they are inconsistent in their grading. The grade for one paper may be affected by the grade of an immediately preceding paper. A "C" paper may be given "B" if it follows an "F" paper; if it follows an "A+" paper it may receive a "D." Moreover, as teachers read down through a pile of papers, the grades they give tend to rise as time passes.

4. The time factor is an important disadvantage of the essay exam. The amount of time and effort expended above that of objective tests is such a limitation that teachers are cautioned to use the essay form only if there are clear and overriding values to be realized. Nevertheless, if essay questions are used because of their real advantages and with proper recognition of their limitations, the time required for grading may be worthwhile.

Certainly the use of this examination form can be improved. Some widely-used suggestions are as follows:

1. Improve the process of grading by reducing the subjectivity of grading. For each question, the teacher should list the specific ideas or points which ought to be included in the answer. This operates as a key which helps to quantify the expected answer and make the grading more objective.

2. Enhance the anonymity of the paper. In order to reduce the effect of past pupil performance and behavior upon the grade, many teachers have students place their names on the back of the paper or assign numbers or symbols for identification. Actually, characteristic

handwriting and verbal expressions soon give clues to the student writer's identity and reduce the effectiveness of this procedure.

3. A number of experienced teachers recommend reading all of the answers to one question before moving on to the next. The reading order can be reversed for the next question. Occasional reshuffling of papers is desirable during this process. This method tends to equalize certain extraneous factors and enables a comparison to be made on the basis of examining one question at a time.

4. Teach skills in studying for and taking essay examinations. This will aid in giving validity to your test and will help to equalize these factors which could penalize some students who have not developed these skills.

5. It is possible to improve this type of examination by increasing the number of questions and reducing the length of discussion expected for each. This is likely to provide a more valid sampling of the pupils' learning.

*Objective Test Forms*

Certain tests are termed objective because the scoring is accomplished by using a key to check correct or incorrect answers. Usually the person doing the scoring does not have to make subjective judgments. Thus, a clerk or even a student may check the papers with extremely high consistency. This is in sharp contrast to the essay examination which requires the teacher to make subjective decisions regarding the quality of the answers. In short, the test form is called objective or subjective according to the process involved in marking the test. However, *"The process of creating items is subjective* whether the items are true-false, essay, matching or multiple-choice."[9] In making up the test the teacher's judgment goes into the formulation not only of the question itself but also of the answers which will be considered acceptable.

Objective tests (true-false, multiple-choice, matching, and completion) have a number of important advantages.

1. This test form lends itself to a wide sampling of the material learned. Within a regular class period, a great variety of content areas may be explored. The objective test, then, is desirable in conserving teacher and pupil time.

2. Objective tests are highly flexible in that a number of different test forms are available for use with different objectives, and many different items may be included in the same test.

---

[9] Thomas, *op. cit.,* 48.

3. The scoring is objective. Answer sheets may be used, machine scoring is possible, and efficient keys are easy to construct. There is no question in the minds of pupils as to whether or not the teacher is showing favoritism, because anyone may check back on the scoring. Moreover, many of the extraneous factors discussed above are eliminated.

4. To a great extent, because of the objective scoring, the test is likely to be highly reliable; a paper receives the same mark, so long as the same key is used, no matter who scores it or when it is scored. In addition, the objective test, because of extensive sampling, is likely to examine the students equally in all the areas concerned, as opposed to the essay examination, for which students might prepare intensively in some areas and only slightly in others. Therefore, while in an essay examination a student might earn several very different scores, depending on what questions were asked, in an objective test, this particular problem can be avoided.

5. Objective questions may be reused. Admittedly, good test questions are difficult to formulate; therefore, some teachers build a file of objective type questions for their subject. By eliminating poor questions and constantly improving others, a reservoir of good items may be accumulated. This file helps prevent hastily constructed tests.

Of course, the objective test is subject to certain disadvantages.

1. Objective tests are likely to emphasize the possession of knowledge and neglect the functioning of knowledge. If you simply establish the fact that your students can recite the Bill of Rights, you may still have to make some uncomfortable assumptions regarding their use of these data in subsequent behavior.

2. Students are likely to study on a surface level, for they know that simple associations and recognition of facts or ideas are usually called for in the test questions.

3. Ability and experience in taking objective tests are sure to be of considerable benefit in dealing with hastily constructed examinations. The test-wise student may receive an inflated score simply because he is alert to grammatical clues, "tip-off" words such as *never* and *always,* and other fairly obvious technical test faults.

4. One disadvantage stems from the tendency of some highly intelligent pupils to ponder over the many implications they see in a particular question rather than taking the most obvious interpretation.

5. Objective tests contain a relatively large number of questions. Therefore, the teacher must spend considerable time and effort in their formulation. However, the objective form allows the bulk of the time to be spent before the test is given and reduces the amount of time required for making the examinations.

6. Because of the nature of the test form, the problem of students' copying from one another may be more pronounced.

*Recall or completion.* This type of examination usually consists of a direct question or an incomplete sentence in which blanks are substituted for the missing part. The student is to recall the answer or associate the proper word or phrase which completes the sentence. For example:

1. What state was admitted as the 49th state of the Union?
2. The 49th state admitted into the Union was _____.

This objective form emphasizes recall rather than recognition. However, unless questions are very carefully formulated, there may be a number of answers which could be accepted. In the example, "Ex-president Eisenhower was born in _____," pupils are likely to ponder whether you want the city, the state, the socioeconomic level or the year in which he was born.

*True-false items.* These tests consist of many statements, each of which the student must read and judge as true or false. The great advantage is that a large number of questions may be typed on a single page. Thus a wide area can be sampled, while, at the same time, economy of test preparation can be achieved. A brief example follows:

> *Directions.* Read the following statements carefully. If the statement is true, circle the "T" before the question; if not, circle the "F." You will not be penalized if you guess.

> T,F 1. The book, *Shuttered Windows,* was written by Florance Means.
> T,F 2. The *Diary of a Young Girl* by Anne Frank is a story about a a teenager living in Boston.

One of the serious limitations of this test is the fact that there is a 50-50 chance of guessing the correct answer. For this reason some teachers use a correction formula which reduces this chance factor. That is, wrong answers are subtracted from right answers, thus penalizing those who guess. However, the directions must warn the students if a correction formula is to be used.

*Multiple-choice questions.* This popular form uses a statement or question followed by three to five possible alternative choices. The pupil is usually asked to select the best answer to the question or the alternative which goes best with the statement given. Occasionally, teachers indicate that more than one of the alternatives may be correct, and must therefore be marked by the student.

> *Directions.* Choose the *best* alternative and write the appropriate letter in the parenthesis to the left of the question.

( ) 1. The President of the United States is the head of what branch
of the government?
   a. Legislative
   b. Executive
   c. Judicial
   d. Monetary

( ) 2. In the forming of our nation the several states came to have
certain powers which they alone could exercise.
   a. A state government may declare war if attacked by an
      enemy power.
   b. A state government has the right to coin its own money.
   c. A state government has the power to control public educa-
      tion within its boundaries.
   d. A state government may engage in the granting of titles of
      nobility.

As you can see, this type of question is more versatile than many
others. For example, often multiple-choice questions are written to require problem solving on the part of the pupil. A situation may be described and several alternative courses of action given. The student must
then think through the situation and choose the best solution.

Probably the most serious disadvantage of multiple-choice testing
lies in the difficult task of constructing fairly logical decoy statements.

*Matching.*    As the name suggests, two columns of items are given and
the pupil must match those items which correspond. Normally the right
hand column is longer in order to prevent students from using the process of elimination. Interesting modifications are sometimes used: for
example, a map might be given with numbers placed at important locations; a list of important rivers, cities, and other geographical features
could be matched with these numbers.

*Directions.* Find the correct English meaning of the Spanish words
in the left column and write the letter of this meaning in the appropriate
blank.

|       |         |    |         |
|-------|---------|----|---------|
| ____1. | arroz   | a. | ticket  |
| ____2. | billete | b. | cartoon |
| ____3. | camisa  | c. | family  |
| ____4. | dibujo  | d. | rice    |
| ____5. | familia | e. | juice   |
| ____6. | jugo    | f. | baggage |
|        |         | g. | shirt   |
|        |         | h. | cabbage |

The matching question is quite useful for quickly checking a number of associations which students may have formed. But because it only indicates association, it does not appraise genuine understanding of the details. Also, many teachers find that students are prone to ponder over the matching section of a test for a disproportionate length of time.

*Test format.*    Once the teacher is satisfied that one or more of the objective types will be appropriate, the question of format becomes important. Certain suggestions appear pertinent.

1. Directions must be carefully worded and placed conspicuously before each test sector. It is helpful to position the directions in the same location above each section of the test.

2. It is essential to group all questions of the same kind together. Students must be able to read directions and form an appropriate mental set in proceeding to answer the questions. It would be highly confusing to mix true-false, multiple-choice and completion items together.

3. The duplication of the examination papers should be carefully checked for errors and for blurred or faint copies.

4. The system to be used in answering the questions should be consistent throughout the various sections of the test. It should not unfairly increase the difficulty of the test and it should be efficient and convenient for scoring.

Although formal tests carry the bulk of the load in the evaluation of learning, they may, as we have seen, involve certain limitations. Some learning outcomes must be appraised by procedures which are more descriptive than quantitative.

*Observing Students*

Many experienced teachers, recognizing the limitations of the formal paper and pencil tests, seek descriptive data through direct observation. For example, if one of your objectives in teaching English has to do with developing student interest in reading for pleasure, the observations you make of students as they read and discuss their reading are probably the most valid and perceptive data which indicate progress toward this goal.

Teacher observation is essentially an attempt to remain alert to student actions displayed in the classroom which are relevant to certain objectives. This is usually somewhat different from test situations which are contrived by the teacher to force all students to reveal pertinent behavior which is then systematically recorded. In the statement of unit or course objectives, most teachers recognize that some of the aims are not susceptible to evaluation through formal examinations. Therefore, they must watch for symptoms of growth in these other areas whenever they might be revealed.

Observing has some significant limitations. Few teachers are trained observers; therefore, they tend to be inconsistent and unreliable in their observations. Pupils often know that they are being observed and behave differently than they might otherwise. In the normal flow of classroom activity, the behavior to be observed may be partially masked by other, non-pertinent behavior. Teachers seldom can give their attention fully to observation and may be distracted by immediate, pressing, and expedient duties and responsibilities. However, teachers may overcome some of these limitations through careful preparation and practice.

Observation is a very important evaluative tool. Instructors who would improve their competence should prepare for the observation. The behavior to be evaluated should be reviewed. It is generally better to watch for one kind of behavior at a time rather than to attempt to observe several kinds in one session. The classroom activity in which this behavior will be revealed should be carefully planned. If certain pupils are to be specially observed, their names may be noted in the daily lesson plan.

The teacher should record the results factually as soon as possible. Some observer errors are systematic, not chance errors. That is, observers tend to have certain mental sets and will see and remember things which are consistent with these. If Eddie has been a persistent troublemaker in class, the teacher may consciously or subconsciously have labeled him a problem student and may tend to note only the behavior which is consistent with this conception. Thus, the teacher must observe as objectively as possible. In addition, it is clear that errors increase with time so it is important that the observation be recorded as soon as possible.

*Observing and recording.*    Several devices have been found to be helpful in observing. Teachers may prepare checklists and rating scales. These are especially helpful in noting changes in behavior. The first step in developing a rating scale is to list the characteristics to be rated. Then a scale is arranged by which these will be rated. Whatever subject area you teach, if you seriously wish to increase pupil interest, you might develop a rating scale which looks something like this:

*Objective 1*:  As a result of this course the pupils should display interest in the study of this subject.

*Ratings:*    a. Alert and enthusiastic in relation to class activities, raises questions, volunteers for extra class work, reads outside material.

             b. Conscientiously does all assignments, usually prepared for class discussions, volunteers comments and pertinent questions occasionally.

             c. Sometimes unprepared for class work, minimal participation in class discussions, never voluntarily does extra work.

             d. Disinterested, never participates in discussion unless called upon, often unprepared.

Such a rating scale may be conveniently used in the evaluation of student behavior in relation to this objective. For each objective of this kind, the teacher writes a series of informal descriptions of behavior which appear to represent levels. It is difficult to judge fine distinctions beyond four or five gradations, thus a relatively simple rating scale is best.

The observer simply notes at what level the student appears to be behaving at various intervals during the school year. One student may start at level "c" and move up to "b" or even to "a" later. Another may already show characteristics of "a" and remain at this level. Still another pupil may display diminished interest and enthusiasm as the study progresses. A coding system may be used with the rating scale to reduce the teacher's clerical work. In the case of the example above, the instructor might write "Ib" in the grade book to indicate that the student has been observed at the "b" level for objective I.

Some form of the anecdotal record is often used to record the observation. This anecdotal record usually consists of two essential parts. First, a careful and objective description of the observed actions is written. Second, an analysis and evaluation of the incident is appended. These two parts—the specific description and the evaluative or judgmental elements of the report—must be kept separate. Other teachers reading the report might evaluate the observation differently and, of course, this would be very difficult if the teacher writing the report injected his interpretive opinions into the account of the observation. The written record is often prepared in duplicate with one copy placed in the student's cumulative file.

After some practice in classroom observation, and given clearly stated objectives of learning, teachers find the descriptive data which result from observing student behavior extremely valuable in regard to evaluation.

## REVIEW

This chapter discusses evaluation as an integral part of teaching, not something which is supplementary or adjunctive. The following questions will point up the main emphases of this topic.

1. For the classroom teacher, the term evaluation is distinctly different from the term measurement. What is this difference in definition? What are the basic principles in the important process of evaluation?

2. The central task of evaluation is an attempt to secure evidence regarding student progress toward instructional goals. What levels of evaluation may be used in the classroom? What basic steps make up this process?

3. Teachers utilize many different devices and procedures in a well-developed evaluation program. A specific test form is chosen because of its special attributes. What are the important advantages and disadvantages of some of the commonly used types?

# Selected References

Alcorn, M. D., Kinder, J. S., and Schunert, J. R. *Better Teaching in Secondary Schools.* 3rd ed. New York: Holt, Rinehart and Winston, Inc., 1970; Ch. 16 "Evaluation Principles and Appraisal Techniques" and Ch. 17 "Teacher-Built Tests."

Beatty, W. H., ed. *Improving Educational Assessment and An Inventory of Measures of Affective Behavior.* Washington, D.C.: Association for Supervision and Curriculum Development, N.E.A., 1969.

Bloom, B. S., ed. *Taxonomy of Educational Objectives, Handbook I: The Cognitive Domain.* New York: David McKay Company, Inc., 1956.

Clark, L. H. and Starr, I. S. *Secondary School Teaching Methods.* 2nd ed. New York: The Macmillan Company, 1967; Ch. 15 "Evaluation and Testing."

Esbensen, T. "Writing Instructional Objectives." *Phi Delta Kappan,* 48:246–47, January 1967.

Gorow, F. F. *Better Classroom Testing.* San Francisco; Chandler Publishing Company, 1966.

Hoover, K. H. *Learning and Teaching in the Secondary School.* 2nd ed. Boston: Allyn and Bacon, Inc., 1968; Ch. 21 "Assessing Learning Experiences: Measuring Instruments and Devices."

Kibler, R. J., Barker, L. L., and Miles, D. T. *Behavioral Objectives and Instruction.* Boston: Allyn and Bacon, Inc., 1970.

Krathwohl, D. R., Bloom, B. S., and Masia, B. B. *Taxonomy of Educational Objectives, Handbook II: Affective Domain.* New York: David McKay Company, Inc., 1964.

Thomas, R. M. *Judging Student Progress.* Rev. ed. New York: David McKay Company, Inc., 1962.

Wilhelms, F. T., ed. *Evaluation as Feedback and Guide,* 1967 Yearbook. Washington, D.C.: Association for Supervision and Curriculum Development, N.E.A., 1967.

# eight

## Grading and Reporting Pupil Progress

One responsibility which teachers periodically face with concern is that of assigning grades to students and subsequently reporting these grades to parents. Certainly, the process of evaluation is set up in part to result in a grade or mark; however, this is but one part of its work. Grading is simply especially visible and often somewhat controversial to the public.

Grading is often the sole contact that the high school has with many parents. Through this medium the school attempts to communicate something comprehensible regarding the students' work in the classroom. Teachers expend a great deal of effort and involve a substantial amount of student time in order that some symbol may be written down in the gradebook, copied on the grade card, and entered in the permanent file. Students and parents ponder these marks at length and presumably gain some sort of communication.

Many authorities verify the teachers' concerns and insecurity over these grades—concerns which most teachers come to intuitively. Without benefit of exhaustive research, school people tend to experience considerable frustration and doubt as they attempt to reduce the multiplicity of learning which each student attains in the classroom to a single grade or mark for the course. The many-sided evaluative process yields certain data which must be averaged somehow in order to arrive at a mark, yet the doubt still persists.

Beginning teachers, as a step toward a possible resolution of the problem, ought to focus their attention on several aspects.

1. A "C" given by one teacher may look the same on the grade card as a "C" given by another teacher, yet what does each grade really mean?

2.  Teachers make many statements regarding their approaches to grading, and these tend to fall into one of several philosophies or basic points of view. Ultimately it is an individual teacher decision—a decision each teacher must make and with which he must work.

3.  After the grades are established, they must be reported to parents. Certain reporting practices are commonly found across the country and their advantages and disadvantages should be understood.

## NATURE OF GRADES

Teachers spend a substantial portion of their time and effort in calculating and awarding grades. Students and parents usually are greatly concerned with grades even though the assumptions with which they interpret grades are often untenable. Grades have important and lasting effects, thus they ought to be the result of a careful and considered application of a defensible educational philosophy.

Read the following description and consider the underlying implications. What does this suggest regarding the nature of grades?

*Description*

Irene was enrolled in English 9. She had been failed twice before so this was her third time through the course. She was a neat, well-dressed girl, quiet, and somewhat withdrawn in class. The cumulative file revealed that her latest IQ score on a group test was 72.

The teacher found her to be a willing though not overly enthusiastic student; she handed in every assignment on time and, in the judgment of the teacher, seemed to be doing a more than adequate job considering her academic aptitude.

Irene enjoyed the out-of-class aspects of high school. She had many dates and sang in the mixed chorus. However, because of her low grades she was prohibited from joining any of the social and service clubs of the school.

Recently the English teacher caught her cheating on the six-weeks examination. In a tearful interview after school, Irene revealed that her parents had put a great deal of pressure on her to improve her grades—specifically to pass English this time—she thought this was the only way out.

Consider this situation a few moments. What are some of the implications which come quickly to mind?

*Implications*

It seems clear that Irene's previous English teachers had been grading on the basis of achievement. They had taken the position that the grade in English ought to represent achievement in the subject. They would agree with the following point of view:

> School marks should not be directly based upon attendance, behavior, effort, or any other characteristic of achievement other than progress or status in the course. Any other procedure is certain to result in or contribute to
>
> a. The misleading of investigators in educational research.
> b. Lack of objectivity and validity of marks.
>   (1) As measures of achievement and progress.
>   (2) As bases for promotion and classification.
>   (3) As data for educational and vocational guidance.
>   (4) As bases for college recommendations.
> c. The misleading of pupils and parents as to pupils' achievement.[1]

Irene found that she could not achieve satisfactorily with her mental equipment.

It appears that some sort of minimum standard concept must be operating here. Students who cannot measure up to this single yardstick must be held back even though this seldom results in increased learning to the student and usually results in the development of a poorer attitude toward the subject, teacher, and school. Her former teachers made the decision that Irene be failed in English even though she apparently did her very best to complete the work. Her lack of intellectual capacity prevented her from meeting the minimum standard. She is required by law to attend school; thus, as indicated in Chapter 7, it would seem to be a certain type of vicious logic that consistently forces her to strive for a "standard" beyond her power to attain, and then, day after day, punishes her for not attaining it. Since society has seen fit to compel her school attendance, what more can anyone ask than for her to try her very hardest to use her capacities and aptitudes to the fullest extent? To fail someone who does this is to admit that society has no place for this person.

Teachers have provided situations wherein students compete with each other for grades. Irene, though taking the course for the third time,

---

[1] Harl R. Douglass, *Organization and Administration of Secondary Schools,* rev. ed. (Boston: Ginn and Co., 1945), 395.

was still unable to compete successfully in this academic area. Actually, out-of-school competition is usually less vicious than the in-class competition which some teachers foster. For example, people with an IQ of 70 very infrequently find themselves competing for success in a group of research chemists. When they do compete in adult life with others who are far brighter than they are, they tend to do so in situations where other qualities are quite important. For example, reliability, industriousness, sincerity, and a good personality are of signal importance, beyond a minimal intelligence, for success in many occupations. On these bases, the slow student often competes fairly well. Irene was competing with considerable success in her social life outside the classroom. Any competition assumes a fair and substantially equal basis upon which to compete. For this reason we would not allow a flyweight boxer to be matched with a heavyweight. We don't let high school football teams play college or professional football teams. Yet Irene, who has an IQ of 72, was forced into competition with the rest of her classmates, probably all of whom had greater academic aptitude than she.

Increased parental pressure is merely another aspect of an impossible situation. In English class, under present conditions, Irene is probably confronted with three alternatives. First, she might try even harder. Of course, this is what she has been doing and, painfully enough, has found it to be ineffective. Second, she might quit. Actually the most intelligent thing to do would probably be for her to withdraw—to refuse to compete in something in which she is foredoomed to failure. If you were abruptly thrust into the ring with the current wrestling champion, an intelligent approach would be to grab a handy towel and throw it in the middle of the ring, or at least make it a very quick fall. However, Irene still has not quit trying. Third, she might cheat in her attempt to please her parents. Teacher and parent actions inevitably led to the cheating. A trained counselor or clinical psychologist would not be surprised at Irene's behavior. It is only a matter of time until she will resort to alternative number two. Hundreds of boys and girls in our high schools have come to this decision through trial and error. Once this alternative is utilized they are likely to be beyond the help of the teacher.

The case of Irene suggests some comments regarding homogeneous grouping and its possibilities, yet far more than half the high schools in America find that they are too small to attempt it. Attention to procedures aimed at individualizing instruction is clearly indicated, because the English teachers in this example (and other teachers before) systematically have destroyed the satisfying self-concept of an innocent student through their oversimplified conception of the grading process.

*The Meaning of Grades*

Grades have meaning in relation to how they are formulated, but they also may be understood through the demands made upon them by society. At present, grades are required to perform a variety of tasks.

*Functions of grades.*    The most obvious functions of grades have been categorized as (1) administrative, (2) guidance, (3) information, and (4) motivation and discipline.[2]

Grades are used administratively by the school in deciding whether or not a student may graduate, indicating he has passed or failed a course, and transferring from one school to another. Colleges use grades in their admission procedures. Often the grade point average of students in the "solid" subjects is calculated and used in screening students. Some businessmen no longer assume that a high school diploma assures high competency in the basic skills and take grades into consideration in hiring.

Counselors and advisors use grades in attempting to pinpoint student strengths and weaknesses, in planning future patterns of courses, and in making predictions about future job or education plans. Student-counselor discussions relating to educational adjustment inevitably center around grades.

Schools must communicate some sort of information regarding student progress and achievement to parents. Grades have customarily been used for this purpose. Students themselves are informed about teacher assessment of their progress by the grades received.

Grades and school marks are often the chief source of classroom control for some teachers. In addition, they are dangled in front of student noses to act as extrinsic incentives to learning. They sometimes form hurdles which boys and girls must clear before being allowed to participate in extra-class activities.

In the overall view, grades are seen to fulfill the demands made upon them only to a limited degree. Actually, among all the functions they are expected to serve, motivation is the only one served to a significant degree.

*False assumptions.*    Many parents and some teachers make certain assumptions regarding the nature and meaning of grades. A number of

---

[2] N. S. Blount and H. J. Klausmeier, *Teaching in the Secondary School,* 3rd ed. (New York: Harper & Row, Publishers, 1968), 419.

these assumptions are at least partially fallacious. Wrinkle's[3] classic discussion suggests the following:

1. It is assumed that a single grade can indicate the student's progress or achievement in a course. High school teachers are quick to see the fallacy here as they recognize the multiple learnings sought in their courses. In English, for example, the classwork deals with a broad subject matter and seeks a variety of outcomes. Does the final grade communicate anything comprehensible regarding student progress? A student who did very well in literature and very poorly in composition might receive the same grade as a student who did well in composition and poorly in literature. Another, who did an average job in both, might also receive the same class mark. Actually most English teachers are concerned with learning in the four communications skills: reading, writing, speaking, and listening. In addition, they seek student growth in the understanding of grammatical concepts, spelling skills, improved attitude toward and interest in books, more mature judgment and perspective in the use of mass media of communication, and the like. Grading practices require that some sort of final average be achieved in order that a single letter or number result. Obviously, the final grade is almost meaningless.

2. It is assumed that a "B" in one school is equivalent to a "B" in another school. Wide differences in student groups from place to place make it impossible to compare grades based upon local school standards. An average mark in a suburban school which draws its students from a highly selected, upper socio-economic population group, is bound to be different from the average grade in a school located in an underprivileged area. A college preparatory high school would differ considerably from the typical vocational high school. Actually, the grade has little meaning for us unless we also have some important information about the nature of the student group in the high school which gave the mark.

3. It is assumed that a "B" in one class is the same as a "B" in another class even within the same school and within the same course. At a joint faculty meeting of elementary and secondary school teachers, a school board member was observed telling the elementary teachers that "You must get tougher in your English instruction. When students come to high school they cannot meet the secondary school standards." The high school English teachers who taught ninth-grade classes then were asked to explain their standards. All said that a 94 or higher on

---

[3] William L. Wrinkle, *Improving Marking and Reporting Practices* (New York: Holt, Rinehart and Winston, Inc., 1947), 36–49.

the final exam meant an "A." They went on to give their conceptions of what ninth-grade English should involve. One felt that the development of student skill in writing was so vital at this stage that he heavily weighted the course in this direction. A second favored more emphasis on oral communication, both speaking and listening, because of its importance in our modern culture. A third believed that a balanced curriculum in general was best, though recent evidence seemed to suggest more attention be given to spelling drill. By this time it had become apparent that the 94 per cent required for an "A" was not the same for each teacher.

Teachers' standards and conceptions of course content vary considerably. In addition, it is obvious that class quality is likely to vary. One teacher may have a classroom group which is quite superior to another. These factors make it difficult to compare grades from one class to another unless the ability and achievement levels of both classes are also known.

4. It is assumed that a pupil can achieve any grade he wishes if he tries hard enough. The competitive marking procedure used in most classrooms is tied to some conception of minimum standards. Thus, the slow student, like Irene in the example given, can work to the best of his ability and still only receive a "D," while a bright student may do little or nothing and receive a "B." In terms of absolute achievement in knowledge of academic facts and understanding of concepts, the latter pupil will consistently outscore the youngster who possesses far less academic aptitude. In this sense, and as long as this grading philosophy is utilized, the assumption that any student can earn any grade he wishes if he puts forth sufficient effort simply is not true. Here, the ability of students to achieve to the maximum of their capacities is not being recognized; it is merely the rewarding of something which happened in the genes.

5. It is assumed that success in school is indicative of success in later life. It is significant to point out that most boys and girls spend about one-fifth to one-sixth of their lives in school (not counting higher education). This means that for a considerable proportion of their early lives young people are required to remain in a non-life-like environment. They are rewarded, punished, achieve success or failure, according to their ability to achieve in academic tasks. The point is, of course, that success in later life depends upon many other things in addition to academic skills.

If we correctly compare the individual to those with whom he associates, we evaluate the success of a truck driver by a comparison with other truck drivers. We do not evaluate him against a background of admirals, lawyers, physicians, and chemists. If we look at it in this way, it should not be such a shock to realize that Wendell, who almost flunked out of high school, is now the leading used-car salesman in town, and that Fern, the brilliant but introverted student, is presently an obscure file clerk in a governmental agency.

6. It is sometimes assumed that the student's grade is analogous to the worker's pay check. Wrinkle explains that the employee gets paid because he does something of value for his employer. Yet the student works for his own good. He studies and learns for his own benefit, not for the benefit of the teacher. Thus, it is fallacious to view the grade as pay for student effort. Actually, it is really a motivational device used by the teacher to impel the pupils to work.

7. It is assumed that competitive grading systems provide a worthwhile introduction to the competitive American culture. Certainly competition is a characteristic of adult society, yet cooperation also is a vital skill and attitude in the American democracy. Teachers with substantial backgrounds and insight in mental hygiene question the effects of stepped-up competition in the schools on the relationship of students in the classroom.

Linda and Nancy were next door neighbors. They had grown up together. However, competition between them, stimulated primarily by their mothers but aided and abetted by their teachers, destroyed the friendship which had existed between them in early life. Each time grade cards came home, the mothers eagerly rushed to compare grades. Linda happened to be a bright student, but Nancy was just a normal, average youngster. Under her mother's goading Nancy tried harder and harder, but was never able to match Linda's grades. Gradually, as Linda was held up as the example to Nancy, the friendship began to break down until by high school the two girls had to be separated. Thus, by forcing them into competition based on an unequal basis, the friendship turned into dislike.

Many teachers feel that self-competition should be emphasized, that a student should strive to improve his previous record rather than to compete with those not his equal. They believe that there is plenty of competition in American life already without the schools adding further competitive pressure on boys and girls.

8. It is assumed that grades may be used as the means to an end without their becoming ends in themselves. Recently a college class in educational psychology was asked to speculate on the results of throwing out grades as typically used and simply giving a mark of pass or fail. The overwhelming majority felt that no one would learn—there would be no reason to learn without grades.

This illustrates fairly clearly the fallacy of the assumption that grades are merely means to an end. As grades are dangled like sweetmeats before student noses in order to stimulate effort, they inevitably come to be seen as the goals of learning. Symptomatic of this development is the effort which students exert in analyzing teachers for hints as to what is likely to appear on the final examination and what sort of term report will please the instructor. The preoccupation is with what the teacher thinks and feels and what he wants them to study because, of course, he awards the grade. This perverts and distorts the real role of the student.

The assumptions with which parents, students, and some teachers view grades are seen to be at least partially fallacious. The false assumptions themselves suggest some modifications in grading and marking practices. Yet the overwhelming majority of parents time after time, in school district after school district, has asserted its preference for the traditional letter or number grading system. Teachers, recognizing the realities of local control of schools, have attempted to provide grades which are helpful and useful to all concerned.

## GRADING PRACTICES

Teachers faced with the necessity of giving grades tend to take one of several positions according to their philosophy of education. Certainly, there are strong arguments for one or another of these. It seems clear however that it is impossible for a single letter or number to fulfill all the necessary demands made upon it.

### Positions

Most arguments in schools tend to revolve around two opposed philosophies: (1) a student ought to be compared with the achievement and ability of his classmates or (2) he ought to be given a grade based upon the progress made relative to his individual aptitudes and capacities. In favor of the first position, it is asserted that students will learn to assess their powers realistically only if they are compared to the achievement of the group. Grades are significant only if they reveal the relative standing in a class. It is argued that the second philosophy implements the task of American secondary education in accepting and seeking to develop the varied potentialities of all boys and girls and, in a democracy under compulsory attendance laws, it is unfair—certainly misleading—not to recognize the degree to which the student makes use of his potential.

Should the student's relative achievement be the sole basis for the mark or should his effort be recognized? It seems evident that if students are graded on the basis of effort the slow student may receive an "A" as easily as a very bright student. There is something repellent about this approach to some adults. After all, a salesman seldom gets paid simply because he tried; he gets paid according to how many sales he makes. A production worker gets paid to produce, and if he can't produce he gets fired.

The achievement approach to grading generally includes some use of the normal probability curve. This assumes that any continuous variable will display a distribution which approximates the bell curve based on the laws of chance. Thus, a teacher who "marks on the curve" may decide to award 7 per cent "A's," 23 per cent "B's," 40 per cent "C's," 23 per cent "D's," and 7 per cent "F's." Or if the teacher recognizes that the high school population is not a normal one, that some selection has taken place because, for example, some of the slow students have already dropped out, he may utilize a different set of proportions— possibly 15 per cent "A's," 25 per cent "B's," 40 per cent "C's," 15 per cent "D's," and 5 per cent "F's." Experienced teachers know that in rather large classes a majority of the marks cluster around the average and spread in decreasing proportions as they approach the extremes. However, the curve has severely limited applicability in small classes, elective subjects, and in the higher grades.

A compromise position is probably more common in practice than a rigid adherence to either of these philosophies. Few teachers are willing to go straight down the line with either of the two approaches. Curriculum workers and supervisors feel that local decisions ought to be made in individual schools depending upon the nature and purpose of the school and the kind of student group enrolled. Thus, the faculty and administration of a high school work toward agreements in the area of grading. This, of course, means that different schools may come to different positions.

A fairly common compromise applies the achievement criterion to the large group of students who cluster in the average, normal range, but the criterion of effort and self-competition is utilized in grading the students with low aptitude and those with high aptitude. Sometimes a faculty will agree that slow students, compelled to attend school by law, may receive passing grades (up to a "C" normally and only occasionally a "B") solely on the basis of effort or self-progress. At the same time, a bright student who is loafing, even though his relative achievement is superior, will receive a "D" or even a failing mark. In any case, careful interpretation is necessary.

*Grading in Ability Groups*

Much homogeneous grouping is found in high schools large enough to accomplish it satisfactorily. In this case, the grading problem becomes multiplied as groups are deliberately set up within the same subject in order to cluster individuals of similar ability. Parents are concerned when two individuals of unequal ability receive the same mark. Students are unhappy when they must work twice as hard to achieve an "A" in the top group as they would to receive an "A" in the average group. The administrator expresses the fear that the academic honors at graduation might be won by students who are not really outstanding. Teachers commonly report the concern that some boys and girls will deliberately try to get into a lower group so that they will not have to work so hard for grades.

Principals and teachers are seeking possible answers. A recommended approach which bases class rank on an accumulation of points through the whole high school attendance was described as follows:

> Students are usually grouped in three to five categories in a required subject such as English. There may be the top section of Senior English designed to prepare students for the Advanced Placement Program. There may be two low ability sections designed for those who do not plan to attend college. The remaining five or six sections would likely be standard college preparatory sections. Under a point system, an "A" would be valued at five points, a "B" at four points and so forth in each section, but the multiplying factor would vary according to the ability categorization. The multiplier for the top section would be six, for the middle groups five, and for the low sections four. Thus, a student in the top section would accumulate 30 points by receiving an "A" valued at five points multiplied by the factor of six for his ability group. The maximum points possible for the middle groups would be 25 and the maximum for the low sections would be 20.
>
> This plan would have the same general effect as raising one letter the grades of those students in the top section and lowering one letter the grades of those in the low sections.[4]

The grade which is communicated to the parents would be that which he received in his particular class. The point system would only affect the student's rank in his graduating class. "It would, however, assure the parents and students that those in the top sections would not suffer in terms of college acceptance."[5]

---

[4] Kenneth E. Michael, "What are Some New Trends in Reporting Student Growth and Achievement to Parents?" *NASSP Bulletin,* 44:148–49, April 1960.

[5] *Ibid.,* 149.

*Teacher Decision*

Every teacher must make some sort of personal decision regarding grading. It is helpful if the high school staff is able to work cooperatively toward a mutually satisfactory position. This contributes to consistency among the faculty. Students are not graded in such a variety of ways in different classes, but rather a consistent policy with which to deal in all classes during the day should be followed. However, ultimately and inescapably each teacher must determine what grading procedure will be followed in his classroom.

Every teacher must take a position and be able to defend it. Sooner or later a parent will come in to see the principal and question a grade. The teacher may be asked to bring his grade book and explain the grade. Some instructors keep a file of papers on each student for this purpose. In addition, it is helpful if the teacher knows what his grade means. Many teachers find that a careful statement of course objectives and an evaluative process which clearly attempts to appraise progress toward these objectives are the best assurance that the grade will mean what they intend it to mean.

The classroom teacher ought to seek to reduce student fear. He may do this by discussing his grading system with his classes. He may explain the objectives, the means of evaluation, and the bases of the grade to them early in the year. Students need to be kept informed of their progress. Some teachers make it possible for pupils to keep an individual record, actually enabling them to calculate their standing at any time. Students have the right to have their grades remain confidential—a matter between themselves and the teacher. This means that there should be no reading of grades aloud, no posting of grades by names, and no comparative progress charts on the wall. The discussion of achievement and self-progress is appropriate for a conference, not an audience situation.

# REPORTING TO PARENTS

The grade card is really the only established line of communication between teacher and parents in most high schools. It is a very important link. Parents have the right to know about the progress and achievement of their sons and daughters in school. Teachers recognize the important influence that parents can have upon the learning of boys and girls, and administrators realize the public relations value of a well-planned reporting system.

*Practices*

An overwhelming majority of secondary schools in the United States use the familiar five point scale (ABCDF) of grades on the report cards which are sent home with the students at the end of every grading period. The student receives a single letter grade for each course in which he is enrolled. A few schools utilize a three point scale—"P," pass; "F," fail; and "H," honors—and a few have reduced this to simply "S" for satisfactory and "U" for unsatisfactory.

Even though the single score or letter grade would seem easy for parents to understand, it has been suggested above that the single mark is almost meaningless unless one has a good deal of additional information. In addition, teachers report that the process of summarizing and averaging grades, keeping track of marks on grade books, and entering grades on grade cards for all the students they have in their classes reaches a bookkeeping and clerical job of considerable significance. Some schools call off classes once every grading period so that teachers may spend the day averaging marks and inscribing the appropriate grade in the proper space on each report card of every student in their classes. It would appear desirable to relegate as much of this clerical work as possible to clerks who are paid less and require far less training. The loss of these teaching days seems an additional high cost to pay for a task which might be accomplished in some other way. A new development may provide real assistance in schools large enough to afford it. The use of district owned, leased, or shared computers and the punch card report cards has given much relief to the human resources of the school.

Occasionally, report cards provide for teacher rating of other outcomes in addition to student achievement and growth in subject matter (for example, social habits, citizenship, work habits). This, of course, compounds the work of grading and reporting.

Because of the obvious limitations of the typical report card, a variety of supplementary reports are increasingly being explored. An "unsatisfactory progress report" is commonly used to notify parents that the student's work leaves something to be desired. The report indicates the nature of the unsatisfactory work and its possible cause. The school mails these reports to parents to insure delivery and requests parental reply. The report often enlists the help and support of the parents while there is still time to alter the situation and also prepares student and parents for the possibility of a low mark when the report cards come out.

A few schools have tried the elementary school practice of sending informal letters to the parents of each student. The teacher makes out reports for one class each marking period rather than attempting to write to the parents of all pupils at the same time.

Once the purpose of the letter is explained and the nature of the class and its basic objectives described, the teacher discusses in detail the student's progress, strengths and weaknesses, attitude toward the subject, and achievement in relation to self and class. While parents are eager to hear something good about their child, they are entitled to an accurate report based on the teacher's professional judgment.

The conference method of reporting, often used in the primary grades, has been attempted in high schools. However, the parent-teacher conference has apparent limitations. Obviously, the great problem lies in the task of scheduling parents' conferences with five or six different teachers who work with their youngster. Each teacher may have to confer with parents of as many as 180 students in all his classes. In addition to the conferences, the school records must be kept up; therefore, this procedure adds considerably to the total work of reporting. Some parents are not enthusiastic about taking the necessary time to meet with the high school teachers.

A promising variation is the parent-counselor conference. Here, the counselor acts as the representative of the school in interpreting test scores and teacher evaluations. Much information on each student needs to be accessible to the counselor as well as a real personal acquaintance with the student. Of course, excellent communication is necessary between teacher and counselor if this plan is to be successful.

*Improving Reporting*

Although a variety of reporting practices may be observed in the schools, most secondary schools use the traditional report card which lists a single letter or numerical mark for each course in which the student is enrolled. Unjustified parental confidence in this reporting procedure and the weight of tradition are probably the two strongest factors in this persistence.

Improvement in reporting practices is likely to be in the nature of some sort of compromise. On the one hand, the school has the vital responsibility for communicating something meaningful and helpful to parents in regard to the learning of their boys and girls in the schoolroom. This single grade has been shown to be almost without meaning and certainly grossly inadequate in this respect. On the other hand, the potentially most helpful technique of parent-teacher conferences is seen to have important and seemingly insolvable disadvantages.

Schools would do well to work with parents in seeking a valid, helpful, and efficient marking and reporting system. Committees made up of teachers and parents have made significant progress toward improved practices.

Productive activity typically involves the examination of purposes to be accomplished by the reporting procedures and the development of an agreed-upon list of aims. The present report card and its marks are evaluated with these in mind. A revised system is sought by the committee which meets the demands and expectations. Following tryout and further refinement a new reporting procedure is proposed to the school administration. The committee assists in implementing the changes after they have been adopted by the school board.

Sound improvement is most likely to come only as teachers and parents work together toward a reporting procedure which will most nearly fulfill the need of both the home and the school.

## CHEATING

Cheating in the high schools has become a problem of considerable magnitude. Experienced classroom teachers, counselors, and administrators indicate great concern over this behavior.

A number of conditions contribute to the problem. For example, the anxiety level in the schools has risen. Many parents exert great pressure on their children to achieve in school (some elementary school educators report cases of ulcers in children at that level presumably because of this pressure). The society in general tends to reinforce the fact that graduation from high school is the absolute minimum expectation for all youth and that college is the route to happiness and success.

Schools may contribute to the situation by excluding "non-academic" subjects from the grade-point average and emphasizing "standards" in the interest of intellectual excellence. One principal prides himself on double checking every "A" given in academic subjects in his school by asking the teacher to justify it. This, of course, results in fewer "A's" being given. One wonders why he doesn't also check up on the "F's" as well.

The advanced placement (college level) classes, seminars, and honors courses offered in the secondary schools have resulted in stepped-up competition among top students. A good student in one of these highly selected groups may find himself the lowest person in the class for the first time in his life and may feel the temptation to cheat to keep up with the leaders.

Some of our teenagers have become over-involved in a wide variety of school-related and community-related activities. When their school-work begins to suffer, some may consider desperate means to maintain their level of achievement in school.

An interesting phenomenon has developed in some schools. Informal interviews with high school students have revealed that for many the question of cheating in school is not a moral or ethical question—it is simply the role of the student to "beat the system," to get through the classwork in any way he can. Of course, some of the adult models of modern American morality which students see around them do little to help the problem. It is reinforced by the fact that the young people may feel that much of the work is not really relevant to their lives.

## Teacher Behavior

It is clear that there is more cheating in some teachers' classes than others. The classroom teacher may *inhibit* or *facilitate* cheating. For example, the teacher with a crowded class who gives an objective test and then retires to the front of the room to read the latest novel is just inviting his students to cheat. Many teachers use alternate forms of the same test or an essay examination in an over-crowded situation.

Certainly, there are some important attitudes toward cheating which the teacher ought to take.

1. The teacher must remain alert. Students expect the instructor to be watchful during the testing period. He should not be overly suspicious —examining shirt cuffs and peering over shoulders—but it is his role to be watchful. The better students especially resent other students looking at their papers. Because of the "student code," many feel that they cannot report the cheating, even though this may diminish their relative achievement in the class. Most of all, they tend to blame the teacher for not doing his best to prevent it.

2. The teacher should move around the room. Students have developed a high degree of skill in screening some of their activities from the teacher's usual position at the front. Simply moving to the side and the rear will tend to minimize cheating.

3. The teacher should set up the physical arrangement and organization to inhibit cheating. When the class is small enough, seat students at every other desk. Plan for an orderly procedure for passing out and collecting test papers. Insist on certain time limits and communicate these to the students. These and similar plans will be more effective than several stirring sermons on the subject.

4. The teacher must be sure before accusing someone of cheating. It is better to let someone go for now (there will be other tests coming up) than to make a false accusation. One junior high school teacher found two essay exam papers were almost identical. They were good papers but one was from a boy who had an average record while the

other boy was a top student in the class. The teacher made the obvious conclusion; she called the average student in and accused him of cheating. It so happened that this time he had really prepared for the test in order to show his teacher he could do it. The other boy had gone skiing, gambling that he would be able to pass the test without studying for it. He admitted later that in desperation he had copied from the paper of the average student sitting next to him. The teacher had obviously acted without sufficient evidence and, as a result, the teacher-student relationships in this class suffered greatly.

Cheating seems to be a problem which no amount of work by administrators, counselors, teachers, and student leaders will completely eradicate. The beginning classroom teacher must accept the realities of the situation and prepare in advance to minimize the problem.

## REVIEW

Chapter 8 explores the difficult and controversial areas of grading and reporting. Teachers are uneasy, parents are unhappy, and students are confused because of the typical practices. The following items will assist you to identify important foci of this discussion.

1. Grades are called upon to fulfill a number of demands yet most parents approach them with certain fallacious assumptions. What are these assumptions and how well do traditional grades fulfill their functions?

2. Grading is often a lonesome task; the individual teacher must make pivotal decisions and live with them.

3. Once marks are established, the school has the task of communicating with parents about the learning of their children. What are typical practices and possible means of improvement?

# Selected References

Clark, L. H. and Starr, I. S. *Secondary School Teaching Methods*. 2nd ed. New York: The Macmillan Company, 1967; Ch. 16 "Marking and Reporting to Parents."

Douglas, L. M. *The Secondary Teacher at Work*. Boston: D. C. Heath and Company, 1967; Ch. 10 "Reporting to Parents."

Grambs, J. D., Carr, J. C., and Fitch, R. M., *Modern Methods in Secondary Education* 3rd ed. New York: Holt, Rinehart and Winston, Inc., 1970; Ch. 14 "A Grade by Any Other Name: Grading and Reporting Student Progress."

Hipple, T. W. *Secondary School Teaching: Problems and Methods.* Pacific Palisades, Calif.: Goodyear Publishing Company, Inc., 1970; Ch. 5 "The Teacher and Cheating."

Hoover, K. H. *Learning and Teaching in the Secondary School.* 2nd ed. Boston: Allyn and Bacon, Inc., 1968; Ch. 22 "Assessing Learning Experiences: Evaluation and Reporting Procedures."

Oliva, P. F. *The Secondary School Today.* Cleveland: World Publishing Company, 1967: Ch. 22 "Marking Pupil Progress" and Ch. 23 "Reporting Pupil Progress."

Risk, T. M. *Principles and Practices of Teaching in Sunday Schools.* 4th ed. New York: American Book Company, 1968; Ch. 21 "Evaluating and Reporting Student Progress."

Terwilliger, J. S. "Self-reported Marking Practices and Policies in Public Secondary Schools." *NASSP Bulletin,* 50:5–37, March 1966.

Weldon, L. L. "Cheating in School: Teachers are Partners in Crime." *Clearing House,* 40:462–63, April 1966.

Wilhelms, F. T., ed. *Evaluation as Feedback and Guide,* 1967 Yearbook. Washington, D.C.: Association for Supervision and Curriculum Development, N.E.A., 1967.

# nine

## Classroom Control

All beginning teachers tend to be concerned about their ability to establish and maintain control in the classroom. Certainly this control is just as essential to teaching now as it was in past years. However, because of greater knowledge of the nature and conditions of desirable learning and insight into the need for optimum mental hygiene in the classroom, the modern teacher uses new and improved control procedures with his students.

In the high school today, the teacher must deal with an ever-increasing cross section of the American youth. Because of compulsory attendance laws and powerful pressures from parents and potential employers, the overwhelming majority of high school age youth attend high school. This means that the students in your classes will represent widely varied socio-economic backgrounds. In addition, some of them may be something less than enthusiastic about studying material which appears remote from their immediate vocational or social goals.

The beginning teacher can best prepare himself through the following activities:

1. Classroom control, like many other aspects of teaching, presents problems of great variability, and occurs within a matrix of subtle and shifting relationships which make a mechanical "cook book" approach impossible. The teacher should gain a deep understanding of certain basic principles which have been identified through research in many areas and long experience in the classroom, and which have been verified empirically in practice.

2. Control measures may only be successfully applied as the teacher comes to have a fuller knowledge of boys and girls. To this end, some

**189**

of the conditions which influence adolescent behavior should be considered.

3. Beginning teachers desperately seek suggestions which may be helpful in the initial stages of their experience. You should assiduously seek tips and procedures which experienced teachers have developed and used successfully over the years. If they seem to agree with the basic principles for classroom control, you ought to think through their possible use with your classes. These suggestions represent a place to begin until you can develop your own techniques.


## CLASSROOM SITUATION

It is difficult to predict exactly the sort of control problems which will occur in a given classroom. However, many of them have certain elements in common. For example, read the following situation, adapted from a case study, and place yourself in the role of the teacher in charge.

*Situation*

> School has been in session for four weeks; it is a Tuesday morning and you have your first class of the day settled down to work on an activity you have specified. You decide to move about the class to help those students who are having trouble, when you see one boy reading a comic book. You ask him to get busy like everyone else.
>
> He says, "I won't do it!"
>
> You say, "Now, Jim, give me the comic book and get down to work."
>
> He replies, "I don't see any reason for doing this stuff anyway. I won't do it!"
>
> The boy is a big (6 feet, 180 lbs.), slow-thinking, school-hating student. However, this is the first time he has refused to do anything. Normally, he would make at least a half-hearted attempt.

What are the possible implications? What are the possible alternative courses of action? What would you do?

*Analyses*

As you ponder the answers to the questions posed, here are the reactions of three beginning teachers.

> 1. *Mary B.* If this happened in my English class, I would hope that I could ignore Jim at first, for he is not disturbing the rest of the class.

However, since I have decided to do something about the situation, I would first try to talk quietly to Jim so as not to distract the other students who are working.

I realize that I would have to proceed with caution. Jim is probably seeking attention and approval from his classmates (he is a slow student and probably hasn't had much academic success in the past), and would like nothing better than to have me help him secure the desired audience. Therefore, I would speak calmly and quietly to him.

Since the assignment had to do with the writing of a short story, I would try to use the comic as a springboard to get Jim to work. I would talk with him about the comic book. What about using its basic plot in his short story? Are some of the characters interesting and useable? Does the beginning or ending give him some ideas?

If these efforts failed and Jim still would not get down to work, I would send him to the principal and let him handle the problem. Certainly, I would inform Jim's counselor about the classroom behavior.

2. *Tim S.* This is a problem that is extreme and must be handled immediately and positively. It is not something that can be ignored because of the serious consequences. If Jim gets away with reading a comic book in class, the next day my whole class might bring comics to read.

I would insist that he give me the comic before doing anything else. I would take it from him, if necessary; I am 6 feet 2 inches tall and weigh 210 pounds, so I *could* take it from him. As the teacher in charge, I must retain control if I want the pupils to respect me. By now they would have heard the conversation, and would be interested spectators to the battle of wits.

After I had removed the comic, I would ask Jim to get out his math book and begin working. If he refused, I would order him to get down to work like everyone else. Rebellion must not be tolerated.

At this point, another refusal would cause me to inform Jim that he was no longer to be permitted to attend my class, and then I would escort him to the principal's office for further disciplinary action.

3. *Ginny T.* I am not sure it would be wise to say, "Give me the comic book." However, it probably would be the impulsive thing to say.

Jim's statement, "I don't see any reason for doing this stuff anyway," would immediately suggest to me that it is just possible that it was *my* fault for not making the assignment clear to him. After all this represents a change in his pattern of behavior—in the past he usually made an attempt at least. Therefore, I think I would forget the comic book and first try to clarify the assignment.

Probably the sudden realization would come to me that I really don't know much about Jim. I haven't been through the cumulative files to dig out information on all my students.

With only this present information to go on, I would proceed to try to help Jim get started on the assignment. If he was still reluctant, I would quietly tell him that since he refused to do the classwork I would have no choice but to give him an "F" for the period. This, then, was his decision.

Finally, I would ask Jim to see me after school. At this time I would try to discover the cause for his refusal to work.

These comments suggest a number of implications and possible alternative courses of action.

### Implications

In this situation, Jim said that he didn't see any reason for doing the work. As Ginny suggested, this could have meant that the assignment was not clear enough for Jim. If so, he might have been punished for something that was initially at least the teacher's fault. This also might have meant that Jim really saw no value in the classwork and needed to be shown why it was desirable or useful to him.

The actions reported represented a break in Jim's behavior pattern. If this reaction was typical, the teacher would expect it and probably would have been prepared to deal with it. Something must have caused this new behavior for, in the past, he at least attempted every assignment. However, there was no time to explore possible causes and, as Tim indicated, something had to be done immediately with only the limited data available. This, of course, suggests that the cumulative files should have been scanned for pertinent information on Jim as well as the other students before the event happened.

The teacher had to consider the effect of his actions on the rest of the class as well as on Jim. As Mary pointed out, the teacher could have, if he was not careful, distracted the other students from their work, or, as Tim indicated, made sure the class was impressed by the teacher's handling of the situation. Certainly, the teacher's actions might have influenced the present and future behavior of Jim and the other students. Whatever was done had to be considered in the light of its effect upon the individual and the group.

Teacher behavior in the control situation was clearly related to the teacher's conception of teacher role. Tim, for example, was concerned with preventing loss of face and asserting the authority which he felt necessarily resided in the teacher. He seemed to see the problem as a "duel-to-the-death," showdown situation. The comic book had to be removed once he had asked for it or he would have lost the respect of the class. Ginny, on the other hand, apparently did not look upon the comic book as such a serious matter. She was much more concerned with causes for the student behavior.

One very serious possible consequence of Tim's treatment of the problem might have been to cause Jim to do something he never intended to do in the first place. For example, by engaging in open combat before the interested gaze of the whole class, Tim might have forced Jim to swear at him or even to strike him—either of which would have been cause for expulsion from school. Mary's insight into a possible cause for the student's behavior—desire for attention and approval—suggests that if the attention of the other pupils was drawn to the teacher-pupil conflict, Jim might have felt it impossible to back down.

Tim's threat to Jim that he would no longer be permitted to attend the class could have backfired if the school regulations did not permit teachers to make these decisions. For example, if the boy convinced the principal that he deserved another chance and appeared in class the following day, Tim's highly prized authority might really have been shaken. The teacher must be careful not to make threats or ultimatums that he may be unable or unwilling to carry out.

The source of control is an important consideration in any situation. Ginny obviously attempted to use grades when she told Jim that it was his decision whether or not he got an "F" for the period. Tim felt that his size and the status position of the teacher were sources. Mary utilized student interests as a source of control. Both Mary and Tim relied heavily on the principal as a secondary source if their efforts were found to be unsuccessful.

*Possible Courses of Action*

The comments by the three beginning teachers reveal or imply several possible alternatives. Some of these are immediate and some are long range.

One course of action in similar classroom control situations would be to ignore the student. Mary commented that as long as Jim was not disturbing the class she would have preferred to ignore him. This is sometimes called "discipline by avoidance." Some teachers try very hard not to notice minor infractions with the hope that they will not be repeated. This may sometimes be justified; however, the incident should always be noted for it may provide clues to subsequent behavior. At best, it is but a temporary expedient.

Tim indicated that removal of the comic book would have been his initial course of action. He felt that the comic was the apparent distracting interest, and its seizure would have paved the way for Jim to get down to work. Moreover, the teacher had asked Jim to give up the comic book, and the teacher's authority was challenged. Certain conditions, however, might have prevented the student from surrendering this symbol of nonconformity. This action by the teacher would have exaggerated the importance of the comic book and actually distracted the attention of both teacher and pupil from the real issue in the situation—why the student could not or would not do the assigned work. Ginny correctly, it would seem, felt that the comic itself was of less importance than discovering causes for Jim's behavior. The removal of the comic by force, as Tim suggested, would have been a dangerous and unnecessary action to attempt.

Both Mary and Ginny made direct attempts to bring Jim back into the work of the class. Mary sought to use the comic book itself as a springboard to get into the assigned lesson. Her goal was to relate the diverting interest to the assignment. Ginny attempted to explain the assignment more clearly in case a lack of understanding was blocking Jim's efforts. Another approach might have been to try to relate the assignment more closely to Jim's personal goals. This would have required an adequate knowledge of the student and often a lengthy conference.

Certainly, an immediate concern was to prevent the incident from interfering with the work of the class. Thus, a quiet discussion in the back of the room, at the teacher's desk, or out in the hall would have been desirable. If classwork is likely to be seriously distracted, the teacher may need to remove the irritating element. The modern public school is involved in mass education; therefore, the individual sometimes may have to be removed temporarily so that the group may continue its work. This is not to say that the teacher ought to abdicate in favor of the principal. Instead, the teacher must institute other efforts, utilizing the counselor and other resources, to deal constructively with the individual.

Discipline situations happen in the present and must be dealt with in some way immediately; however, long-range activities will seek to find causes for the student's behavior. Mary said that she would have reported the incident to Jim's counselor. This would not only have provided the counselor with added information about Jim, but also presumably would have set him to searching for causes. Teacher-counselor cooperation is necessary for the effective performance of both roles.

Ginny recognized the inadequate information possessed by the teacher in the situation, and she suggested that the cumulative files might have offered pertinent data which could have been helpful in dealing with Jim. Other teachers who had him in their classes and Jim's parents could have been contacted for possible clues to his behavior.

If the teacher has retained a wholesome relationship with the offender, a personal interview might provide that most valuable setting in which to discover causes. This might be arranged for after school or during the teacher's planning period. If possible, it should be set up so that it is not perceived by the student as punishment, but as an opportunity to discuss the episode with the teacher involved.

Discovery of apparent causes will lead to measures which promise some remediation. These may be instituted by the teacher alone or through the cooperation of counselor, principal, other teachers, and parents. Of course, not all causes will be within the school's power to correct. However, often just the knowledge of the conditions which led to the behavior will make the teacher more understanding and helpful in his treatment of a situation.

## BASIC IDEAS IN CLASSROOM CONTROL

Study of similar classroom discipline situations, results of research in many areas, and experience in the classroom have led to certain concepts and principles which are basic to the handling of control problems.

*Nature of Discipline*

The word discipline is confusing because it is used in so many different ways. Sheviakov and Redl[1] suggest three meanings as teachers use it. Discipline represents (1) the degree of order established in the classroom, (2) the method by which order is established, and (3) an euphemism for the word punishment. In discussing classroom discipline, one must be careful to recognize which meaning is used.

As you think about classroom control, what do you want students to do? How do you want them to behave? The word control implies conformity, docility, and obedience to the directives of the teacher. Is this what you would strive for? From the point of view of the student, the most desirable discipline in our society is *self-discipline* or the "organization of one's impulses for the attainment of a goal."[2] Within the context of a class, "group discipline involves control of impulses of individuals composing the group for the attainment of a group goal."[3]

The teacher's concept of the nature of discipline is very important for it may determine the kind of control possible in the classroom. If the teacher visualizes discipline as basically the teacher's responsibility to impose rules and regulations, the result is bound to be a constant battle

---

[1] George V. Sheviakov and Fritz Redl, *Discipline for Today's Children and Youth* (Washington, D.C.: Association for Supervision and Curriculum Development, a Department of the National Education Association, 1944, 1956), 21–22.

[2] *Ibid.,* 4.

[3] *Ibid.*

of enforcement. If the teacher recognizes the teleology of discipline, he will emphasize the importance of student held goals and provide for student effort toward the attainment of these goals. This teacher facilitates self-discipline oriented toward the satisfaction of pupil purposes. Of course, in the teaching situation this is not an either/or thing. Sometimes you will need to use your own control measures so that order may be established in the group. However, the objective is to increase opportunities for student self-control.

*Aim of Classroom Control*

In the schoolroom, what is the purpose of classroom control? Certainly control is not sought as an end in itself.

To be very realistic it must be pointed out that principals prize very highly the teachers who can establish and maintain order, and this may be a partial justification for control measures. Effective control is one of the characteristics of successful teaching. However, the only real justification for classroom control is *to facilitate learning.* The teacher's primary task is to provide learning experiences for his students, and the great importance attached to discipline is derived from the necessity to establish order in the group so that the learning may occur. This implies that all efforts directed toward class control must be subject to evaluation according to whether or not they facilitate learning.

*Discipline in a Democracy*

The modern American high school exists within the context of the American democratic society. Thus, it must help prepare youth to participate in this society and it must utilize processes which are consistent with the democratic beliefs held by this culture.

Democratic discipline attempts to preserve the healthy self-concept of each individual as a person of worth and dignity. It strives to benefit the majority, yet respect the rights of the minority. It seeks to provide opportunity for students to participate in their own control. It is oriented toward the progressive attainment of self-direction.

This means that both the teacher and students must come to prize behavior characterized by respect for the property of others, decisions made for the benefit of all, importance of majority opinion, self-direction, respect for the rights and integrity of the individual, and the like. This is not to suggest that classroom democracy is not without limits. For example, the students and teacher in a mathematics class cannot through majority vote, decide that they do not want to study mathematics any more this semester, and would prefer to study arts and crafts instead during this class time. Certain decisions are beyond the control of teacher and pupils. In this case, they have been assigned to deal with the area of mathematics during this particular period. Thus, the freedom to operate democratically exists within a framework. Certain goals are appropriate, although there may be considerable room for decision among pertinent goals, and certain activities may be relevant to the subject area to be studied.

In the classroom, democracy operates within limits. However, instead of seeking conformity, docility, and automatic obedience, the teacher should provide for the development of pertinent pupil goals and establish democratic processes which will allow self-direction in the accomplishment of these goals.

## Sources of Control

Orderly, controlled, student behavior in any class situation is derived from one or more sources. These sources of control may be either intrinsic or extrinsic to the learning itself.

*Intrinsic sources.* Certain, highly effective sources for control lie within the learning process itself. Obviously, the factor of interest is important. The lesson may be so interesting to some boys and girls that they would rather participate in the learning activity than do something else. Thus, the teacher seeks to make lessons as interesting as possible to students because this in itself is a powerful source of discipline.

The learning process as it is set up may facilitate control. If the class procedure is tightly organized, there may be little opportunity for students to engage in activities which are unrelated to the classwork. As the teacher's planning takes into consideration the factor of length of attention span and provides for variety in teaching procedures, the teaching-learning process will enhance classroom control.

Research in learning indicates that, as students develop realistic self-expectations and are kept appraised of their progress, better attitudes toward the learning and sustained effort are developed. The classroom learning atmosphere is also important. Pupils learn more readily and display more cooperative behavior in a class in which there is a favorable feeling tone.

*Extrinsic sources.* Most teachers seem preoccupied with the sources of discipline which are essentially external or outside the learning process itself. One of the most prevalent extrinsic sources of control is the grade. A common approach involves the teacher with the grade book in one hand and a red pencil in the other striving for class control by using grades as a club. This usually works with most students who come from middle-class homes where grades are highly prized. However, occasionally one may meet a student who has little if any concern for grades. One high school student told a teacher, "I wish you would give me an 'F'; the principal told me that he would kick me out of school if I failed another course, and I want to get a job." Certainly, grades have long been used in an attempt to secure class control.

A few teachers use sarcasm and razor-edged wit to make students conform. This is grossly unfair, for the student would be severely punished if he replied in kind. It would certainly not improve class morale or facilitate subsequent discipline attempts.

Sometimes in the elementary and junior high school grades, teachers resort to physical fear in establishing control. This was a common source of discipline in schools until twenty-five or thirty years ago; however today actual use of physical force is fairly rare and when used is usually reserved for the principal to administer. Any teacher who finds himself threatening to use physical force should be sure he is able and willing to carry out his threat. Beyond this, he ought to consider the possible effects upon the students in the class.

The peer group may operate as a powerful influence upon standards of behavior. Most youngsters, especially adolescents, want to be accepted by their peers. Therefore, the behavior expectations of the peer group are important determiners of pupil conduct. Teachers must study the mores of the student group for the program of discipline must operate within this framework.

Other extrinsic sources are often noted in use in the schools; for example, fines for misconduct (the legality of this procedure may be questionable), point systems leading to automatic suspension or punishment, student courts, and the like.

Behind the teacher stands the principal and his administrative staff as secondary extrinsic sources of discipline. Beyond this the legal structure of society exists as a tertiary source. These normally are not called into action unless the teacher's efforts are ineffective or unless the behavior of the pupil is very serious.

It should be obvious that intrinsic sources of control are preferable. By their very nature they are an integral part of the process of learning. They tend to be ultimately more effective and longer lasting than extrinsic controls.

*Behavior Is Caused*

One of the most significant insights which teachers gain as they work with youngsters is that behavior is caused. If Charles is sleeping in the back of the room, if Nancy snaps back at the teacher, if Sam habitually cheats in examinations, there are some logical reasons to be discovered if possible. Some teachers are too quick to place "labels" on students. The student is "lazy," "just plain mean," "no good," or "bad." This is a dead end because once the student is labeled he then may be marked for special treatment in the classroom and forgotten. However, if the teacher really believes in the causality of behavior, then he must constantly be searching for causes for the misbehavior and, utilizing all the available assistance, attempt to remove the causes.

The behavior observed in class may be viewed, in most cases, as symptomatic of deeper problems. The symptom itself is often treated without any attention to the underlying conditions. Obviously, if the deeper problem still exists even though the particular undesirable classroom behavior is eradicated, some other kind of behavior is likely to appear which may prove to be even more undesirable.

## POSSIBLE CAUSES OF ADOLESCENT MISBEHAVIOR

Student behavior is the resultant of the human organism interacting with the environment in which it exists. The youngster must deal with many forces and pressures, some arising within himself and some exerted upon him by the society into which he has been born.

Adolescents especially become concerned about their health problems. Often they develop intense concern regarding normalcy. Defects or illnesses which, in themselves, are not incapacitating may have serious social and emotional impact. Thus, boys and girls come to feel they are abnormal, different from their peers, and hopelessly inadequate. Actually, it is estimated that at least one-third of the students in our schools have a serious defect of some kind (for example, heart murmur, poor eyesight), and an additional one-third have minor defects (for example, teeth which need attention, nutritional deficiencies).

Some diseases are so debilitating that the pupil may be unable to exert the expected amount of effort in the classroom. Other conditions, such as hyperactivity, may make it difficult for the student to remain quietly in his seat for the entire period. However, the psychological concomitants often have serious implications. For example, our society has fully accepted the wearing of glasses to correct defects of eyesight. This is not true as yet for devices worn to correct hearing defects. The high school student who must wear a hearing aid often puts it on in the morning but removes it before reaching school. He would rather not be able to hear all that goes on in the classroom than to display his abnormality so obviously as a hearing aid requires him to do. Sometimes the hearing or sight loss is so gradual that students and their parents are unaware of the deficiency. Thus, student inattention in class may actually be caused by not hearing or seeing what is going on.

Young people have taken up a frightening array of drugs. These range from the sniffing of glue to the use of hard narcotics. Many school and government authorities increasingly are engaged in the study of the causes of the problem and possible means of prevention and control. Of course, communities vary greatly in the nature and severity of drug usage by youth, but it is clear that educators must become more aware of the effects of hallucinogens, stimulants, depressants, and narcotics on the mental and physical health of boys and girls.

Teachers must seek to understand health factors in the behavior of their pupils. A very important function which teachers perform is to roughly screen students for obvious defects. In this way, they train themselves to observe students carefully for signs of sight and hearing problems, illnesses, and symptoms of drug use and to refer them to the nurse, school physician, or principal.

*Academic Aptitude*

Students come to the school with varying degrees of academic aptitude, and behavior problems result as the classwork proves unsuited to their levels of ability. The bright youngster who is not challenged and stimulated by the work may utilize his intellectual powers in devising ingenious ways to disrupt the class. As the teacher pitches the assignments to the level of the average student without any real attempt to plan for individual differences in ability, the pupil with substantially greater potential may be bored, restless, and sometimes contemptuous of the teacher and his fellow pupils.

The boy or girl of lower academic aptitude often finds little success experience in the classroom. He has constantly been "punished" for something largely beyond his control. He didn't choose to be born with an IQ of 70, yet he may find it impossible to meet the teacher's *minimum standards*. Therefore, he seeks other avenues to success since he is required by law to be in school. He may uncritically follow the suggestions and examples of other, more clever, mischief makers.

*Home Environment*

Much of what the individual is, is a result of his home environment. Parental standards of conduct are accepted uncritically by young children and become modified somewhat as the peer group culture becomes important. In some families, stealing is perfectly acceptable, "as long as you don't get caught," and certain four-letter words are standard means of communication even at the dinner table. Thus, some youngsters may be reflecting simply their acceptance of their parents' standards when they exhibit undesirable behavior in the classroom.

The child who comes from a home in which parental control is over-strict may carry a built-in resentment toward all authority. Therefore, the teacher, as the authority figure in the schoolroom, may be automatically resented no matter what he does. In other homes with too little control, youngsters may learn lack of respect for all authority. In this case, the teacher's authority initially may be ignored.

Parental attitudes toward school are reflected in the behavior of their children. If parents do not prize a high school education, their sons and daughters are unlikely to be highly motivated toward earning a diploma. Other youngsters may be motivated beyond their ability as parents hold goals for them which they find difficult or impossible to achieve.

Occasionally, a pupil who appears dull and confused in class may come from a home in which family quarrels and impending divorce result in his being caught in cross currents of violent emotion. He may be "emotionally bruised" and unable to function adequately in school.

Some students are allowed to stay up very late watching television or attending a movie. They may simply be sleepy and not purposely in-attentive or lazy. Others may be working to help support the family, and have expended so much energy that they find it difficult to complete the work required in school.

In a period of increased militancy in the United States, boys and girls from minority races often are caught up in the struggle for equal op-portunities, more integration, less integration (e.g., "black schools for black students"), problems of busing to achieve racial balance, recogni-tion of racial contributions to the American culture, and the like. They bring their powerful emotional positions into the classroom and some-times use them as excuses for misbehavior. Other youngsters may be similarly affected by parents and family having strong feelings; for example, liberal, reactionary, anti-draft, anti-war, pro/anti-integration. Our nation is involved directly in epic stresses and, of course, they find their way into the life of the school.

Persons who have a more talented brother or sister, or are afflicted with "momism" are other examples of students bringing with them the possible causes of misbehavior. Certainly, the learning which goes on in the home and neighborhood environment is an important contributing cause of behavior in the schoolroom.

*Teacher-Caused Problems*

Classroom behavior, desirable as well as undesirable, is, of course, partially the result of teacher action. One important contributing factor is the almost universal teacher attitude long referred to as "mind-body dualism."[4] In the classroom, the body is treated as an intruder. Even though boys and girls must bring their legs and arms with them into the classroom, the noise made by the awkward adolescent shifting his feet, the tapping pencil which is symptomatic of building tension, and other such noises made by a healthy, active, growing individual temporarily caught in a sedentary environment are considered to be out-of-place. Teachers should not insist on an unreasonable degree of physical inactivity even in the classroom which must of necessity deal primarily with things intellectual.

The majority of teachers are from middle-class homes, and they often find it difficult to understand students who come from upper and lower socio-economic backgrounds. Typically, the school insists upon rather rigid and severe standards of conduct based on middle-class values. This may not facilitate acceptance and adjustment of the pupils from the extreme socio-economic levels.

Teachers themselves have problems, and occasionally seek to work out their maladjustments on the boys and girls in their classes. In interviewing students who had been referred as major discipline problems, one school psychologist recently estimated that in the case of a majority of these children, the problem was really the teacher's problem and that by transferring them to another teacher's class the discipline situation would be cleared up.

These have been some of the causes for students behaving as they do. If the teacher believes that boys and girls are not simply "lazy," "no good," or "just plain bad," but rather that behavior is caused, he would refrain from labeling students and look for similar underlying, causal factors.

## SUGGESTIONS TO THE BEGINNING TEACHER

The beginning teacher can best approach this complex and troublesome responsibility in the classroom with the assistance of practical suggestions tested and verified in use. Teachers must inevitably work out their own control procedures which are consistent with their own personality and

---

[4] John Dewey, *Democracy and Education* (New York: The Macmillan Company, 1916), 164.

adapted to the particular situation in which they must work. However, these borrowed procedures offer a starting point.

*Plan for "Red Line Areas"*

Every school calendar can be analyzed for its "red line areas." The day before and the day after Thanksgiving and Easter vacations and the week preceding Christmas vacation are obvious periods of time when special planning should be undertaken. Other such "red line areas" are the day of the football game with the rival school, the day or so leading up to the all-school carnival, and the afternoon of the junior-senior prom. These should be marked on the calendar for special planning. Certainly, other interests and enthusiasms are operating in competition with the class-work, and high-interest lessons and activities must be sought which will minimize discipline problems.

*Organize Routine Efficiently*

A considerable amount of classroom activity might be classed largely as routine. The collecting of papers, passing out materials, taking attendance, and making daily assignments are examples of typical class activities which ought to be organized as efficiently as possible. Occasionally, teachers are observed spending ten to fifteen minutes of the period taking roll while the students sit idly talking and playing in their seats. Sometimes teachers move about the room collecting papers from each student instead of having them passed forward or being collected by a student. If the class is allowed to come forward en masse to secure supplies, confusion is bound to result. Actually, the students as well as the teacher benefit as the routine activities are tightly and efficiently organized.

*Overplan at First*

Beginning teachers invariably benefit from overplanning. A certain degree of confidence is derived from knowing exactly what you are going to do each period. Of course, the plans must be flexible; however, specific, detailed plans are essential at first. It is wise to lay out more work than you think you possibly can accomplish in a single class period in order to avoid the experience which happens only once—the daily lesson plan has been used up, it is still fifteen minutes until the end of the period, and you stand before thirty-five expectant faces with your heart in your throat, perspiring profusely, grasping wildly for something to do. Some teachers keep an emergency activity plan handy for use in just such a case or when the normal plan doesn't go well.

*Know the School Routine*

When you first start teaching, one of the initial tasks is to familiarize yourself with the normal school routine. For example, find out how attendance is checked and picked up by the office, what the procedure is for handling tardy students, whether or not students may go to their lockers for forgotten materials, what the procedure is for sending a student to see the principal or counselor, what to do when a pupil is sick or hurt, how books are checked out of the library, what is involved in taking your class to the library or other school facility, how to secure and use audio-visual machines, what to do when you need a custodian to clean up something which has been spilled or broken, and when and how all-school announcements are made. You can minimize confusion and remove uncertainty if you know how to take care of these matters and are ready for them when they come up.

*Learn Names Quickly*

The use of a seating chart will help you in the essential job of learning the names of the pupils quickly. Most persons intuitively know how important an individual's name is to him, and it simply is a clear demonstration of your interest in your students if you rather quickly are able to call each of them by name. In addition, it is considerably more effective to say, "Now, Sally, please pass your paper in" than "Will the girl in the green dress pass her paper in?"

*Know Your Students*

Every possible source must be tapped in order to get to know more about your students. Some school districts help new teachers in this task by providing bus tours around neighborhoods from which students come. In this way, you can secure an insight into the general home backgrounds of individuals as you place their home addresses in the area. Cumulative files are available and should be studied. Information about the academic achievement, academic aptitude, extracurricular involvement, health status, parental situation (divorce, separation, occupation of father and/or mother), number of siblings, mobility of the family, and the like is vital to knowing and understanding your students. Student conferences, observation inside and outside school, home visits, and discussions with teachers and counselors are other sources.

*Handle Your Own Discipline*

Each teacher should seek to handle his own classroom control problems as they arise in his class. There is little doubt that the teacher himself is most likely to provide the most constructive and ultimately the most effective discipline as he works with his pupils in the day-to-day teaching-learning situation. As soon as the teacher sends the recalcitrant boy or girl into the principal's office, he admits that he cannot handle the student or the situation. Of course, there may be a few students who justifiably must be referred to the administrator; however, the teacher who sends a steady stream of pupils to the office is demonstrating his inability to teach.

Often the instructor simply reaches the "point of no return" too quickly. For example, the normal and healthy exuberance of youth and the understandable inclination to chat with friends about something interesting are seldom serious enough to justify sending students to the office unless the teacher falls into the trap of saying, "Ted, if you make one more sound I shall send you to see the principal." Then, if Ted does make another sound, he must be sent to the office. Actually, the problem is one of class disturbance and/or inattention to the lesson. A more constructive approach would be in the direction of making the lesson so interesting that Ted would rather participate than chat, or to break up seating combinations which tend to produce disturbances. If Ted and John always seem to have a great deal to chat about and seem unable to keep from talking, then one or the other might be moved to another seat where the chances of disturbance are less. In this way the problem is resolved constructively without the danger of losing contact with the student and without making something serious of a relatively normal and healthy tendency.

## Keep Your Radar Swinging

One of the simplest and most effective techniques which teachers use is to keep eye contact with the class. As the teacher sweeps his gaze about the group, he learns to spot discipline problems before they start or as they begin to develop. He senses how the lesson is going, how the pupils are reacting to the classroom activity. Often this awareness will allow him to modify and make more effective his class procedure and thus reduce control problems. At any rate, this technique will help the teacher to identify and deal with discipline situations before they gather momentum.

## Underreact

Self-control is just as essential for the teacher as it is for the students. The teacher should strive to display self-control as an example to his class. Actually, the safest thing to do in any classroom conflict is to underreact. Above all, try not to become angry. Of course, students are likely to forgive if they realize that their instructor really likes them. But the teacher who cannot control his emotions is less able to deal constructively, objectively, and intelligently with the situation. Impulse expression is immature, unprofessional, and ultimately ineffective.

*Project Your Personality*

The successful teacher is one who is able to come across to the pupils as a real, live, human being. If they realize that he is a warm, friendly, accepting person who has his good days and his bad days, good points as well as faults, but who is sincerely interested in them as individuals, they are more likely to accept and try to work with instead of against him.

Occasionally, a teacher, because of a misconception of teacher role or teaching method, may adopt an aggressive, threat-producing attitude. Threat in the classroom leads to rigidity of perception and reduction in intelligent behavior on the part of the students. It reduces the inclination and ability of pupils to adapt to changing conditions. Thus, it interferes with learning as well as leads to discipline problems. The teacher who possesses a good, healthy personality and who is able to operate naturally and consistently with it, is less likely to have discipline problems.

One experienced teacher utilizes this common-sense approach with his classes. He says, "You are stuck with me as your teacher and I am stuck with you. We might as well make the best of it and in the process all of us may learn something about the subject." Actually, the great majority of students are interested and naturally curious about a great many things. They are quite willing to cooperate with an interesting person in order to learn more about the subject matter.

# REVIEW

This chapter discusses classroom control against the background of a classroom discipline situation. From the analyses, implications and possible courses of action, certain principles are pointed up. Before you go on to the next chapter check yourself with the following questions.

1. Do you understand the basic ideas of classroom control? Do you see how the treatment of the discipline situation could be improved by their application?

2. Assuming that you believe that behavior is caused, do you have a better idea of where and how to look for possible underlying causal factors when faced with a behavior problem in the classroom?

3. After reading the suggestions for the beginning teacher, do you feel more certain of yourself in preparing for classroom teaching? Do you have some fairly specific things in mind which you intend to do as you begin teaching?

# Selected References

Ackerly, R. L. *The Reasonable Exercise of Authority*. Washington, D.C.: National Association of Secondary School Principals, 1969.

Blount, N. S. and Klausmeier, H. J. *Teaching in the Secondary School*. 3rd ed. New York: Harper & Row, Publishers, 1968; Ch. 15 "Promoting Mental Health and Self-Discipline."

Clark, L. H. and Starr, I. S. *Secondary School Teaching Methods*. 2nd ed. New York: The Macmillan Company, 1967; Ch. 17 "Classroom Management."

Douglas, L. M. *The Secondary Teacher at Work*. Boston: D. C. Heath and Company, 1967; Ch. 14 "Discipline."

Hoover, K. H. *Learning and Teaching in the Secondary School*. 2nd ed. Boston: Allyn and Bacon, Inc., 1968; Ch. 25 "Maintaining Effective Class Control:: Discipline Problems."

——. *Readings on Learning and Teaching in the Secondary School*. Boston: Allyn and Bacon, Inc., 1968; Ch. 22 "Discipline Problems."

Madsen, C. H. and Madsen, C. K. *Teaching/Discipline: Behavioral Principles Toward a Positive Approach*. Boston: Allyn and Bacon, Inc., 1970.

Muuss, R. E. "First Aid for Discipline Problems." *N.E.A. Journal,* 52:9–11, September 1963.

Oliva, P. F. *The Secondary School Today*. Cleveland: The World Publishing Company, 1967; Unit 6 "Discipline and Control."

Risk, T. M. *Principles and Practices of Teaching in Secondary Schools*. 4th ed. New York: American Book Company, 1968; Ch. 12 "Effective Classroom Management."

# ten

# Extra-Class Activities

An extremely visible part of the total work of the secondary school is the extra-class activity program. Most schools are evaluated, to some degree, by the public according to these student activities. The typical parent knows a great deal more about the status of the varsity football team than the status of the English curriculum.

The more familiar term is extra-curricular activities. However, this program is part of the curriculum of the school. As pointed out in Chapter 3, the "planned activities and experiences which students have under the direction of the school" embraces the organized courses which carry credit toward graduation as well as the student extra-class activities of the school. Thus, the term extra-curricular is less desirable because it implies that these student activities are outside the curriculum and not really a part of the school's educational program.

Certainly, the modern high school is much concerned with extra-class activity; indeed some critics charge that it is too preoccupied with this program. They say that it tends to pervade the entire school, and that all teaching is affected by the extra-class events. Thus, the beginning teacher needs to explore several aspects of the subject.

1. Extra-class activities are looked upon as a legitimate part of the work of the school, contributing in many ways to its purposes.

2. The extra-class program involves a wide variety of activities and typically is plagued with a number of problems.

3. Teachers are often called upon to contribute to the extra-class program. They especially need to be prepared for the role of sponsor.

## NATURE OF EXTRA-CLASS ACTIVITIES

Extra-class activities must contribute to the educational objectives of the school. Only in this way can they be justified. If they fall within the accepted definition of the curriculum, then they become a legitimate activity of the staff and, at the same time, become subject to the same sort of evaluation as any other part of the curriculum.

### Definition

The extra-class program refers to those activities under the direction of the school for which no credit is given toward graduation and which are not a part of the regularly organized instructional program. This includes a wide variety of activities such as student government, social clubs, subject-matter clubs, assemblies, school publications, music and drama, intramural and interscholastic athletics.

### Values

A number of possible values are likely to accrue as desirable student activities are organized.

*Need groups.* During the adolescent years, boys and girls feel the urgent need to belong to a meaningful group, and they will find some kind of group to join. One very significant value of the high school's extra-class program is the establishment and maintenance of socially acceptable groups to which students may belong. The school attempts to provide interesting and desirable group activities under the supervision and guidance of professional personnel.

*Special interests.* Students are likely to have a wide variety of interests not all of which are satisfied in the classroom program of the schools. Extra-class activities perform an important function in helping boys and girls fulfill special interests and aptitudes. For example, groups of students interested in astronomy, fencing, short story writing, reading, automotive mechanics, stamps, puppets, advanced mathematics, and the like form clubs which bring together young people who enjoy sharing a common interest.

*Exploratory experiences.* The extra-class program provides an opportunity for students to sample many different experiences without having to take a year or semester survey course in the subject. They may try out for the school plays, work on the paper or yearbook, attend meetings of various subject-area clubs, visit some of the hobby groups, or join one of the vocational clubs. In this way, they begin identifying interests and capacities in various fields. This may aid the individual considerably in deciding upon further educational plans and making wise occupational decisions. It may also increase the individual's enjoyment of constructive leisure-time activities.

*Motivation.* Through the student activity program of the school, real interest and motivation in school subjects may be developed. The very bright students, for example, may be bored with the normal pace of the classroom learning but, because of the science club which meets on Saturday morning and which has the use of the laboratory facilities, some of them may be motivated to participate in the science classes and secure the basic material which will enable them to do even more of the challenging things they enjoy in the science club. Students working on the school publications, seeing their writing and bylines in print, are stimulated to greater effort in improving their spelling and English usage. Thus, the student activities may actually provide for more effective in-class learning.

*Holding power.* The holding power of the school may be increased through extra-class activities. Even though some students find few satisfying experiences inside the classroom, many of them will continue in school because they secure satisfactions in the student activities. Some boys may stay in school primarily so that they can participate in athletics or, perhaps, because they like to sing in the school choir. Other students find the social activities so attractive that they prefer not to drop out. At any rate, students tend to remain in school longer when there is an effective extra-class activities program.

*School loyalty.* As students belong to specific school-sponsored organizations, they tend to feel an increasing identification with the school. When boys and girls work for the school, they become part of it. Membership in the total student body or freshman class is less meaningful than participation in the school band, the rifle team, the school paper, or the pep club. When students are members of specific school activities, they are likely to develop strong allegiance and thus feel a commitment to support their school.

*Integration of social groups.* Although some aspects of the extra-class program may increase the social distance between certain socio-economic groups, many student activities provide students of all socio-economic levels experiences in working and associating with each other. In sports, no one checks the socio-economic credentials of the boy who runs a kickoff back for a touchdown or who has just opened a hole in the opposing team's line. The members of a school dance band are preoccupied with the absorbing feeling of operating together in the interdependent performance of the music and are probably not even aware of social status or level. Many clubs are concerned with sharing and enhancing certain interests rather than the snob appeal of the activity. In this way, extra-class activities may provide increased opportunities for all students to learn to understand and appreciate each other.

*Development of certain traits.*    The extra-class activities afford unique opportunities for the development of desirable traits of personality and character. Through participation in the student government of the school, students may learn a variety of citizenship skills. Other student activities may facilitate the development of leadership, social intelligence, facility in social relationships, and skill in the use of group process.

*Guidance.*    Extra-class activities allow the teachers to work with students in an especially desirable atmosphere. Teachers and students are not concerned with grades, "covering the textbook," minimum standards, or discipline; instead, the situation is informal and relaxed. The attention is focused on the activity and the interests of the students. This provides an excellent opportunity for guidance and often leads to informal counseling. Many activities have vocational significance, and group guidance in terms of occupational and educational planning is desired. Social and personal guidance may be needed. In addition, the informal relationship between sponsor and students provides the opportunity for the teacher to learn a great deal about his pupils.

*Interpret the program.*    The school may use the extra-class activities whenever possible to help interpret the total program of the school to the community. Regardless of what one does, the public will evaluate the work of the school through the activities which it is shown. Thus, the school personnel ought to plan carefully to give the parents valid insights into the total curriculum. School publications describe, report, and interpret aspects of classroom experiences along with other student activity. Music and drama performances can be related to pertinent parts of the classroom program. Every extra-class activity, when placed before the public, can help to show how it fits into the total program of the high school and upon what bases it justifies its existence. Parents and townspeople may be involved in the assemblies and the club program at pertinent points and in appropriate roles. In this way, they tend to get clearer insights and more accurate information about the school.

The extra-class activity program is a part of the curriculum of the secondary school, and it possesses a wide variety of possible values which may justify the time and effort expended. Such an evaluation is properly the task of the local school staff and must depend upon the degree to which the activities contribute to the educational objectives of the school.

## THE EXTRA-CLASS PROGRAM

Student activity programs vary greatly from one size school to another, from rural to urban areas and from community to community. As you look back on your experience, what activities did you participate in? What activities did you enjoy most? Least? Why?

Although specifics may differ among schools, there tends to be a common pattern of extra-class activities. Most schools have established some kind of student activity in each of the following categories.

### Student Government

Most high schools attempt to provide for some degree of student government. Commonly, an elected body called the student council or school council is organized to allow students to participate in the control of some phase of the work of the school. The school council, which may include students, teachers, administrators, and parents in its membership, is delegated with authority over some area of the school by the principal. For example, the council may be given responsibility for the general supervision of the extra-class program, enforcement of established policies, and the chartering and rechartering of clubs. The amount and nature of authority varies from school to school; however, the council has the right to a careful definition of areas of authority and non-authority. It ought to involve some real elbow room for decision making and not become simply a rubber stamp for the wishes of the principal. Ideally handled, the school council offers a rich experience of participating in democratic self-government.

### School Clubs

One of the interesting characteristics of the modern secondary school is the quantity and diversity of school clubs. Most schools have some clubs which are closely related to the subjects which students study in the classroom. For example, the Latin club, Spanish club, science club, and art club may extend the work of specific courses beyond the classroom and provide related experiences which appeal to students interested in a particular subject area. Service clubs have been formed to provide service to the school and to the community. The Red Cross, safety patrol, library assistants, pep club, and student secretary club are examples of clubs which provide valuable services and, at the same time, enable the members to gain significant satisfactions from these activities. Another large and popular group is the hobby clubs. Photography, radio, electronics, rocket, hot rod, and fly tying clubs are examples of the many groups which may be formed in order to satisfy student interests and needs for hobby activities. Athletic or recreational clubs may include fencing, hiking, mountain climbing, skiing, bowling, modern dance, boating clubs, and the like. Another group of organizations are frankly organized as social clubs. High school fraternities and sororities have widely been prohibited[1] from operating as school organizations, yet social clubs of all kinds flourish. Honor societies are organized to recognize academic achievement.

Actually, the proliferation of school clubs is difficult to control without some machinery being set up to analyze applications for new clubs and to re-examine existing clubs. For this purpose, some schools require that every new club be chartered by the school council and that all clubs be subject to periodic rechartering. Carefully considered criteria which clubs must meet in order to be chartered are established. These criteria may include such items as: (1) The club must have worthy purposes, (2) It must set reasonable standards for membership which are explicitly stated, (3) It should not require an unreasonable expenditure, (4) It must demonstrate that a real interest exists, (5) It must submit to school regulations, (6) It must have a capable and reliable school person willing to act as sponsor, (7) It should schedule its meetings and place them on the school calendar, (8) It should generally meet on school grounds, (9) It should contribute to good variety and balance in the club program, and (10) It must submit to periodic rechartering (for example, every three to five years).

The club program is generally considered a very important aspect of the total program of the secondary school. Parents, teachers, and students typically support school clubs if they are well conceived and

---

[1] See, for example, Gerald M. Van Pool, "The Case Against High School Secret Societies," *NASSP Bulletin,* 45:5–19, May 1961 and Virginia Hamilton, "Secret Societies in American High Schools," *NASSP Bulletin,* 40:22–34, October 1956.

administered. The professional staff must continually seek ways to vitalize and improve the clubs in order that students and school might realize the maximum benefits.

*Assemblies*

One of the few extra-class activities which brings together the entire student body is the all-school assembly. For a variety of reasons all students convene in the school auditorium at periodic intervals. Assemblies are planned and are justified because they (1) provide wholesome entertainment, (2) educate, (3) enable certain school problems to be discussed before all the students (for example, good sportsmanship at basketball games, smoking on the school grounds), (4) provide experience for students in appearing before the large group, (5) furnish opportunities to enhance the unity of the school, (6) enable segments of the school student body to inform others of their achievements, and (7) develop students who are able to act as an intelligent audience.

It seems increasingly clear that assemblies ought to be free and open to all students. If the activity is educationally justifiable, then the school should pay for it in the best tradition of free public secondary education. In addition, the school administration must insist upon assembly programs of high quality and interest, adequate supervision of the assemblies, wide student participation in preference to outside speakers and entertainers, and continuous evaluation of the assembly programs to provide for improvement.

*Publications*

Secondary school publications are likely to include a school newspaper, yearbook, literary magazine, student handbook, and certain specialized publications such as the student and alumni directory. Through these media many boys and girls are given the opportunity to practice and to display their special talents and to exercise their special interests. In addition, some of the publications disseminate necessary information, chronicle the on-going events of the school, and may serve to unify the school.

Publication sponsors or advisors must be careful that the result is truly a student production and not their own creativity being shown through the efforts of the pupils. Sometimes the excellence of the product becomes so important to the sponsor that he usurps the job of the editor and directs the efforts of the staff sometimes going even so far as to rewrite student material before it is published. Problems of financing the publication, including the time and effort involved in selling advertising space (actually this is more nearly in the nature of soliciting donations than selling advertising), must be resolved in terms of the benefits to be realized by the entire school.

## Music, Drama, and Speech

An important cultural contribution which some high schools make to their communities results from the music, drama, and speech performances. Smaller communities especially, find student operettas, band concerts, music festivals, class plays, variety shows, debates, interpretive readings, and discussions of various kind significant competitors to the only movie house and the usual television programming on the single available channel.

Although not necessarily an either/or proposition, the directors of these activities must make some decision regarding whether or not the activity is to be mainly performance oriented. If the decision is made in favor of performance, a very few, gifted students may be spotlighted time after time, and opportunities to bring in a large number of boys and girls with somewhat lesser abilities but considerable interest may be neglected.

The values of these programs to pupils are realized as the activities are enjoyed by the students as spectators and as participants. Their evaluation must depend upon the degree to which they achieve the educational objectives of the school, and their finances should be determined on the same bases.

## Intramural Sports and Games

In the spectator culture of today there is a tendency to emphasize the interscholastic sports and to neglect the intramural program which seeks to provide competition and participation for all interested youth. Such a program in the schools should seek the involvement of a large proportion of the student body, provide for the satisfaction of present recreational interests, and foster the establishment of future leisure activities. Thus, the intramural program ought to include all types of sports and games (for example, checkers, quoits, table tennis, chess) and be open to anyone who is interested.

The organization might be placed in the hands of an intramural council or committee which is responsible for scheduling, publicity, records, appointment of varsity players as referees, coaches and managers, selection of officials, provision for printed rules and regulations, and recognition of winners. Time for scheduling the competition is always a problem. Practices include time (a) before or after the school day, (b) at noon, and (c) during the school day. Before or after school is often desirable, for teachers may be free at this time to supervise. After school, the students are eager to release their pent up energy through the program. However, schools which transport a substantial proportion of the pupils to and from school find this time almost impossible to use. The noon hour is a popular time for intramural activities, especially when the entire student body has a common lunch period. A very serious limitation develops, however, as some students bolt their usual lunch of a hamburger, several soft drinks, and a handful of candy bars and then proceed to play a rousing game of basketball. During the school day, the activity period may be used for intramurals or a regular intramural period may be scheduled before the first bus leaves in the afternoon.

The intramural program of sports and games seeks to broaden the participation base, utilize fully the sports facilities in the interests of the total group, develop interest and experience in worthwhile leisure activities, and to stimulate more students to improve their skills.

### Interscholastic Athletics

"Of all the activities included in the school's program, none draw more attention or cause more controversy than the interschool athletic program." It is designed for the athletically gifted and is set up so that "the most skillful of one school meet the similarly skillful from another under well regulated competitive conditions."[2] Unless the athletic program can fulfill this purpose without limiting the opportunities for the great mass of students or producing other undesirable, concomitant effects, it may be considered overemphasized.

As an example of some of the abuses which may develop in the search for glory via interscholastic athletics, the following hypothetical description is given. It represents a collation of observations made in many different high schools over a number of years. Its main purpose is to set down for analysis some fairly common symptoms of overemphasis.

### Description

"X" high school is very interested in basketball and it has a long tradition of winning basketball teams. Its trophy case is heavily laden with cups. The townspeople consistently have backed the team; attendance has always been good at the home games. In addition, the town business-

---

[2] Edward Masonbrink, "Physical Activities and the Secondary Educational Program," *NASSP Bulletin,* 48:34, October 1964.

men enthusiastically supported a school board decision to tear down the old gym and construct a new fieldhouse which would seat 10,000 spectators. This would enable the school to sponsor the sectional basketball tournament each year.

However, the girls' physical education instructor is not too pleased. During basketball season the girls are prohibited from using "the floor" once it is prepared for interscholastic competition. Barricades are placed around "the floor" and no one is allowed to use it except the varsity basketball squad. Thus, if it rains or snows outside, the girls' physical education program is greatly curtailed. Plans are being drawn for a girls' gym, but no one is sure how soon it may be built.

The band director feels it is good experience for his students to play at all the basketball games. However, he is still waiting for the new band uniforms which were promised three years ago. It seems that in a burst of expansiveness the year the basketball team was runner-up in the state tournament, someone promised the team new, scarlet, warmup suits. Somehow there wasn't enough money left when it came time to buy the band uniforms.

The principal is concerned because the basketball coach has convinced the school board that there should now be a separate budget for athletics. In effect, this budget has been removed from the control of the school administration. It is negotiated between the coaches and the school board.

Recently a group of students was asked about the school spirit in "X" high school. They replied, "Well, we lost about half our basketball games this year, and without a winning team the school spirit is very poor."

Teachers have mixed feelings about the athletic program, especially the sectional tournament which the high school now puts on each year. Many of them are asked to sell tickets and to help patrol the grounds. Classes are disrupted; student interest and effort are focused on the games; teaching and learning are secondary. Some report pressure to insure the scholastic eligibility of the varsity players.

Think of your high school experience. Did your high school embody any of these characteristics? What effects did they have on the total program of the school?

*Effects.*    Of course, basketball is not the only sport which may be overemphasized. In Pennsylvania it is likely to be football, in Colorado it might be skiing, in California it might be tennis or swimming, and in one town in Oregon, it is wrestling. In any event, some of the effects are fairly obvious.

1. Even though it is currently becoming more respectable to achieve high academic standing, for many years more prestige was to be gained by athletic prowess. A student was elected president of the student body

because he was the star forward on the basketball team, and not because he was the best person for the job. Varsity athletes learn to enjoy the wildly cheering crowds, the recognition given in the mass media, and the hero worship of those younger than they. All persons need and strive for success experience, but for a group of young men in high school and college, a particular exciting kind of success experience is attained through interscholastic athletics. However, for most people superior athletic ability does not make for success in later life. It may make adjustment difficult as the great proportion of these athletes, who are not good enough to make the grade in professional sports, face the adult world. It is only too true that people soon forget the great touchdown play, the scoring record, and the all-state champion.

School spirit becomes identified with interscholastic athletics. It is unfortunate when the spirit of the school is identified solely with the success or failure of the varsity teams. Both students and townspeople perceive the status of the school as dependent mainly upon the coaches and the athletes.

2. Unless controlled, interscholastic competition may result in incalculable cost to the school. Certainly, it is expensive to provide field houses, stadia, olympic-sized swimming pools, transportation to and from the games, as well as all the equipment needed to compete in the program. Much time is spent by the participants and the spectators, some of whom might be engaged more profitably in other things. For example, prior to each game all-school assemblies are scheduled and cheerleaders, teachers, coaches, and principal combine their efforts to exhort all students to attend, often broadly implying that they are something less than good citizens of the school community if they do not help cheer the team to victory. Teachers are pressed into service selling tickets, patrolling restrooms, and directing traffic in the parking areas. This is often considered part of the teacher's normal duties.

A very serious cost to the school is the tendency to sacrifice other parts of the program for the sake of interscholastic athletics. Unless the gymnasium facilities are duplicated, the girls' physical education program may be greatly curtailed. "The floor" is reserved for the use of the varsity team, and the physical education program of the entire school must utilize other facilities until after the season is ended. The physical education of the total student body is sacrificed so that the few on the team may enjoy optimum conditions. When the varsity sports receive top priority for money to purchase equipment and facilities, other aspects of the total program of the school may be neglected.

The emphasis on interscholastic sports by the community and the school has typically resulted in a distortion of perspective. When classes are disrupted to sell tickets, all-school assemblies or pep rallies are scheduled before each game, the victory celebration following the conference championship cancels the morning classes, and all homework is prohibited on the eve of the game with the town rival, there is little doubt in the minds of the students which activity is more important— schoolwork or sports. Teaching effectiveness is reduced as pupils are caught up in the excitement and understandably become preoccupied with the coming athletic contest.

3. As the school becomes involved in interscholastic athletics, it tends to be forced into a role which appears incompatible with its basic purposes. The school administrator becomes an *entrepreneur*. He acts as a matchmaker whose job it is to arrange athletic contests. And if the townspeople convince the school board and superintendent that the school should sponsor the district or sectional tournament, the school becomes even more an agent of commercial entertainment. In view of the tremendous demands upon the school for other services and functions, it would seem undesirable to have it accept the role of professional athletic promoter.

Of course, overemphasis of interscholastic sports is not found everywhere; most high schools have them fairly well under control. However, these are a few of the deleterious effects which may result if a proper perspective on sports is not established.

*Causes.* Who is responsible for overemphasis when it is found? Today's culture has increasingly become spectator minded, and most people tend to enjoy watching the athletic competitions. However, few administrators and even fewer teachers promote the increasing emphasis upon varsity sports. Relatively few coaches desire the tremendous pressure to win. Actually, it appears that the adults in the community deserve a good deal of the blame. They want entertainment. They enjoy the football and basketball games especially when their town is winning, and of course, their attitudes influence the youngsters in school. Townspeople are interested in their community becoming well known. A championship team will secure publicity and renown for the school and the town. The businessmen are interested in the games and tournaments because this will bring more money into the community.

When school officials attempt to make certain that the interscholastic athletics are self-supporting and thus will not use money needed for other aspects of the school program, pressures then accrue to make every student and townsperson an enthusiastic supporter and regular spectator at the games. In this way, the assemblies and pep rallies become justified in order to increase the boxoffice take.

*Constructive measures.*     There are some positive steps which a school
can take to reduce or prevent overemphasis of interscholastic athletics.
Secondary schools today usually hold membership in state and national
athletic associations which have formulated policies and guidelines. All
interscholastic leagues now have developed regulations and standards
which govern competitive conditions. Thus, the group support which
comes from belonging to an association will help the school counteract
unhealthy local pressures.

Schools can attempt to dilute the prestige. They can work to develop
other activities to publicize the school and provide the desired competition. One high school principal waited until the basketball team had experienced several poor seasons and then began to build up the band.
He brought in a young band director who put new vitality into the music
program. An increasing number of people came to the games just to see
and hear the band, and the students looked upon participation in the
band as a prestige activity. A junior high school administrator developed
a group of interested youngsters into a mental arithmetic team. After
some exhibitions before service clubs and civic organizations, they
challenged a neighboring school and a new competition was initiated.
Other schools have sought to provide enhanced recognition for the writing of short stories, poetry, and essays by publishing a school literary
magazine which is attractively printed and given a wide circulation. One
school district presents academic "Oscars" for excellence in school
achievement. In these ways, schools seek to raise the prestige of other activities besides athletics. It is simply an attempt to provide other respectable and desirable ways for students to gain recognition and prestige.

In areas where they have control, school people can make sure that
athletics are not overemphasized. Teachers and administrators can see
to it that athletes receive no special considerations in their academic
work. For example, there will be no special examinations in order to
bring up a grade so that eligibility is retained. Varsity athletes should
not be discriminated against; however, neither should they receive special
considerations.

In the use of facilities, the school personnel must be certain that the
best interests of the entire student group are served. For example, the
basketball court might be used by the boys' and girls' physical education
classes for instruction, for practice sessions of the tap dancing club, to
polish the formations of the marching band, for pre-season conditioning
of the ski team, as well as for practice sessions by the varsity basketball
team. All facilities of a school ought to be available for legitimate use
by the students and faculty in the best interest of the total program of
the school.

School money must be spent with the perspective of the overall task of the school in mind. School personnel can exert pressure so that needed books for the library receive priority over a new electric score-board for the football field. No one activity of the school should receive amounts of money disproportionate to the number of students which participate.

The base of participation in athletics may be broadened. One high school asserts, "The important question is not what the boy can do for athletics; it is what athletics can do for the boy. To this end any boy who reports regularly, and who is willing to cooperate and be a regular fellow, is never cut from any squad."[3] Thus, all interested boys are able to participate as members of the varsity squad.

*Values.* In spite of the threat of overemphasis, the program of inter-scholastic athletics has certain positive values to the student body and community. It may be of benefit in the following ways:

a. By developing an understanding and an appreciation of the place which interscholastic sports occupy in American culture and developing sound, educational attitudes toward them.

b. By educating the student body in the appreciation of sports and the best way to enjoy them from the point of view of good sportsmanship.

c. By serving as a focal point for the morale, spirit, and loyalty of the students by providing a common meeting ground and enthusiasm which is shared by all.

d. By providing a wholesome program of sports in which students, parents, patrons, and friends of the school may share, to the end that the loyalty of these groups to the school may be constantly renewed, strengthened, and united.[4]

School athletics do sometimes suffer from commercialization and preoccupation with winning. However, they are usually viewed as an indispensable part of the extra-class activities program. They enable the physically gifted youth to utilize special talents and to receive recognition for them.

Considerable disagreement[5] obtains in regard to the question of inter-scholastic competition for junior high school youth. Practices vary, with many junior high schools playing a full schedule of games in football,

---

[3] *A Statement of the General Policies, Curriculum and Services of Community High School* (Blue Island, Ill.: District 218, n.d.), 38.

[4] Ray O. Duncan, "Scope of Interscholastic Athletics," *NASSP Bulletin,* 44:91, May 1960.

[5] Masonbrink, *op. cit.,* 35:41.

basketball, and baseball. This practice is, of course, encouraged by the senior high school coaches who look upon the "feeder" junior high schools as farm teams. Probably the majority of the authorities in secondary education recommend against interscholastic competition prior to senior high school.

The activities mentioned are the major ones which make up the extra-class program in most secondary schools. The need for sufficient quantity and variety so that, in theory, all students have the opportunity to participate in something must be joined with the problem of attaining balance in the program.

*Participation*

The extra-class activity program of the school should be established for the benefit of the interested students, not to enhance the reputation of certain coaches, sponsors, or directors. Often, the nature and extent of pupil participation provide a meaningful index into the quality of the program. However, most schools are concerned with encouraging participation on one hand with controlling participation on the other.

Participation is insured if an "interest questionnaire" is periodically circulated among students to assure that their interests are met by the extra-class activities. Moreover, the basic motive for continued active membership is closely related to the degree to which the individual receives satisfactions from this membership. Participation may also be enhanced if the school is able to develop student approval and enthusiasm for the activity.

Point systems which attempt to quantify the extra-class participation of the students may be used to limit as well as encourage participation. Each activity, such as membership on the varsity football squad or serving as vice-president of the student body, is given some point value. Attainment of a certain number of points may entitle one to an award. At the same time, a maximum number of allowable points may limit the students' participation. This procedure obviously necessitates a great deal of time and effort if the point totals are accurately kept up to date. While it obviously possesses certain advantages, it seems highly inflexible and may ignore other important factors in the life of the student. For example, some students vary considerably in the amount of extra-class participation which they may handle without interfering with studies. Other out-of-school involvement might change the actual activities load of the student without the knowledge of the school.

Use of an activity period is likely to encourage participation because the alternative to attending a club or other school organization would be a study hall. Even though it is not the most desirable motivation, most students would join some extra-class activity rather than spend the period in a study hall. At the same time, the activity period makes available only so many activities to the student. His participation may be limited by the fact that all meetings are held during this period.

Careful records of the extra-class participation of each student ought to be maintained. Data regarding membership, offices held, athletic competition, and some evaluation of the participation are desirable. With these data included in the cumulative files, advisors and counselors are better able to help students make intelligent decisions in regard to the amount and nature of their extra-class involvement.

## ROLE OF THE SPONSOR

At this point, the teacher is likely to ask, "Where do I fit into this picture?" Probably he will be asked to sponsor an extra-class activity. Principals almost universally take the position that a reasonable extra-class assignment is part of the usual teacher load. If these activities fall within the definition of the curriculum, then they are a legitimate part of the work of the school and of each teacher. He may be expected to accept the sponsorship of a student activity in which he has some interest, background of experience, or pertinent training.

Actually, the job of the sponsor is vital to the success and achievement of worthy outcomes. As the only adult present, he is able to operate in order to give leadership which helps build successful school activities. The sponsor should lead through his ability to guide students rather than as a dictator. Only if he is thoroughly interested and enthusiastic about the activity is he likely to contribute fully to its success. The effective sponsor must feel that the extra-class activity is a legitimate part of the school program—indeed that it is a part of the curriculum. He should recognize the potential values of the extra-class activity to the students, to the school, to the community, and to his work as a teacher.

Teachers tend to have ambivalent feelings toward participation in extra-class activities. On one hand, they feel that this is "extra" and is simply more work, time, and trouble for them. On the other hand, the informal relationship with boys and girls, the focus upon student interests, the absence of classroom discipline pressures, the increased responsibility accepted by the pupils for planning, organization, and evaluation all make the sponsor's job stimulating and enjoyable.

An important factor in the teachers' attitudes toward extra-class assignments is directly related to the school policy for extra compensation. In some school systems, extra-class duties are considered part of the teacher's job and nothing extra is paid even to athletic coaches. Instead, a real effort is made to attempt to equalize the load by reducing classroom assignments for teachers with above-average activities involvements. Other schools pay modestly for certain activities which are judged to claim an excessive amount of the teacher's time. Athletic coaching, advising on publications, and drama coaching are examples of these time-consuming activities. A very few schools accept the theory that all extra-class assignments are extra work, and thus they have had to set up schedules of payment for all teacher involvement in the extra-class program.

Principals must be very careful, regardless of the policy for extra-compensation, not to seriously overload the teacher. As one person somewhat acidly put it:

> It should be relatively easy for the true educational leader, however, to recognize that the payment of an extra two hundred or two thousand dollars will not make the assignment one iota less of an overload.[6]

Thus, the extra-class sponsorship plus the regular classroom commitment ought to be within the reasonable energy demands of the teacher in order that he may do the best possible job in both areas.

A significant problem with which the faculty sponsor must be concerned is the handling of funds. Casual and poorly organized methods of handling receipts and disbursements must be avoided if the sponsor and student organization officers are to be protected. Local conditions should be considered in setting up some sound accounting process, but large petty cash accounts and the holding of dues receipts in an empty cigar box are to be avoided. Important suggestions emphasize centralized accounting, acceptance of the responsibility for keeping accurate records by student treasurers, a system whereby all withdrawals are countersigned by the sponsor, receipts given for all dues taken in, establishment of a budget system for all organizations, periodic reports, and an annual audit of treasurers' records. Normally, the money handled by most school club treasurers is not great; however, in some cases the annual total may run into the thousands of dollars. In any case, in the interest of good public relations, sound training for the students, and as a protection against dishonesty and carelessness, a businesslike process must be established.

---

[6] Arthur C. Hearn, "Consider the Position of the Activity Sponsor," *The Clearing House,* 31:241, December 1956.

If the teacher is asked to sponsor an extra-class activity, one of the richest sources of assistance for him is the periodical, *School Activities,* which contains articles[7] giving specific tips and suggestions based on experience in the schools today.

The school administration ought to provide certain facilitating conditions which will assist sponsors to make maximum contributions to the program. For example, the school administrator should:

1. Provide coordination of the total program in the interests of balance and less competition with the regular classroom activities.

2. Plan the total extra-class program utilizing the experience and suggestions of the sponsors.

3. Assist sponsors in securing publicity and recognition for their organizations.

4. Secure help for inexperienced activity sponsors.

5. Protect the faculty sponsors from inordinate demands upon their time and energies.

Teacher participation in student activities at the high school and college level provides a desirable background of experience. Hobby and leisure time interests, skills, and achievements may assist the teacher in choosing an extra-class activity which he might enjoy as a sponsor. Such college courses as guidance and counseling, audio-visual materials, and the nature of extra-class activities would be helpful in preparation for sponsorship of a high school extra-class activity. During student teaching, the prospective teacher may be able to get many insights and some experience in the role of the sponsor. He should take every opportunity to secure additional knowledge and understanding about this facet of his job.

## REVIEW

The extra-class program of the school falls within the definition of the curriculum. Thus, it becomes a legitimate activity of the staff and at the same time becomes subject to the same sort of evaluation as any other part of the curriculum. Only insofar as the program contributes to the objectives of the high school can it be defended. Read the following questions before moving on to the next topic.

---

[7] See for example P. J. Sleeman, "Science Club Film Programs," *School Activities,* 39:20, April 1968; Noel Bullock, "Program Possibilities for Aviation Clubs in Secondary Schools," *School Activities,* 39:5–7, January 1968; J. S. Smith, "The School Rifle Club," *School Activities,* 38:8–9, March 1967; Earl Reum, "A New Student Council for a New School," *School Activities,* 38:3–5, May 1967; Bernice Samalonis, "Sponsoring a Dance," *School Activities,* 36:20–21, 25, September 1964.

1. How are extra-class activities defined? What values are they said to possess which contribute to the educational aims of the school?

2. What sorts of student activities are commonly found in the extra-class program? What are the factors involved in the related problem of student participation?

3. What is likely to be your involvement in the extra-class program? How do most school administrators look upon the teacher's role in extra-class activities? What are some of the things a sponsor may do to make the student activity more successful?

# Selected References

Bent, R. K. and Unruh, A. *Secondary School Curriculum*. Lexington, Mass.: D. C. Heath and Company, 1969; Ch. 6 "The Curricular Program."

Davis, E. D. *Focus on Secondary Education: An Introduction to Principles and Practices*. Glenview, Illinois: Scott, Foresman and Company, 1966; Ch. 9 "Extraclass Activities in the Secondary School."

Douglass, H. R. *Secondary Education in the United States*. New York: The Ronald Press Company, 1964; Ch. 17 "Extrasubject Learning Activities."

————. *Trends and Issues in Secondary Education*. Washington, D.C.: The Center for Applied Research in Education, Inc., 1962; Ch. IX "Guidance and Extracurricular Organizations."

Dumas, Wayne and Beckner, Weldon. *Introduction to Secondary Education: A Foundations Approach*. Scranton, Pennsylvania: International Textbook Company, 1968; Ch. 8 "The Curriculum: Extraclass Activities."

Faunce, R. X. and Munshaw, C. L. *Teaching and Learning in Secondary Schools*. Belmont, California: Wadsworth Publishing Company, Inc., 1964; Ch. 12 "Student Activities."

Frederick, R. W. *Student Activities in American Education*. Washington, D.C.: The Center for Applied Research in Education, Inc., 1965.

Hipple, T. W., *Secondary School Teaching: Problems and Methods*. Pacific Palisades, Calif.: Goodyear Publishing Company, Inc., 1970; Ch. 6 "The Teacher and Extraclass Activities."

Lee, F. H., ed. *Principles and Practices of Teaching in Secondary Schools: A Book of Readings*. New York: David McKay Company, Inc., 1965; Ch. XV "Extraclass Duties" and Ch. XVI "Sponsoring Student Activities."

Oliva, P. F. *The Secondary School Today*. Cleveland: The World Publishing Company, 1967; pp. 105–9 "The Supplementary Curriculum."

# eleven

# The Classroom Teacher
# and Guidance

The public school shares the responsibility for the total education of youth with other educative agencies in American society. However, in recent years the schools have been called upon to carry an ever-increasing portion of the burden in the job of guiding youth. With the resources available and the training and experience possessed by the school staff, it would seem logical to utilize such a well-qualified agency for this important task. Moreover, it has been discovered that teachers and counselors often are more able to deal objectively and constructively with the problems of young people than parents and friends, who find their very emotional attachments prevent them from seeing the problems clearly and identifying the significant factors involved.

The current impetus for guidance services stems from a variety of factors. The shift from the farm to the city has accompanied the industrialization and specialization of our labor force; later came the movement of great numbers to the suburbs. Modern American society has become infinitely more complex than the predominately rural culture of yesterday. Thus, significant changes in modes of living and complexities in occupational structure have brought added problems to young people.

Our nation is unique in its insistence upon implementing the objective of education for all. However, this means that today many boys and girls are in high school who in previous years would not have gone beyond the basic three R's. When multiple curricula became necessary, assistance in choosing appropriate academic programs became essential. At this point, the great public school system, which had developed and become committed to mass education ascertained the need for the guidance point of view which prizes the individual and seeks to help him adjust and find himself among the group.

Another indication of the need for a guidance program in the public schools stems from the fact that during the current power struggle among nations it has become clear that the human resources of America must be more wisely utilized. If the United States is to survive, our society must make it possible, hopefully probable, that every young person may make the maximum contribution which his potentialities will allow. Rather than dictate the positions our youth should hold, thereby denying them of their heritage of free choice, we in a democracy would prefer to guide them toward a decision which would benefit both the individual youth and the nation. This is an essential service that the function of guidance seeks to perform.

As you prepare for teaching you need to recognize the part you must play in the guidance services of the school, for the classroom teacher has vital responsibilities here which he must be prepared to carry out. You should consider the following:

1. Within each school, a point of view is represented by the guidance-oriented personnel. You ought to know in advance the aims of the guidance program and the problem areas with which it deals.

2. Fully developed guidance programs offer a variety of services. You should discover the nature and extent of these services.

3. As a classroom teacher, you will have a strong stake in the guidance program and will be expected to participate according to your training and background. You ought to explore the dimensions of this probable involvement.

## NATURE OF GUIDANCE

Modern guidance has its roots imbedded in the psychological developments which gave impetus to the study of children and the recognition of individual differences among youth, and in the mental hygiene movement which spotlighted the need for preventing mental illnesses and improving their treatment. Actually, the widespread utilization of guidance services in public schools is a fairly recent development. Nevertheless, specialized guidance workers have come to some careful agreements regarding the nature of guidance and most teachers generally recognize a fairly well-defined guidance point of view.

What does the word guidance mean? What does the concept include? With what kinds of problems is public school guidance concerned?

*Meaning of Guidance*

Guidance in the public schools may be thought of as assistance offered to an individual by competent personnel in order to help him solve his problems and develop his talents to the maximum so as to benefit himself and society. This definition clearly has a number of important implications as we think it through.

Guidance is *assistance*. This is a fundamental part of the guidance point of view. Guidance is neither making decisons for someone else, nor telling someone else what to do. Rather than imposing ideas or answers, guidance is committed to preserving freedom of choice within appropriate maturity limits, so that an individual may be better prepared to make other decisions on his own at a later time. Thus, guidance aims toward making the individual more mature and thereby increasingly competent to handle his own life problems, rather than prolonging his dependency on others.

This assistance is offered by *competent personnel*. Although any and all of the school's certificated and non-certificated staff may be called upon to contribute in some way to the total program of guidance, it is recognized that guidance is a vital service which demands as much training and experience as possible. Formal, planned guidance requires professional expertness. With this in mind some school systems have recently begun requiring that all classroom teachers complete a minimum number of hours in guidance so that they will have at least a minimal level of competency.

Guidance seeks to help the *individual*. The American public school system is necessarily committed to the goal of mass education. Because of this, the schools have sometimes become preoccupied with big business methods and assembly line processes as enrollments have grown. As a consequence the public school staff has often lost sight of the uniqueness of the needs and potentialities of the individual student.

> Thus, instead of laboriously producing a beautiful hand blown goblet, we prepare a battery of blowpipes; dip them in homogenized, molten glass; press the bellows to force a carefully measured amount of air into the pipes; and, presto, we have some reasonable facsimiles. Occasionally a glass bubble ruptures and out comes a spurt of hot air—a suitable tribute to our process.[1]

---

[1] Robert C. McKean, "The Nurture of the Modern High School Teacher," *News and Views,* 1:6, March 1960.

Someone needs to remind us of the limitations of mass education. Within the school context, guidance operates both as a set of special services and as a point of view in the interests of the individual.

Each individual is aided in developing *his talents to the maximum*. Guidance seeks to avoid the minimum-standard concept and attempts to facilitate the development of the maximum potentialities of all youth, with the clear understanding that these potentialities vary widely. Today, a high school education is the common expectation for every youngster; the guidance worker seeks to know as much as possible about the emerging talents of each individual and to provide learning experiences which will enhance their development.

The development of the individual should *benefit* both *himself* and *society*. This implies that in a democracy there is no necessary conflict in interest between individual and society; guidance works to promote growth which will be of optimum benefit to both.

*Kinds of Guidance*

Of course, the guidance program is concerned with all aspects of the individual's personality. School and classroom are only one part of his environment; he also associates with other peer groups, community, and family. As his situation must be seen in its entirety, so his problems and his development must be conceived of and dealt with as a whole. However, for convenience, the assistance which is offered may be categorized according to the major focus of the different problems.

*Vocational guidance.*     A vital task for all youth is the selection and preparation for an occupation. Students in high school present a great opportunity and challenge for the guidance worker who would help them in this important process.

Vocational decisions are difficult today for a number of reasons. The occupational structure of the United States is tremendously complex; the comprehension and the attainment of some perspective of this structure is difficult in itself. The presence of greater specialization requires extended training and careful preparation in more and more occupations. Because of this, an early and intelligent vocational decision is almost imperative today. But increasingly fewer youth have a clear conception of and a familiarity with a variety of occupations. In fact, many boys and girls in modern suburbia have very little idea of exactly what their own father does for a living.

Typically the non-college-going high school student finds his first job largely through chance. After an appropriate period of rest following graduation, one morning the young man appears downstairs, dressed and ready to go out. He spends some time analyzing the help wanted columns in the morning paper as he eats his breakfast. Then, armed with some likely addresses he sets out to find a job. Often he accepts the first opening he is offered. As simply as that he may make a decision which is likely to be of inestimable importance to his happiness and future welfare. Fortunately, however, this experience is becoming less prevalent because guidance workers in the schools offer their services to all.

*Educational guidance.*   As boys and girls progess through school, many questions may arise in their minds about their present educational experiences as well as their possible educational plans for the future. Certain problems are immediate, pressing, and vital to the student. For example, some students are concerned about academic achievment, teacher-student relationships, and improvement of study habits. Others need help in making curricular adjustments, course choices, and evaluation of educational experiences.

Related to vocational planning are the long-range educational guidance considerations. In a period when college enrollment is rapidly growing, admission to institutions of higher learning is becoming progressively more difficult. Moreover, college choice is assuming greater importance in relation to college success. This problem area is certain to receive increasing attention. Simply keeping current records of college scholarships available and assisting students with their applications is a big job in the modern high school. In addition, opportunities for further training in trade schools and in various branches of the service must be considered for a sizeable number of students.

*Personal-social guidance.*   Most adolescents sometimes have problems which are personal-social in nature. Family problems, often made acute because of the individual's desire for increasing independence, plague the teenager. Boy-girl relationships, dating, and planning for marriage often loom larger in the student's life than the threat of war or riots in Asia. The establishment of sound friendships, the concern over manners and morals, and the careful observance of current fads are other examples of problems in this category that call for serious and carefully considered assistance.

*Emotional guidance.*   Some students have serious problems of adjustment. Many others need help in coming to grips with their fears, worries, conflicts, concerns, and frustrations. All youth must learn to handle their emotions at increasingly more mature levels. This problem area requires, in many cases, a high degree of professional training and experience if the results are to be most helpful and constructive.

At present, the total program of guidance in the public high school is likely to emphasize educational guidance and vocational guidance above the other forms. This is probably due in part to tradition. These problems may be felt to be more legitimately the concern of the public school. Moreover, the background of some guidance workers causes them to be understandably reluctant to deal with the deeper and more complex problems. School personnel recognize the high-level training necessary to offer extensive assistance with problems of this kind. Students themselves tend actively to seek out teachers and counselors for aid in problems closely related to school and also for advice about future plans. However, these students are sometimes more likely to turn to non-school persons for help with problems of a personal-social and emotional nature.

## GUIDANCE SERVICES

As you begin teaching you will quickly become aware of the diverse nature of the total guidance program in the public schools. Although there has been a considerable upsurge of interest in guidance recently, you are likely to find the organization of these services in various stages of development, depending largely upon the length of time guidance has been stressed in the district and on the quality of educational leadership present. Any well-planned program ought to include some degree of service in each of the following areas.

### Counseling

Although at the core of the guidance program itself, counseling is but one of several kinds of services offered. The term usually refers to the assistance offered by a staff member who is definitely assigned counseling as a major responsibility and is scheduled for a certain part of his working day to provide this service.

Counseling generally involves a one-to-one relationship between the counselee and the counselor which focuses upon the individual's problems, concerns, choices, and plans. Basically, it is a provision by the schools, otherwise committed to mass education, for assistance to the individual student by a specially trained professional. In the face-to-face counseling situation, the counselee is aided in exploring the various facets of his problem and is helped toward self-understanding and self-decision. The counselor performs a process role in the counseling relationship; he operates to help the individual student solve his own problem.

Obviously this is a service which requires special skill and preparation. Many schools employ well-trained professional guidance workers to do full-time counseling. Others schedule teachers who have considerable training as part-time counselors. If you would become a trained counselor you should probably count on fulfilling the following requirements. You should:

1. Be a mature, well adjusted person.

2. Possess a valid teaching credential.

3. Have completed several years of successful teaching at the high school level and preferably have other work experience as well.

4. Have completed a year's study beyond the A.B. degree which will include courses calculated to help you understand the individual student, comprehend the nature and organization of guidance services, develop skill and knowledge of actual counseling procedures and resources, know the use and sources of informational materials in guidance, understand testing and statistical processes, and experience actual, practicum counseling under the supervision of highly trained and experienced personnel.

Many counselors in our schools fall short of such a preparation. However, many others have gone beyond the desired minimum. All attempt to work with the individual student within certain limitations. If a problem emerges requiring assistance which goes beyond the counselor's training and experience, he immediately seeks to make a referral to more qualified personnel.

## Group Guidance

In addition to offering assistance to individuals through the counseling program, the school provides for guidance in groups. Of course, good teaching is guidance. However, in practice, the high school teacher, due to his orientation and training, often emphasizes intellectual growth above adjustment. Therefore, the organized guidance program provides the setting for group work in guidance and encourages teachers to bring guidance into the curriculum of their courses.

Secondary schools are increasingly planning *orientation* activities in order that the transition between elementary and secondary school levels is facilitated. The new student is assisted in becoming acquainted and feeling at home in the school. Sometimes orientation may be emphasized in freshman English class, freshman guidance class, or homeroom. In these cases the students are provided information about the school and are given the opportunity to raise questions which are important to them. Some schools select upperclassmen who act as "big brothers" to groups of new students through conducting tours of the school, explaining rules and regulations, acquainting students with their new teachers, and answering questions. Assemblies and orientation handbooks are also used to enhance adjustment to the new school.

*Homerooms* are an old but still popular device for group guidance. In certain schools, the homeroom period is used almost completely for administrative purposes—making announcements, selling tickets, making a careful attendance check, filling out forms, and the like. However, with careful planning and organization, the homeroom may provide the setting wherein students are encouraged to discuss matters which concern them. Examples of the areas which are often dealt with include vocational planning, understanding the emotions, physical health, mental hygiene, study habits, boy-girl relations, etiquette, opportunities in college, and juvenile delinquency.

Special *courses* are sometimes set up for guidance. At the ninth grade, courses such as high school orientation, occupations, group guidance, career planning, and self-appraisal are occasionally offered. At the twelfth-grade level such special courses as psychology, mental hygiene, and senior problems may be taken on an elective basis. These kinds of courses usually utilize counselors or guidance directors as teachers and stress self-understanding and preparation for effective living.

Student visits to businesses, colleges, and trade schools are often arranged in order to give students exploratory experiences. College and university conferences, career days, and school assemblies are planned to help students secure information and answers to their questions. Beyond this, every teacher is encouraged to be guidance-minded. When a significant problem or concern is expressed by a substantial proportion of the class, and if the teacher is qualified to deal with it, the problem might be made the focus of profitable class discussion and study. The course content may be replanned so as to include the exploration of recurrent pupil problems and concerns.

## Testing

An important part of a guidance program is the testing service. Tests are used in the following ways by the groups indicated:

*Teachers* use tests as one basis for grouping pupils within the classroom; as a means to secure information on student interests, values, and concerns; and as a way of analysing student academic problems.

*Guidance workers* seek test results as essential information which they must have in order to understand and work with individuals. These results help them diagnose individual difficulties, assist in making realistic decisions, and facilitate self-understanding.

*Students,* with assistance, may use tests to discover their own strengths and weaknesses, and assess realistically their present achievements and potentialities in relation to other boys and girls.

*School administrators* use tests to place different students in appropriate courses and groups, and to study the effectiveness of school organization and curricular arrangements.

Thus, the testing service is supportive of guidance and instructional activity in the school. Although other testing may be done upon the request of counselors or for special purposes, three kinds of tests are most commonly given to all students at the high school level.

The *academic aptitude* test provides a prognosis regarding a student's possible success in the academic situation. It seeks to assess the individual's potential to achieve in school. High school testing programs usually use one or more of the group academic aptitude tests. This means that the tests may be administered to large numbers of students at a time. The tests may yield results expressed in a single measure (IQ), they may offer scores for quantitative as well as for verbal aptitude, or they may provide multiple scores for such areas as verbal, spatial, rational, and numerical ability. In using the results of group tests, teachers and guidance personnel should recognize that a variety of factors may cause error: extreme nervousness, misunderstanding of directions, illness, reading handicaps, and the like may contribute to a low score. Thus it is desirable to have several test results for each pupil. When test scores are in doubt, the student is sometimes given an individual academic aptitude test. Here, a trained examiner administers a test to a single student. An important part of this examination involves the careful observation of the subject himself during the testing period.

*Achievement tests* provide a standardized measure of scholastic attainment in a number of fields such as reading, written expression, various foreign languages, general mathematics, algebra, geometry, trigonometry, general science, biology, chemistry, physics, American government, American history, and world history. Some of these tests are highly useful as diagnostic measures. For example, an area may be divided into sub-tests (as an achievement test in arithmetic might be divided into sub-tests of addition, subtraction, multiplication and division), and, in additon to the total score, the teacher is provided with sub-test data which may enable him to localize learning difficulties and plan remedial work to correct them.

*Interest tests* attempt to secure an indication of the likes and dislikes of students. The vocational interest inventory is based on the observation that different occupational groups have recognizably different interest patterns. Thus a student may be able to discover which occupational pattern most nearly fits into his own pattern of interests and, in this way, presumably, may identify the occupation he would enjoy most. One widely used test, the Strong Vocational Interest Blank, may be scored for thirty-nine different occupations ranging from accountant to YMCA director.

*Records*

In the process of working with a particular student over the years, the school is able to gather a great deal of information about him which is valuable to preserve for easy reference when needed by teachers and counselors. To this end, most high schools use some form of cumulative record. This record may be simply a large envelope or folder in which important data are kept; it may be a card or folder upon which the important data are recorded, or it may involve some combination of the two. As the name suggests, the cumulative record provides a procedure for collecting significant information about the pupil as it is secured, and making it readily available to those who need it. This record is likely to encompass a great variety of data. It provides personal information, including the name, birth date, birthplace, sex, nationality, and residence address of the student. Home and community background information most likely includes the names of parents or guardian, parents' or guardian's occupation, birthplace, and marital status, and number of brothers and sisters. A careful record of academic achievement as revealed by grades, subject by subject, semester by semster, is found. All scores of standardized tests are included in the file. Information is provided regarding school attendance—days absent each year and different schools attended. Some health data are included, such as results of physical examinations, nature and extent of physical handicaps, and inoculation record. Other information may include brief accounts of significant teacher observations, extra-class participation, vocational and educational plans, and employment record.

*Library of Information*

The guidance program requires a variety of materials which provide information helpful to students in securing answers to their vocational, educational, personal-social, and emotional problems and questions.

This information is sometimes used in group guidance in the systematic study of a common problem, it may be placed in the hands of an individual student who needs it as the result of a counseling interview, or it may simply be made available to students who may be interested on their own.

This library of information must cover a wide range. In the vocational area, pupils need accurate, up-to-date data on a wide variety of occupations. In the study of a particular occupation, the student is likely to need such information as (1) the nature of the occupation, (2) some of the advantages and disadvantages of this kind of work, (3) current salary or earnings, (4) requisite training, (5) length of time needed to learn the job, (6) age limitations, (7) status of labor supply, and (8) industry trends. Materials on vocations are probably best grouped into "occupations" sections in the school library. Unbound publications, such as occupational briefs, pamphlets and monographs, should be filed systematically and made readily accessible.

Students with questions about education beyond the high school need an extensive collection of catalogues and bulletins from colleges, universities, junior colleges, trade schools, and business schools. In addition, there are many valuable books and pamphlets available which help to answer student problems and questions in the personal-social and emotional guidance areas.

*Placement*

An increasing number of secondary schools are directing attention to the need for placement. The concept goes beyond simply job placement. It also involves assisting students in discovering rewarding extra-class activities and in finding appropriate educational experiences in high school, university, trade school, armed service, or apprenticeship. As pupils make vocational and educational decisions, the guidance program seeks to facilitate their placement along the lines of their considered choice.

The entire professional staff is involved in educational placement. However, some schools have organized vocational-placement services headed by a director of placement. The director's job is to work with the town businessmen who look to the school as a major source of new labor, and to attempt, with his knowledge of the pupils, to place the right young man or woman in the right job. A carefully planned placement service is, of course, a great benefit to graduating students and to dropouts, since it seeks to place them in their first job. It also benefits the employer by making wise selections, and finally, it enhances the public relations of the school.

*Follow-up*

The high school guidance staff seeks "feed back" information from former students in order to improve the educational program of the school, evaluate the guidance services, and offer some post-graduate guidance service. For this reason, guidance personnel engage in follow-up activities. Former students are interviewed at homecoming, or are sent questionnaires. Employers are queried about successes and failures of the high school graduates. College and university records are studied, and reports on students requested. Discussions are planned with graduates and dropouts. Through these procedures, valuable data can be obtained to help improve the high school.

This section has sketched out the nature of the diverse services likely to be found in a well-organized guidance program. If these are to operate successfully, the cooperation and participation of the teaching staff as well as the efforts of certain guidance personnel are required.

What is the role of the classroom teacher regarding guidance? How will you be expected to fit into this picture?

## ROLE OF THE CLASSROOM TEACHER

Every teacher is a member of the guidance team. As you work toward your goal of being an effective teacher, you are likely to find yourself participating in many ways as a matter of course. In addition, your students are almost certain to come to you with guidance problems. Previously in this chapter, counseling was described as a specialized and highly important aspect of the guidance program. You should realize that counseling also involves certain personal restrictions and obligations. School counselors have patently accepted these attendant responsibilities and so are presumably aware of them. However, the typical classroom teacher may find himself faced with the professional decision of accepting or rejecting the counseling role, often with little knowledge of what may be involved. For example, think about the following situation. What are its implications? What would you do in this situation?

*Situation*

You are sitting in your room after school grading papers when one of your students comes in to see you. "May I talk with you?" he asks. "I am in trouble and you are the only person I feel I can tell."

You reply, "Yes, of course, I'll talk with you."

He continues, "Before I tell you, will you promise not to tell anyone? Will you keep it a secret?"

You can see that he is clearly disturbed about something so you answer, "Yes."

He then tells you that this very night he and some of his friends plan to steal a car and run away to California. "What shall I do?" he asks.

Think carefully about this situation. Reread it. What have you let yourself in for? What are the implications in this matter (a) for the boy and (b) for you? There are several courses of action possible; what are they? What would you do?

*Implications.*[2] This situation follows a fairly common pattern. Boys and girls with problems are drawn to warm, accepting teachers. Students may one day come to you asking that you help them, asking that you counsel them.

In the above and similar situations the implications are clear: (a) you have accepted a student's confidence, (b) you have given your word that you will keep this secret confidential, (c) you have come into possession of information that an illegal act is about to be committed, and (d) you have accepted, as far as the boy is concerned, the counseling role—probably before you realized it.

In this situation what would you, as a classroom teacher, do? It would seem that you could choose between two alternatives:

1. You might keep the confidence inviolate and try to help your student see that there are, in fact, several alternatives for him, each having certain probable consequences. He would then have to make his decision based on these data.

2. You might try to dissuade him from participating in the plan and, failing this, subsequently report the anticipated action to the administrative head of the school, the police, or the boy's parents.

Actually the basic conflict here seems to be between (a) the role of counselor and (b) the role of teacher and private citizen. As a private citizen you have the duty to prevent an illegal act against society. However, as a counselor you have accepted a clear and overriding obligation. The welfare of your student, the client, is paramount. Within professional limits, you commit yourself to place his welfare before that of society or that of yourself; to do otherwise suggests that you are operating at something less than a professional counseling level.

---

[2] This section is adapted from Robert C. McKean, "The Teacher in a Counseling Role," *The Clearing House,* 33:176–7, November 1958.

Thus, only if you can make the considered decision that it is in *his* best interest to reveal his confidence would you do so.

The consequences of either alternative action are fairly certain. If you break your promise and violate your student's trust in you, you may very well destroy his faith in all professional workers, and thus he may find himself forever unable to accept help from them. If then, he is caught in the act and sent to the reformatory, he may return a confirmed criminal. However, if he decides to commit the act and you *do not* go to the authorities, you might be charged as an accessory to the crime. Even though there is the possibility (although evidence for this is not clear) that officially designated counselors in some states are neither compelled to reveal confidential information, nor are held liable for it,[3] as a classroom teacher you would not have this protection. Furthermore, besides the legal action which could be taken against you, the school board may feel justified in dismissing you from your position.

Thus the nature and legal status of the relationship of confidential information to the counselor hangs upon one vital point.

> The members of the legal profession, the ministry, and medicine usually have legally defined, privileged communication relationships with their clients. Privileged communication means essentially that the professional member cannot be compelled to reveal information which a client has told him in confidence. Certainly a counselor has a highly intimate relationship with his client and may be in a position to find out much personal information about the client during the interview. However, he often does not have legally defined privileged communication.[4]

Teachers must think through the nature of the counseling role and its attendant obligations and restrictions. Some may find themselves unable or unwilling to perform this role. Certain persons may recognize that they possess a personal moral code so rigid that they would immediately reject any act in conflict with their own standards whether such an act might be in the best interests of the counselee or not. Some teachers may lack the ability to operate in the process role of counselor. Others may wish to reject this role out of fear of losing their

---

[3] See Carol E. Smith, "Development of Ethical Standards in the Secondary School Counseling Relationship for the Use of Counseling Information," Unpublished Doctor's Thesis (Los Angeles: University of Southern California, 1956) and Alexander A. Schneiders, "Problems of Confidentiality," *The Personnel and Guidance Journal* 42:252–254, November 1963.

[4] H. B. McDaniel, J. E. Lallas, J. A. Saum, and J. L. Gilmore, *Readings in Guidance* (New York: Holt, Rinehart and Winston, Inc., 1959), 243.

job. A few may be willing to meet the difficulties and the possible personal jeopardy involved in the counseling, in the interests of helping the individual.

All teachers should be aware of the *point of decision*. This is the point at which you must declare your intention as to what role you wish to play. In the above situation, the crucial point of decision came when the student said that he was in serious trouble and asked for your confidence. At this point there were roughly three choices: (a) to tell him to go ahead—thus accepting the counseling role, (b) to tell him that if this involves something illegal or immoral, the conversation may have to be revealed (a compromise position) or (c) to tell him that you cannot accept confidences—thus rejecting the counseling role altogether.

In the day-to-day process of working with boys and girls, many classroom teachers are confronted with similar situations (usually less dramatic ones) which call for a decision to accept or reject the role of counselor. We should not quarrel with whatever decision is made so long as the teacher involved understands the inherent implications and demands.

## The Teacher and Counseling

Teachers have the right and the opportunity to counsel, if they choose to accept the counseling role. However, they must clearly recognize the serious limitations within which they work. Teachers seldom are qualified through specialized education and experience to counsel students with difficult problems. The actions of well-intentioned but untrained persons may actually make the student's difficulty worse and less amenable to later professional treatment.

If a classroom teacher makes the considered decision to go ahead with the counseling sought by a pupil, he must accept the following imperatives: (a) place the welfare of the counselee first, (b) recognize the need to retain confidences, (c) seek to embody the objectivity and maturity of an adult who is genuinely interested in the person, and (d) be careful to seek referral at the first hint that the difficulty requires more professional competence than he possesses.

Given some control over the counseling interview you should attempt to utilize some of the following suggestions.

1. Prepare for the interview. You should seek to provide the greatest degree of privacy possible and to anticipate unwanted interruptions. Pertinent information regarding the student should be studied in order to better understand your client and his possible problems.

2. Build a friendly relationship. Everything from the relaxed, friendly atmosphere to the warm, sincere personality of the counselor will contribute to the establishment of rapport.

3. Listen to the problem. The skillful counselor listens more than he talks and allows the pace of the student to set the pace of the interview. He seeks to understand the feelings, attitudes, and reactions of the student as they are being revealed. The problem as initially stated may not at all be the real problem of concern to the counselee. The counselor attempts to understand the problem both as his client sees it and also in a wider, more mature perspective.

4. Decide on *possible* solutions. Ultimately, the decision is made by the counselee himself. The counselor has the responsibility of making sure that the student sees the problem with all the important factors delineated and recognizes the possible alternatives with their probable consequences.

5. Follow through. The student may desire assistance in carrying out his plan of action or may need further help of some kind. At any rate, the counselor must keep careful notes which form the basis for follow-up activity and subsequent evaluation of the interview.

## Screening

The classroom teacher has many very important contributions to make to the guidance program. One of these is screening.

As the teacher works with boys and girls in the day-to-day process of teaching and learning, he is in a position to "rough screen" for obvious defects. Certainly he is not qualified to diagnose illnesses, sight and hearing losses, or psychological maladjustments. However, the alert teacher can often spot obvious defects which ought to be called to the attention of someone qualified to diagnose them and give remedial treatment.

This is a crucial contribution which teachers alone can make to the total guidance program. No one has the opportunity to detect emerging maladjustments and physiological disorders that teachers do in their daily work with their students. Only the personal daily contact between teacher and student makes this important screening role possible.

## Referral

When obvious illnesses and defects are identified, appropriate referral must follow. The teacher must know whom to call in to deal with the problem. The school nurse, the physician retained by the school district, the school psychologist on the county superintendent's staff, the psychiatrist, the oculist, the dental consultant, the principal, the dean of boys, the dean of girls, the guidance director, and the counselors are some of the persons to whom the teacher may refer.

A student may experience sight or hearing loss without himself or his parents being aware of it. Teachers may detect the condition and refer the student to the school nurse, who will arrange for careful testing and diagnosis. A boy or girl occasionally comes to school seriously ill. If this happens, the student should be sent to the school nurse for his own protection as well as that of the other students. Behavior which is symptomatic of serious psychological maladjustment may be identified, and referral made to the director of guidance, the principal or the clinical psychologist. As teachers counsel pupils they may uncover problems which they are unqualified to deal with. These students are then referred to the more experienced counselors. In this way, teachers attempt to see that the resources of the school are utilized by those who need them.

*Mental Hygiene in the Classroom*

If the guidance point of view is to be implemented, high school classrooms must not contain unhappy, tension-ridden, threatening situations. This means that all teachers must strive to promote good mental hygiene in their teaching.

In a real sense, the learning atmosphere is part of the curriculum, for it is inseparable from the total experience of the student in the classroom. The classroom must be a warm, friendly place where learning is felt to be pleasant, even fun sometimes.

The individual must be prized by the teacher so that differences among individuals will be taken into consideration.

> The forces which make for relative inflexibility in classroom work are appreciably greater in the secondary than in the lower school. The high school teacher's training as a subject specialist makes it especially difficult for him to feel comfortable about varying his expectations to insure a better "fit" with the capacities, interests and needs of individual students.[5]

The minimum standard concept, where a level of achievement is set up and all students are held to this level, is incompatible with the guidance point of view. As students differ from one another physically, so they also differ intellectually. You don't expect Sammy, who is five feet two inches tall and weighs ninety pounds, to jump as far or as high as

---

[5] *Guidance in the Curriculum,* 1955 Yearbook (Washington, D.C.: Association for Supervision and Curriculum Development, N.E.A., 1955), 10.

Michael, who is six feet tall and weighs one hundred and seventy pounds. It should come as no great shock, then, to find that the intellectual abilities and academic aptitudes of a given class are widely distributed. Similarly, no teacher should be alarmed to find that one-half of his students are below the class average and one-half above it. This is simply to be expected.

The danger comes, however, when teachers fall into the trap of thinking an average score or norm is a minimum standard to be applied to all. As a result, some students are held to a goal which they find quite impossible to achieve. Furthermore, if they do not achieve that goal, the teacher may use coercion to "motivate" them. This produces a situation in which certain youngsters are punished day after day for something completely beyond their control. They simply do not have the intellectual equipment with which to measure up to the teacher's definition of success. For these students the classroom can be an unhappy, frustrating, even terrifying place.

Every person must come to think of himself with some degree of satisfaction, must believe in himself, must be convinced that he can improve himself and succeed in something. No matter what the reason, the guidance-minded classroom teacher cannot, in good conscience, use procedures which will make his students feel otherwise.

*Group Guidance*

The classroom provides the setting for a significant amount of group guidance. Alert teachers watch for opportunities to deal with common problems and questions expressed by the group, especially problems and questions which have some relevance to the subject at hand.

Teachers in every subject area should provide opportunities for exploration of the vocational possibilities open to a student who has considerable interest and ability in that subject. For example, if you are a music teacher you should be prepared to help interested students arrive at a valid and realistic appraisal of future job possibilities in music. Educational concerns such as the value of a college education or trade school, study habits, homework, test taking skills, and note taking, are other legitimate topics for group guidance in the classroom. Certain personal-social problems may be investigated through discussions, projects, reports, papers, or other activities in English class, homeroom, or guidance class.

Group guidance may also be used in various extra-class activities. Sponsors of subject area clubs and social clubs may help make arrangements for tours, field trips, speakers, discussions, and the like which seek to answer the questions and alleviate the concerns of club members.

*Information Gathering and Sharing*

Teachers often have occasion to discover many highly important things about their pupils, things which may be significant to other teachers and to guidance personnel. In some classes, the schoolwork itself may reveal such information. For example, in English classes the writing of autobiographies is often assigned to obtain pertinent material which will help teachers and counselors better understand the boys and girls. Student art may also be revealing to a trained interpreter. Papers and projects in social studies, guidance, home economics, and other such classes may provide valuable insight into the thinking of students.

Teachers must train themselves to watch for significant student comments, actions, attitudes, and interests in the flow of class activity. How do students behave as individuals compared to their overall pattern of behavior? How do students respond to others? How do they respond to you, their teacher? Do they talk abut significant out-of-school conditions? Do they reveal feelings about school situations? Are there unexplainable fluctuations in the achievement of some students?

When significant information is gathered it must be shared with other, interested persons. Anecdotal records or written reports based on student observation, student papers, and other records of vital information are placed in the student's cumulative file so that they will be readily available. Sometimes a case conference is called by the director of guidance or by the counselor concerned with the case. In this event, all staff members who have had an opportunity to learn to know the student in question are called together to pool whatever information they have in order to help the counselor in dealing with the problem.

Thus, the classroom teacher is an important and active member of the guidance team. He works in many ways, responding to the needs of other guidance personnel as well as to the needs of the boys and girls in his classes. He makes a real and indispensable contribution to the success of the guidance program in the high school.

# REVIEW

This chapter discusses guidance as it relates to the classroom teacher. In the high school, the guidance program is seen as a point of view as well as a set of specialized services in which the teacher, himself, is likely to be involved in many ways.

1. Can you define guidance? With what areas of problems must it deal?

2. How does guidance strive toward its general goals? What kinds of guidance services may be offered in the high school?

3. Recognizing that teachers are vital to the guidance program, in what possible ways are they likely to be involved?

# Selected References

Blount, N. S. and Klausmeier, H. J. *Teaching in the Secondary School.* 3rd ed. New York: Harper & Row, Publishers, 1968; Ch. 16 "Guidance and Counseling."

Brown, D. "Pseudo-Guidance Programs in Our Schools." *NASSP Bulletin,* 50:43–48, September 1966.

Dinkmeyer, D. "When Guidance and Curriculum Collaborate." *Educational Leadership,* 25:443, 445, 447–448, February, 1968.

Dumas, W. and Beckner, W. *Introduction to Secondary Education: A Foundations Approach.* Scranton, Pa.: International Textbook Company, 1968; Ch. 10 "Special Services."

Faunce, R. C. and Munshaw, C. L. *Teaching and Learning in Secondary Schools.* Belmont, Calif.: Wadsworth Publishing Company, 1964; Ch. 7 "Guidance and the Teacher."

Grambs, J. D., Carr, J. C., and Fitch, R. M., *Modern Methods in Secondary Education,* 3rd ed. New York: Holt, Rinehart and Winston, Inc., 1970; Ch. 17 "Is Anybody Listening? Counseling Individuals and Groups."

Green, J. A. *Fields of Teaching and Educational Services.* New York: Harper & Row, Publishers, 1966; Ch. 13 "Guidance and Pupil Personnel Services."

Johnston, E. G., Peters, M., and Evraiff, W. *The Role of the Teacher in Guidance.* Englewood Cliffs, N.J.: Prentice-Hall, Inc., 1959.

Miller, C. H. *Guidance Services: An Introduction.* New York: Harper & Row, Publishers, 1965.

Ohlsen, M. M. *Guidance Services in the Modern School.* New York: Harcourt, Brace & World, Inc., 1964.

# twelve

# The Effective Teacher

The success of the public high school is dependent upon the work of the classroom teachers. In reality, the efforts of the superintendent with his central office staff and the principal with his administrative and supervisory personnel are supportive to the teachers. The special services personnel of the school seek to facilitate the job of teaching which is the central consideration. The school exists so that classroom teachers may guide youth to constructive, desirable learning. Thus, the test of whether or not the high school is doing an effective job will be made through an evaluation of the results of the teachers' work in the classroom.

The job of the classroom teacher, strangely enough is a lonely one. Of course, he works along with a group of colleagues and he deals with large numbers of boys and girls, yet the role is lonely because so much depends upon him as an individual. Major decisions at all stages of the teaching-learning process are his. He must make pivotal decisions, often on the spot, without consultation and assistance.

In the teaching career of an average secondary school teacher, it is estimated that he will have touched the lives of literally thousands of students. Therefore, society invests a great deal of trust in the teachers of its youth.

Beginning teachers justifiably approach this profession with some trepidation. They have some real concerns regarding their ability to measure up to the demands made upon them. This chapter seeks to explore and provide understanding of the following areas of concern.

1. The teacher's role is difficult to describe. One profitable approach to assist a better understanding of this role is through the opinions of parents, students, administrators, and teachers themselves.

2. A successful teacher must possess a number of competencies. What are some of the characteristics which make for effective teaching?

3. To be most effective, teaching seems to require a considerable degree of commitment. What are practices which distinguish the professional teacher from the unprofessional teacher?


## TEACHER ROLE

Few beginning teachers have the opportunity to secure any real insight into the role of the secondary school teacher. When they attempt to recall the situation that existed when they were students in high school, they find that, because of the time which has elapsed, their relative immaturity then and the fact that they usually were not observing with the idea of becoming a teacher, they cannot remember significant things about the teacher's role. During student teaching and observation, the sampling experiences are so limited that it is impossible to generalize broadly.

Most beginning teachers would like to know more about the role which teachers must assume. They want to know what parents think about teachers. They want to know what students like and dislike about teachers. They want to sample administrator opinion about teachers, and especially they want to know what teachers think about themselves.

A college class in secondary education was engaged in discussing what it thought was the role of the teacher. This exploratory discussion quickly showed that the students had little real data to go on; they had read autobiographical accounts of rural teachers of several generations ago, witty discourses about the trials and tribulations of a college professor, glowing descriptions of the challenges of teaching in brochures aimed at recruiting teachers, facts and figures compiled by teachers associations, and even a delightful report about teaching in the days of saber-toothed tigers. But they wanted to know what people think about the present job of the teacher. What are current attitudes toward the teacher's role?

The professor suggested that the class do some informal research— go out and talk directly with the people. Four committees were formed; one which would interview parents at random around the community, one which would catch students after school outside the high school and ask them questions, one which would make appointments to see administrative personnel in the system, and one which would contact secondary school teachers for their comments. They worked out an open-ended question which seemed likely to encourage these people to talk about characteristics of teachers and their role today, and all agreed to use the same question and general approach in the interviews.

A few weeks later the student committees brought the reports to class. They had condensed the responses into succinct statements representing each of the four groups of people who were interviewed.

*Parents.* We haven't thought much about it, but in general the teachers seem to be doing a good job in spite of considerable handicaps in our school district. Most of them are fine, dedicated, sincere people, although there are a few who are just teaching for the paycheck. Teachers are underpaid but they do have long vacations and good working hours. The teachers ought to be an example to boys and girls. They need to be interested in their students and be able to get them interested in the school work. We would encourage our daughter to become a teacher, but we're not sure about our son.

*Students.* We think teachers are a necessary evil. We like a teacher who controls the class, who knows his subject and can make it interesting to us. We have some teachers who play favorites, are too strict or not strict enough, who don't really seem to like their subject or their job, and who aren't concerned about us. The teacher who has a good sense of humor, a good personality, and who is really interested in us as persons is our favorite. In general, we favor young teachers over older teachers. We feel sorry for our instructors and don't think we want to become teachers.

*Administrators.* Today's teachers are better prepared than ever before. We still have a wide range—from excellent to very poor—however, the quality is rising. Our teachers must not only be well prepared in their subject and know how to teach it, they must also act as guidance personnel, work with extra-class activities, and represent the school in the community. The teacher has to get along with his students, fellow teachers, and the parents and lay people in the community. We are looking for teachers who have the ability to make school a challenging and enjoyable experience for all students.

*Teachers.* Most high school teachers, we feel, are doing an adequate job in spite of handicaps. We teach because we want to be of service to the youth of America. Most of us like to work with boys and girls, and we enjoy working in the academic atmosphere. Our teaching loads are too heavy, classes are too crowded, many facilities are inadequate, there are too many distractions in our culture competing with us for the time and energies of our pupils. In general, society does not prize intellectual things, the teacher is not respected, and we are not paid commensurate with our level of education and degree of responsibility. If we had better backing and assistance from parents, fewer distractions in school, and more status in the community, we could do a far better job.

*Implications*

The composite statements which represented the comments received by the students in their interviews with the four groups, even though they were the result of very informal research and subject to some sampling error, provide a basis for a number of significant and insightful implications. In the ensuing discussion, some of these implications were pointed up.

*Parents.*   The parents' comments revealed that they generally felt teachers were doing well considering the growing enrollments, crowded classes, and lack of facilities. They felt that present criticisms of teachers may be true in some other school district, but not in the local one. There were some exceptions and qualification, but general satisfaction was reported by the parents interviewed.

Although the parents indicated that they really hadn't given it much thought, they seemed to be evaluating the work of the teacher from three sources: (a) through the eyes of their sons and daughters in school, (b) from recent publicity about teaching conditions and criticisms, and (c) through their memories of their experiences in high school years ago.

The statement that teachers ought to be an example to youth is an old and invalid conception of teacher role. As a matter of fact, high school students often report that some of their teachers are attractive, interesting, vital persons, but they seldom want to be like them. Teachers, by their very choice of occupation, where money is not the prime motivating factor, are deviates in this culture, and thus are not objects of imitation for secondary school youth. For example, a few years ago a high school teacher was approached by one of his better students. The boy spoke very seriously and with obvious sincerity, "Mr. Mack, I think you are the best teacher in the whole school. We all know about what salary you get. You are much smarter than my dad and he makes five times more than you do. I've talked to him and he will get you a job with his company if you want it. How about it?" This young man was not being sarcastic; he liked his teacher and was simply trying to assist him. He wanted to be helpful, but he did not want to imitate his teacher. A teacher must not be expected to be some sort of impossible paragon of virtue, for he does not operate as an example to modern youth.

The real insight into the parental conception of teacher role comes through the statement that teaching might be all right for their daughter but probably not for their son. They feel teachers are, by and large, dedicated and sincere. The teacher seems to have nice vacations and good working hours, yet this occupation is not an attractive lifetime expectation for their male offspring.

*Students.*  Students tolerate teachers. The teacher comes as part of the school, and usually the compulsory school experience is accepted as a necessary part of growing up. Actually, they feel teachers have a tough job working with boys and girls all day, and few students indicate that they want to prepare for this profession.

High school pupils evaluate a teacher by his human relations characteristics. The way a teacher works with students—his sense of humor, fairness, enthusiasm, liking for the work, ability to control the class, and his personality are important to them. The classroom teacher must know his subject and possess the methods to make it understandable and interesting. Above all, the students seem to prize a teacher who is really interested in them as persons. Such an instructor is friendly, helpful, patient, and fair.

In general, young teachers are preferred by students over older teachers. Apparently this is because the younger instructors tend to have more vitality, enthusiasm, and a fresher point of view. At the same time, most students are likely to point to a senior teacher who is respected and admired as an important bulwark of the school.

*Administrators.*  Administrators, from the perspective of their positions, commented on the present range in quality of teachers. They asserted that the preparation is getting better and better. Certification laws, improvement in teacher training, recent research in learning and methodology, superior screening of students who would become teachers, and more general commitment of all departments of the college or university to teacher training are some of the probable reasons for this improvement.

The broad demands of the teacher's job were pointed up by the principals. The need for teachers to accept and deal constructively and helpfully with all youth who are required to attend school was highlighted. Beyond this, they mentioned such areas of responsibility as guidance, extra-class activities, and public relations.

Administrators seemed to emphasize the "get along" qualities of the teachers. As the persons charged with the smooth running of the school, they want instructors who can get along with the students, fellow staff members, and parents. The average principal would look with disfavor upon a teacher who sends a steady stream of students into the office for discipline or who had a large number of the parents of his students storm into his office protesting grading inequities or harsh and unfair treatment of pupils.

*Teachers.*   The high school instructors themselves expressed general agreement that they are doing at least an adequate job. This does not mean that they saw no room for improvement. A few years ago a pollster asked a number of teachers if they were satisfied with the teaching job they were doing. The great majority replied in the negative; therefore, he concluded that the quality of teaching was abysmally bad. Actually, it is quite a different question to ask if teachers are satisfied with their teaching than it is to ask if they think their teaching is bad. Good teachers always tend to feel that they can improve their work. This group of teachers indicated that, in the main, the level of teaching was satisfactory.

Teacher comments revealed that a basic motive for their going into and remaining in teaching was the opportunity to be of service to youth and their country. Satisfactions grew out of the enjoyment of working with maturing boys and girls, and knowing that they had a part in their growth.

Teachers rightly feel that the public takes them for granted and doesn't really understand them. For example, they often react defensively to the public's idea that teachers work "bankers hours" and have long, enjoyable vacations. For example, a teacher was spending the summer tending his garden. After a few weeks, the next door neighbor felt compelled to lean over the fence and remark that he was envious of teachers and their long vacations. The young high school teacher calmly replied, "I don't have long vacations. Actually teaching is seasonal work! I'm laid off now until September!" This, of course, is the truth. Even though some school districts will spread salaries over twelve months, the fact is that the teacher is paid for only nine months. Many teachers work at other jobs during the summer to supplement their income from teaching; others return to college for advanced work to help keep up with the rapidly changing developments in various subject areas or prepare for guidance and administrative responsibilities.

Some resentment over lack of status was evident from the comments. In American society today, knowledge and wealth seem to be the bases for prestige; the teacher has only knowledge. Teachers invest substantial amounts of time, money, and effort in preparing to teach, they accept vital and overriding responsibilities as a part of their professional duties, and they fulfill a task of great importance to the nation. Therefore, teachers feel that they should receive more respect and more money.

It is obvious that significant differences in opinion exist among the various groups. These differences are related to the different frames of reference from which the work of the teacher is viewed. Beginning teachers should think through these implications and others for the effect upon the sort of work they feel they can enjoy spending a lifetime doing.

## Teacher Image

For a variety of reasons, a certain conception of the nature and role of the teacher[1] has evolved in the public mind in America. This image has come from publicity which repeatedly has emphasized the sad lot of the teacher, his dedication to his task even under great difficulties and in the face of sizeable obstacles, his financial plight, and the need to support him in this thankless task. It has resulted from the traditionally low station of the teacher, an attitude which goes back to colonial days. It has also grown from the almost anti-intellectual flavor of American culture; the great and approved image has long been the poor boy who, through hard work and shrewd application of common sense, worked his way to the top and to financial success. The person who was preoccupied with intellectual pursuits was considered an "egg head" and somewhat under suspicion. Even though there is some evidence that this attitude may be slowly changing, it still is a factor.

Although there is no rigid teacher stereotype existing today, several qualities were characteristic of the generally unappealing image of the teacher in the mind of the public.

1. The teacher was felt to be more at home with books than with people his own age. Teaching was somehow thought of as a woman's occupation, and any male teacher, except for coaches, was assumed to be effeminate or else he would have chosen some other line of work. Parents expected teachers to be restrained and conservative in behavior.

2. Teachers were considered submissive and even somewhat masochistic. They were observed to endure the critics and attackers without replying except in very careful, objective terms. The teacher was long-suffering and greatly put upon. In the past, the school boards and administrators seldom had much trouble dominating the staff. Teacher requests for salary raises and improvement of working conditions were often summarily rejected or ignored.

3. The instructor was judged to be unsure and ineffective. America's system of local control placed the will of the people, interpreted by the school board, as the significant authority. This resulted occasionally in lay persons determining what was to be taught. In a possible conflict

---

[1] See Arthur Foff, "Scholars and Scapegoats," *English Journal,* 47:118–26, March 1958 for an analysis of teachers as pictured in novels.

between local mores and the teaching of experimentally verified facts, the authority of the school board sometimes negated the authority of truth. The classroom teacher who possessed a real measure of expertness in his field was likely to be dominated by lay people. Teachers sometimes agreed with parents and submitted to pressure groups in the interests of good public relations. As a consequence they were considered to lack assurance and self-confidence.

4. Because teachers were dedicated and committed to serve youth, they were admired and often classed with clergymen. The feeling was that teaching was a function which was desirable and necessary to the welfare of our society but one which someone else could do. Youngsters today generally are encouraged to look for an occupation with rewards which are more material than spiritual.

Even today, some teachers themselves are apologetic about their choice of occupation. They marshal their reasons (for example, long vacations or inside work) when they talk to their friends. Many feel that somehow they are something less than a success in life if they go into teaching. Teachers, too, have been affected by the prevailing image.

Since World War II, a countertrend has emerged within teaching itself. This trend was initiated by a sizeable number of returning veterans who had decided while in the service to teach. Many of them made up their minds about two important things. First, they wanted to be of continuing service to their country and particularly its youth, and second, they wanted to live a normal, well-rounded life while doing so.

These young men were assertive, self-confident, and even slightly cocky. They were deeply serious about their desire to teach and they did very well in college work. They were equally sure that they would not teach unless they could live a normal life.

These young teachers were accustomed to defending their beliefs, and teaching began to take on a slightly new look. For example, one young teacher of social studies accepted a position in a school district where ninety per cent of the adults were Republicans. In his first lecture of the year, he pointed out that he was a registered Democrat and that the students should evaluate his statements with this knowledge in mind. After a brief furor, the parents accepted him and his unorthodox approach. Other young teachers joined community service clubs and lent their considerable talents to the work of the organizations, incidentally demonstrating to all that they were human beings too. Some became involved in community projects of all kinds. Many made friends with people in the city, played bridge, went to dances, and generally lived as any respectable citizen might.

Following this early group came many, many more like them so that today the old teacher image is changing. During the 1960's, teachers increasingly used their power through collective negotiations to affect profoundly the decisions made in great numbers of local school districts. Moreover, today teachers are no longer restricted by artificial and impossible expectations in their personal life style.

## THE SUCCESSFUL TEACHER

Even though definitions of the successful teacher vary widely as school districts seek to work out some practicable solution to the issue of merit pay, supervisors and administrators must operate with some sort of conception of the effective teacher in mind. Teachers are hired, fired, achieve tenure, receive promotions, are selected to work on committees, and the like. People in the school district are making judgments day after day in regard to these considerations. Actually, experienced school people engaged in school surveys and accreditation visitations find high agreement among administrators, supervisors, state department personnel, and college professors in selecting the best teachers and the worst teachers in a school. The middle group of just average to poor teachers is less clearly agreed upon. In discussing the effective teacher with these people, certain qualities tend to stand out.

### Qualities of the Successful Teacher

A number of approaches[2] have been made to the identification of traits. Some writers have used an armchair approach to the problem and have listed a challenging set of qualities. Others carefully analyzed the literature on the subject and condensed the results into a manageable list. Involved, highly organized research projects have attempted to explore this problem. However, an informal distillation of the opinions of the personnel who find themselves regularly engaged in judging teacher competence would seem likely to provide a helpful listing of characteristics to be found in the successful teacher. The following qualities are descriptive of the teacher who is judged to be effective.

*Concern for the individual.*   The teacher works with students, recognizes that the student is the most important element in the teaching-learning process, and, to be really effective, must focus upon the individual learner. The successful teacher cares about what happens to his students. He is not aloof, distant, or immersed completely in his

---

[2] See for example B. J. Biddle and W. J. Ellena, eds., *Contemporary Research on Teacher Effectiveness* (New York: Holt, Rinehart and Winston, Inc., 1964).

subject. He is interested and concerned about the fears, the enthusiasms, the learning problems of the individual student. He may perform two functions: at times he may be first of all a scholar and student in his subject specialty, but in the classroom he knows his work as a teacher is with and through the learner.

*Expertness in a subject.* To be effective, a teacher must possess a real measure of expertness in his subject area. A secondary teacher will usually be less highly specialized in a narrow aspect of his subject than a doctoral candidate at a university—one reason being that his preparation and teaching assignment in the high school are more diffuse. However, he must have perspective and knowledge of his field which allow him to teach confidently and well. For example, a high school English teacher may not be qualified to engage in advanced research in structural linguistics, yet he knows the field and how it is related to traditional English grammar. Good teaching may be characterized by a kind of pervasive validity which is derived from this expertness in the subject.

*Understanding of youth.* Successful teachers know youth. For example, junior high school teachers understand the early adolescent and are prepared to deal helpfully and constructively with his immaturities. Successful teachers plan and teach according to the realities of the situation. They know that certain kinds of behavior are normal and to be expected. They accept the immature actions and employ a guidance point of view in seeking to promote progressively more mature behavior patterns. The effective teacher understands the motives and needs of youth and uses these in teaching.

*Skill in teaching processes.* Teachers who are effective have developed skill in planning and executing effective processes of teaching. A study[3] of employing officials' reasons for terminating the employment of teachers revealed that more teachers fail because of poor teaching techniques than for any other reason. When these same officials were asked about qualities of their superior teachers, they placed knowledge of effective teaching methods first in importance to success. The best teachers have developed procedures for making material interesting and promoting effective learning. Because classroom learning occurs in a group situation, most successful teachers are skilled in the group process.

*Physical health and stamina.* A teacher who remains in teaching must have good health and physical resources. The usual teaching assignment

---

[3] M. E. Stapley, "A Study of Teacher Effectiveness," *The Teachers College Journal,* 30:41–42, December 1958.

in high school would wear down all but the most robust. Studies[4] made of the teachers' work week indicate hours substantially above the usual forty-hour week of industry. Moreover, coffee breaks are not provided. It is not uncommon for a high school teacher to be assigned six classes a day with a half-hour for lunch. This means that the teacher is faced with a demand for sustained performance the like of which no professional entertainer is likely to meet. Problems of sustaining enthusiasm, vivacity, concentration, and sensitivity throughout each class during the day are almost impossible to overcome. Such demands made upon the teacher have caused one writer to comment, "It is not an exaggeration to say that it tends to be a breathless, continuous expenditure of energy, from the first bell to the last."[5] Teaching is a difficult demanding job, and physical health and stamina are needed.

*Mental health and emotional stability.* Of course, good mental health is a desirable characteristic for all teachers. This is especially important because of the pervasive influence of the teacher's personality upon the learning atmosphere of the room. Teachers need to be mature, well-adjusted, and accepting. Superior teachers tend to manifest superior emotional adjustment. Teachers need stability and sufficient adjustment so that they can help boys and girls with their problems; teachers should not use the class to work out personal problems.

*Enthusiasm and drive.* Effective teachers tend to exude contagious enthusiasm toward their subject. The drive and vitality of these teachers often help carry the class into the work. This is one reason why students often express a preference for younger teachers. The younger teacher sometimes brings freshness, interest, and motivation for a subject. This very enthusiasm and drive help to make the subject meaningful to the student.

*Sensitivity.* The gifted teacher is observed to have great sensitivity to the feelings and reactions of his students. In his teaching, he may revise, replan, and generally adjust his methods and materials according to the feedback which he receives from his pupils. The teacher knows when the lesson is going well or poorly and he makes appropriate changes which he hopes will improve the learning. The insensitive teacher is forced to approach his teaching in a mechanical fashion, for he lacks the essential quality of awareness.

---

[4] See for example *Teaching Career Fact Book* (Washington, D.C.: N.E.A., 1966), 4–5.

[5] Robert E. Jewett, "Why the Able Public-School Teacher is Dissatisfied," *Educational Research Bulletin,* 36:231, October 9, 1957.

*Verbal facility.*    The work of teaching requires considerable verbal facility. The superior instructor is able to explain clearly, describe accurately and vividly, and generally use words easily and effectively. The process of education in the classroom is much preoccupied with the written and spoken word, for this is the basic medium of instruction. Thus, essential attributes of the successful teacher are a rapid and flexible reading skill, effective speaking ability, and competence in writing.

*Attractive appearance.*    Students respond well to an attractive person. This attractiveness may be related to physical appearance, dress, absence of serious defects, personal charm, sense of humor, or some combination of these attributes. The highly successful teacher tends to be perceived as an attractive person in the eyes of his pupils.

*Self-confidence.*    The effective teacher is poised and self-assured. He makes decisions with confidence derived from the expertness which he possesses both in his subject and in his knowledge of youth and the principles according to which they learn. He is self-reliant, independent, and courageous in his beliefs. The really effective teacher has the self-confidence which will allow him, when necessary, to respond to a student's question with, "I don't know the answer but we can find out." He does not feel compelled to bluff some sort of answer, for he knows that no single teacher can be the "fount of all knowledge." He is not cocky but speaks with the authority and assurance of one who is competent and is aware of his abilities.

These qualities are related to the work of the teacher in the classroom. In addition, the successful teacher needs to work well with his fellow teachers and his superiors. He must deal tactfully with parents and townspeople. He also may need to consider the obligations of his profession.

## THE PROFESSIONAL TEACHER

Teaching is generally conceded to be the largest profession in America. That is, the number of persons engaged in teaching is far larger than in any other occupation normally classed as a profession.

Teachers at all levels commonly speak of their teaching profession. Educational journals and convention speeches are full of references to the "profession." As a matter of fact, the long-standing debate between the American Federation of Teachers and the National Education Association has not hung on this issue. National teachers' organizations are agreed that the continuing professionalization of teaching is an important aim.

The general public seems quite willing to admit to the profession of teaching; however, it still ranks teachers behind such occupations as physicians, engineers, architects, and dentists in professional status and provides somewhat less compensation. It may be that one of the basic motives for people going into teaching is "a chance to climb from the blue collar to the white collar class,"[6] and this sort of motivation is behind the great insistence for professional status and recognition. The fact is clear that the bulk of teachers are eager to be members of a professional group and are interested in continuing and enhancing their professional position.

*Teaching as a Profession*

Writers have variously defined the characteristics of a profession and then analyzed the occupation of teaching to discover whether or not it has attained the professional status. Most of them[7] have concluded that much is left to be desired.

Teaching in America (a) requires personnel who have mastered a body of specialized knowledge, (b) demands a substantially long period of training to fulfill requirements, (c) employs persons who declare their motive to serve mankind, and (d) involves strong professional organizations. On these criteria, teaching ranks relatively high in its progress toward professional status.

However, it only partially fulfills conditions related to (a) the control of standards for entrance into and membership in the profession, (b) the establishment and enforcement of codes of ethics, and (c) the lifetime career expectation of people engaged in the work. Because teachers are mainly publicly employed, they have not been able to exercise the same amount of control over standards for entering members of the profession as have other, privately employed occupations. As with other professions, the licensing requirements are usually determined by state legislatures, but teachers as a group have traditionally had less influence upon the formulation of these requirements than other professional groups have had on their licensing standards.

The large education associations have been leaders in the careful formulation and publication of codes of ethics which presumably provide guidance for teachers in determining right and proper conduct. How-

---

[6] Myron Lieberman, *Education as a Profession* (Englewood Cliffs, N.J.: Prentice-Hall, Inc., 1956), 218.

[7] See for example T. M. Stinnett, *Professional Problems of Teachers,* 3rd ed. (New York: The Macmillin Company, 1968); Ch. 3 "The Profession of Teaching" and R. C. Phillips, "How Does Education Measure Up as a Profession?" *The High School Journal,* 51:158–164, January 1968.

ever, in the past, enforcement has been almost totally absent. In 1960, Firth was impelled to write that teaching has had some sort of code of ethics for many, many years, "yet only one member has been expelled from the National Education Association for violation of its ethical code since the adoption of that code in 1919."[8] More recently, the organized teachers at the local, state, and national levels have begun to face up to the problem of enforcement of ethical standards through the control and discipline of their colleagues.

Teaching is becoming less a stopgap, temporary occupation. The spread of career salary schedules will do much to encourage youth to think of teaching as a career. At this point, however, many young teachers do not have lifetime expectations when going into education.

It seems fair to characterize teaching as at least substantially a profession. There is much improvement to be made in some areas, yet in the perception of the public and on the basis of the criteria of a profession, it rates status as a professional occupation.

### Professional Behavior

In many ways, the actions of persons engaged in teaching provide the most revealing index to the degree of professionalization existing in the great mass of educational workers in America.

Some principals comment privately that one of their greatest problems is the unprofessional teacher. By far, the majority of teachers do not fall into this category, yet a substantial minority behave in ways which are unethical and distinctly unprofessional. Some of these unprofessional acts are included in the following discussions.

*Confidential information.* Most codes of ethics are quite explicit regarding the obligation of teachers to respect a student's right to have certain information remain confidential unless its release is required by law or requested by authorized agencies. One high school teacher, under the hypnotic influence of the hairdryer at the local hairdresser's shop, told a group of women that one of her students had confessed to her in confidence that she thought she was pregnant. Of course, the whole town knew about it by the next morning. Another thoughtless instructor discussed the IQ scores of some of her students with a neighbor, with the result that this information became part of the neighborhood gossip.

---

[8] Gerald H. Firth, "Teachers Must Discipline Their Professional Colleagues," *Phi Delta Kappan,* 42:24, October 1960.

*Criticism of colleagues.* Too many teachers are prone to criticize fellow teachers in conversations with parents and students. For example, one parent came in after school to discuss his son's mediocre academic achievement in English. The teacher quickly resolved the situation, to her satisfaction at least, by blaming everything on the English teacher who taught the boy the previous year. Another example would be the high school counselor who was asked to speak before a community service club regarding the current criticisms of public education. During his talk, he managed to criticize everyone from the superintendent down to the newest teacher.

Critical examination of school practices is, of course, highly desirable *within professional circles.* However, teachers who criticize the teaching of colleagues to parents and pupils, usually without full knowledge of the situation at that, are performing a disservice to their own profession and the school within which they work.

*Job seeking.* Some beginning teachers, through ignorance of the ethics involved or because they have been accustomed to operating according to usual practices in business and industry, may be guilty of unprofessional, job-seeking behavior. Ethical codes specify that teachers should not apply for a position unless they have information that there is a vacancy. Picture this situation. A beginning teacher has been hired to teach general math and algebra. Another teacher, with eight years of experience and work beyond the masters degree in math, knows that the new teacher has been struggling along making adequate progress for the first year, and applies for the job stressing his qualifications and the other teacher's inexperience. Here, is a teacher trying to displace another teacher from his position. The teaching profession would hope to avoid bidding between teachers for a position. Years ago, teachers, with considerable urging from a few school boards, actually sought to underbid each other by naming a lower salary figure than the others. Ethically, an application for a position cannot be made unless there is a vacancy. However, it is permissible under certain conditions to write a letter of inquiry to a school system stating qualifications and making inquiry regarding the possibility of a future vacancy.

A few teachers attempt to have important and influential friends or relatives exert pressure on the school board and school administrators in order to secure a teaching position in the school of their choice. Of course, this sometimes succeeds, yet employment which is secured on the basis of factors other than competence tends to be less than satisfactory from the point of view of the pupils and the employee himself.

*Professional contracts.* A teaching contract is a legal and ethical agreement entered into by the teacher and the school district. Unprofessional teachers, however, sometimes sign more than one contract and then break all but the most advantageous one. A common situation facing beginning teachers is closely related. You have been interviewed by two high school principals and received encouragement from both, but no contract has been offered you as yet. Privately, you feel that the teaching assignment, salary, and general appeal of the position at Alpha High School is somewhat better than that at Beta High School. However, you would not be unhappy with the latter. In the mail, you receive a contract from Beta High, you wait a week for some word from Alpha High, and finally you feel, in fairness to Beta High, that you must sign the contract and place it in the mail. The next day you receive the contract from the principal at Alpha High School. What do you do? Ethically what can you do? Obviously you would prefer this latter position. You might:

1. Return the contract to Alpha High School expressing your regret but informing them that you have already accepted a teaching position for fall.

2. Sign and return the Alpha contract and inform the principal at Beta High School that you cannot teach there because you have decided to go to Alpha High School instead.

3. Go to the Beta School board and request that they release you from the signed contract so that you can accept a position in another school.

It seems clear that the first alternative is ethical and probably sound if there is no great difference between the two positions offered. The second is unprofessional, unethical, and illegal. In this situation, the teacher simply breaks the unwanted contract. The third alternative is the proper procedure if you can make a good case for your preference of Alpha High School. You would go to the principal at Beta High and justify your request for release from the contract in order to accept a position which offers greater professional challenge, presents the opportunity to teach in areas of your greatest strength and interest, or some other convincing reason. Unless this request is made a few weeks before school is due to open, almost all school boards would be quite willing to give you the release. School officials do not want to employ you if you are going to be unhappy in the position; they, of course, are concerned about filling the vacancy with a competent and interested teacher.

These are a few of the areas in which unprofessional behavior of teachers is observed. Great damage to teaching as a profession results from the few who do not observe professional standards of conduct. In an occupation such as teaching, with its tremendous number of workers, it is difficult to identify and control those who make this type of behavior a problem.

*The avocational teacher.*    At present, the great need for teachers allows many who are not fully qualified or fully committed to remain in the profession. A difficult problem is the avocational teacher. "The semi-professional or avocational teacher may be defined as one who teaches, but considers teaching a secondary occupation."[9] This refers to the man who owns and runs a dude ranch or a sporting goods store and teaches on the side. His major income comes from the business; his major interest is in the business. Teaching is an avocation. Some people sell insurance, operate cattle ranches, organize travel bureaus, lead a dance band, or provide accounting and tax services and also teach. Some housewives teach primarily to help pay for the new car, to finish the party room in the basement, to secure a down payment for a new house, to purchase a deep freeze, or to save up for a trip to Europe.

The real issue, of course, is where the focus of a person's interest rests and what he feels to be his primary commitment. It is quite possible for a man to own and supervise the operation of a business and still remain primarily and wholeheartedly committed to teaching. Many women successfully perform their roles as wife and mother to their families and, at the same time, fulfill the demands of professional teaching. The fact is that teaching, if it is to be professional, demands full time, fully involved men and women who are willing to give their primary interest and allegiance to work which they have chosen as their lifetime career. Professionals seek to improve the education of youth, better the working conditions for themselves and their colleagues, continue the search for knowledge, and enhance the profession of teaching through their support of professional associations as well as professional standards of conduct.

## REVIEW

Teachers have long sought increased prestige and status in America. They sometimes look longingly at reports from Europe which depict teachers as persons who are respected highly in the community. Students stand when the teacher comes into the room and remain standing quietly

---

[9] John R. Rogers, "The Avocational Teacher: A Professional Problem," *Journal of Teacher Education,* 10:390, December 1959.

until the instructor gives them permission to be seated. American education has moved toward the concept of teacher as guide to learning and friendly advisor to students, rather than stern taskmaster.

Some observers have felt that the American movement toward professionalization of teaching is a result of teachers wanting to make up in prestige some of the inadequacies they face in salary. At the same time, the realities of public employment, control by lay boards of education, formulation of certification requirements by state legislatures, great shortages of qualified teachers, and a traditional conception of teachers have inhibited this development. In spite of this, substantial progress has been made and more appears to be forthcoming in the future.

This chapter has sought to examine the role of the teacher in light of typical questions and concerns of the beginning teacher.

1. The work of the teacher touches parents, students, administrators, and fellow teachers. What do they think about the role of the high school teacher?

2. The effective teacher performs many functions in the classroom and must possess a number of important qualities. What are some of the traits which are said to be characteristic of the successful teacher?

3. Teachers as a group are working to secure and enhance the status of teaching as a profession. What are common areas of behavior in which some beginning teachers are unprofessional? What does professional teaching demand from you?

# Selected References

Adams, R. S. and Biddle, B. J. *Realities of Teaching: Explanations with Video Tape.* New York: Holt, Rinehart and Winston, Inc., 1970.

Alcorn, M. D., Kinder, J. S., and Schunert, J. R. *Better Teaching in Secondary Schools,* 3rd ed. New York: Holt, Rinehart and Winston, Inc., 1970; Ch. 1 "Orientation to Teaching as a Profession" and Ch. 20 "Advancement in the Profession."

Anderson, R. H. *Teaching in a World of Change.* New York: Harcourt, Brace & World, Inc., 1966.

"The Beginning Teacher," *NASSP Bulletin,* 52 (entire issue), October 1968.

Biddle, B. J. and Ellena, W. J., eds. *Contemporary Research on Teacher Effectiveness.* New York: Holt, Rinehart and Winston, Inc., 1964.

*Careers in Education.* Washington, D.C.: National Commission on Teacher Education and Professional Standards, National Education Association, 1968.

Green, J. A. *Fields of Teaching and Educational Services.* New York: Harper & Row, Publishers, 1966.

Lieberman, Myron and Moskow, M. H. *Collective Negotiations for Teachers.* Chicago: Rand McNally & Company, 1966.

Stinnett, T. M. *The Profession of Teaching.* Washington, D.C.: Center for Applied Research in Education, Inc., 1962.

_____. *Professional Problems of Teachers.* 3rd ed. New York: The Macmillan Company, 1968.

# thirteen

# Historical Antecedents

The United States, in less than two centuries of existence as a nation, has developed a system of secondary education which is peculiarly its own. The nature and organization of today's high school have their roots buried deeply in Western European culture, yet this young, idealistic nation has fashioned an institution which, until now, has maintained a high degree of flexibility and adaptability to meet the demands of a swiftly changing day and to remain sensitive to the public which it serves.

Young people who would spend their lives teaching in the secondary school need to understand its evolution. They need to look at historical antecedents in order to better know the modern high school and its possible future. Accordingly, this chapter is organized around the following points.

1. Colonists, soon after they became settled, worked to establish educational opportunities. What was the earliest form of secondary education in America?

2. Changing conditions in the new world led to changing needs for secondary education. What was the second distinctive educative agency which appeared and why?

3. The public high school was a tertiary development in secondary education. What conditions led to its emergence? What transitional developments have occurred between the early high school and the one we know today?

The historical development of the secondary school is a long and interesting story. To cover this in a single chapter means that only a few of the high points may be included.

## EARLIEST SECONDARY SCHOOLS IN AMERICA

The growth of a secondary education in America is, of course, closely related to the traditions which the colonists brought with them. It also reflects the motives which impelled them to come and the conditions with which they had to deal when they arrived.

Naturally, the people who brought their families and settled in the colonies to live were most concerned with the problem of education. Because of the predominance of English colonists, it was quite reasonable to expect English educational patterns to be imported. New England imported the Latin grammar school and very early established the first secondary school in the colonies. The southern colonies were British in their point of view toward education, but in a different way. They felt that private control and support of education were right and proper. Free schools were only for children of the poor and orphans. Parents of any substance hired private tutors for their children. The middle colonies were mixed in the early developments. Because of differing religions and racial backgrounds, these colonies moved toward private and church control of education.

Life was hard in the New England colonies, and a system of compact town communities grew up. Farmers often lived close together for mutual protection and support and worked the land which spread out in all directions around the population center. A close knit community spirit emerged which gave a distinctive flavor to the political developments which followed. In contrast, the southern colonies, especially after 1680, developed the plantation system in response to the demand for tobacco. By the very nature of the large land holdings, the population was thinly scattered and the plantation rather than communities of people became the unifying force. The land owner in the south sought a great supply of cheap, unskilled labor while the landowner of New England worked his own land and looked to skilled workmen in the town to supply many of his needs. The economic life in the north became diversified and the community far more self-sufficient.

New England religious beliefs placed emphasis upon ability to read the Bible and the right of private decision. Institutions were needed which would provide for the education of religious leaders (for in a theocracy the religious leaders were also the civil leaders) and also offer training which would allow each person to read the Bible for himself. Secondary education became important because it was indispensable in preparing young men to enter college and thus be trained for the clergy. The southern colonists had no conflict with the Church of England;

therefore, ministers could be imported or young men could be sent to England for training.

For these reasons, it is understandable that the earliest secondary schools in America should develop in the New England colonies and thus form the basis for the evolving system of secondary education.

## The Latin Grammar School

Actually, the first attempt to establish a Latin school came in the south.

> Early in the history of the colony of Virginia, funds were raised and lands set apart for the endowment of a Latin Grammar School. But these promising beginnings were swept away by the Indian massacre of 1622, and the school seems never to have been opened.[1]

The first Latin grammar school was set up in 1635, only fifteen years after the Puritans landed at Plymouth, by the town of Boston in the Massachusetts Bay Colony. This school, which is still in existence, is judged to be the first secondary school in America.

It is significant for the future of American education that a town meeting was the setting for the public expression which resulted in the establishment of this first secondary school. Townspeople voted to support the school by rent from certain islands in the harbor. Private funds were also donated to keep the school going. Other towns in New England followed suit and soon the initiative for establishing schools and partially supporting them clearly belonged to the civil authorities. Typically, money from rental of town lands, fines, licenses, some property taxes, and tuition charged those who could pay went to support the schools.

*First school laws.* The legislature of the Massachusetts Bay Colony soon took an important step to encourage the futher expansion of education. In 1642, a law was passed which gave town officials the authority to require parents to see to it that their children received elementary education. In 1647, another, broader education law was adopted. In this legislation, every town of fifty families was required to hire a teacher for elementary education, and every town of one hundred families was compelled to set up a Latin grammar school. The legality of the authority of towns to tax for support of the school was confirmed. The importance of these two legislative acts rests in the establishment of the

---

[1] Nicholas M. Butler, ed., *Monographs on Education in the United States* (Albany, N.Y.: J. B. Lyon Co., 1904), 144.

authority of the state over education, the recognition of the principle of public support of schools, the requirement compelling parents to educate their children, and the compulsory establishment of elementary and secondary schools in communities of a certain size. Other colonies soon followed with similar legislation.

*Nature of the Latin grammar school.*    As the name implies, the Latin grammar school was simply a transplantation of the English secondary school of the day. Its curriculum consisted mainly of instruction in Latin, some elements of Greek, and religion. Later some of the schools made provision for the teaching of English, composition, and arithmetic. However, the Latin grammar school was almost entirely a college preparatory institution. The entrance requirements of Harvard University, established in 1636, stipulated that applicants must be able to translate Latin classics into English, speak and write acceptable Latin, and know basic Greek grammar. Thus the Latin grammar school attempted to take boys from the upper-class families who had some training in English and help them meet these prerequisites for college. College then prepared those who completed the course for the clergy.

The Latin grammar school enrolled boys at about seven years of age and retained them until they were accepted into college or chose to leave school. The usual span of years was close to seven; therefore, the boys usually began college work at about the age of fourteen. The school day was long and discipline was stern. Memory work and drill were typical methods of instruction.

*Passing of the Latin grammar school.*    Latin grammar schools never really became greatly popular. The need for additional clergymen was soon met, and thereafter only a relatively small number of additional churchmen were required. A curriculum which was largely Latin, Greek, and religion had little appeal for a struggling frontier society. "In the state of American society at that time, the ministry, the magistracy, or teaching in a Latin school were virtually the only occupations in which Latin was very helpful."[2] Young men who were interested in law and medicine had to apprentice themselves to prepare for these professions. The rising merchant class sought a more practical training than the Latin grammar school offered.

The clergy gradually lost its powerful hold over New England colonies. A growing middle class, which had never been to Latin grammar

---

[2] R. Freeman Butts, *A Cultural History of Education* (New York: McGraw-Hill Book Company, Inc., 1947), 301.

school and which was not convinced that its children ought to go to such an institution, reacted against this school which had largely been for the upper class. Towns refused to establish Latin grammar schools and sought relief from the fines imposed.

For these and other reasons, the earliest form of secondary school in America began to pass. By the end of the Revolutionary War, the Latin grammar school was rapidly being supplanted by another educative institution.

*Significance of early secondary education.*    This first period in the development of secondary education in America is significant because of a number of important achievements. During this time:

1. The first secondary schools in America were established. These had little relationship to existing elementary education and served as "fitting schools" to the colleges.

2. The civil authorities took the initiative in developing and supporting the Latin grammar schools in the New England colonies. This led to the eventual principle of public control and support of secondary education.

3. Early colonial legislation asserted the authority of the state government over education. It confirmed the right of civil governments to tax for the support of schools.

4. Compulsory education was promulgated. This was not compulsory attendance, but it referred to the requirements that parents educate their children and that communities establish schools.

The Latin grammar school had competition from certain schools established as private business ventures by some schoolmasters. Such schools offered instruction in practical subjects which had appeal to the youth of the day. Arithmetic, surveying, navigation, reading and writing in English, astronomy, and modern foreign languages were some of the areas in which courses were taught. However, these schools had no organized support and thus did not survive. They were really transitional between the Latin grammar school and the academy.


## THE ACADEMY

The secondary institution which emerged in the middle of the eighteenth century and which lasted to the end of the nineteenth century became known as the academy. These schools resulted largely from private subscriptions and were controlled by boards of trustees.

## The Academy Movement

The academy movement is generally calculated as starting with Benjamin Franklin's Academy which was established in 1751 as a result of a pamphlet which he wrote and published. In this publication, he called for a broadening of curriculum. The practical subjects were to be included as well as some of the elements of the curriculum of the Latin grammar school. Three departments were organized at first—an English department, a Latin department, and a department of mathematics. It seems clear that his proposal was a sort of compromise between his ideas of a desirable offering of practical subjects and the learning demanded for admission by the colleges of the day. This compromise was necessary in order to secure financial support for the new school.

Other academies were started by wealthy men who put up the money, chose a board of trustees, and gave the school their names. Some academies were established and run as businesses. In addition, certain church groups sponsored academies for the benefit of their own religious sects.

During the academy period, large numbers of these schools were organized throughout the nation. Although they were generally replaced by the high school, a few academies remain in operation to this day.[3]

*Nature of the academy.* As this secondary institution became firmly established, it tended to display several characteristics. Usually the academy was not publicly established and controlled by town authorities as was the case of most of the Latin grammar schools. Boards of trustees were selected to control the school, and private money typically was used for support.

A great many of the academies became boarding schools, and elaborate rules and regulations were promulgated to control the behavior of students in school and in the dormitories. Sports and games became a part of the school life, and various clubs and societies grew popular. A much wider range of ages was evident in the student groups. Students were usually admitted at the age of nine or ten years with the requirement that they be able to read common English. However, not all pupils were planning to enter college and vocational preparation in some academies was an important aim; therefore, many older students were in attendance. The academy at first opened its doors to the middle-class

---

[3] In illustration Harriet W. Marr (*The Old New England Academies,* New York: Comet Press, 1959, 289) reports, "Several Schools in Massachusetts retain the name of academy, and are under the control of the academy trustees, but serve as free public high schools for the town. Among these are New Salem Academy, Hopkins Academy at Hadley, and Sanderson Academy at Ashfield."

youth as well as the upper-class youngster and made some provision for preparing students for college and for life.

The curriculum of the academies typically displayed the compromise position formulated by Franklin. Two divisions came to be important. The classical department retained the general qualities of the program of the Latin grammar school. Great emphasis was placed on Latin and Greek. Later, in response to the changing college entrance requirements, the classical department commonly offered instruction in history and various areas of mathematics. The English department of the school stressed a wide variety of new and more practical subjects. The use of the English language—reading, writing, grammar, rhetoric, and public speaking—was emphasized. The study of mathematics, including surveying and navigation, exploration of natural sciences, instruction in geography, history, and modern languages, all typically were available.

Girls were enrolled on a large scale for the first time in secondary education. For years, they were believed to have inferior intelligence and the rigorous secondary and college work was considered too difficult for them. However, some academies began to admit girls, separate female seminaries were established for girls, and in 1835 the first women were admitted into Oberlin College.

*Passing of the academy.*    As the years passed, the academy became less and less committed to the broad educational aims with which it started. The classical, college preparatory curriculum became more and more emphasized. The classical sequence of courses became the standard program and the parallel English offerings were de-emphasized. The upper-class, college-going youth was the dependable student; he enrolled and had the money and motivation to continue on through the program. Therefore, the academies began to cater to this student, and many of these schools became more and more exclusively college preparatory in aim. Others gained status in the eyes of the public as substitutes for college and accordingly began to offer a different curriculum. In fact, many later became colleges and universities.

During the nineteenth century, the great westward expansion created a moving frontier which affected the lives of a great number of persons. Frontier life was a great social equalizer. For example, survival skills were often far more important to status in the community than material possessions, position, or family lineage. The extension of the right to vote to a greater proportion of the male citizens and even some movement to allow women this privilege resulted in a greater demand for a more democratic educative agency which would offer secondary education to the potential voters. As a result of the changing social and political conditions, a new educative institution emerged. The new institution was more compatible with the democratic ideals than the academy which had become upper-class, college preparatory education.

*Significance of the academy.*    The academy emerged with great promise. Because it became fossilized it was gradually replaced by the public high school. Yet, even though the academy became rigidly college preparatory and exclusive in later years, it is significant because of a number of contributions.

1. It broke with the traditional curriculum of the Latin grammar school and laid the basis for a broadened program of studies.

2. It provided secondary education to the rapidly expanding middle class.

3. It extended secondary education to girls.

4. It implemented the idea that secondary education might be desirable for others besides those going on to college.

5. Although religious and private control and support were common, public contributions to the support of education were continued during this period.

6. It assisted in the improvement of elementary education and built its program on the curriculum of these elementary schools, thus leading to the ladder concept.

7. It initiated the first teacher training courses as the elementary schools sought academy graduates for instructors.

8. It prepared the public mind for universal secondary education in the United States.

## THE PUBLIC HIGH SCHOOL

In 1821, with the Latin grammar school almost out of existence and the academy just approaching its peak, the first public high school appeared. Again Boston led the way with the establishment of a school which became known as The Boston English High School.

> The Latin Grammar School . . . represented an extension *downward* from the college. When the people of Boston requested the establishment of a new secondary school they were asking that educational opportunity be extended *upward* from the existing primary schools for their sons who had no desire to prepare for college.[4]

---

[4] *The High School Curriculum*, 2nd ed., edited by Harl R. Douglass (copyright 1956 The Ronald Press Company), 26–27.

A few years later, in 1827, a Massachusetts law was enacted which required such a high school to be organized in each town of 500 or more families. This and similar state legislation led to the gradual growth of the public high school during the middle of the nineteenth century.

## The Early High School

At first, the high school movement faltered. It had some real support yet the academies were adequately preparing upper-class youth for entrance into college. The demand for education for a larger segment of American youth was slow in coming.

*Nature of the early high school.* The first high schools seemed to be a reaction against the exclusive college preparatory orientation of the academies. Accordingly, the curriculum was largely practical in its emphasis. However, the high school soon added a program of studies which led to college entrance. Thus, it became the institution in which the upper-class, middle-class, and some upward-mobile, lower-class youngsters could be served. It developed a broad curriculum which contained the subjects which met college entrance demands and also subjects which were suitable for youth who would terminate their formal education upon high school graduation. The Western European inheritance of a school which was aristocratic, religious, and humanistic had been subordinated to the vision of a new, idealistic, vigorous nation. New ideals of democracy, emerging concerns for the developments in science and technology, the developing industrialization, and the emerging nationalistic pride all led to the expansion of the public high school.

The college preparatory subjects rapidly came to dominate the total program of studies; however, with the tremendous expansion of courses offered, the elective system became necessary. A single required course of study was not possible to maintain. Industrial arts, home economics, business courses, agriculture, fine arts, and physical education began to be included in the high school curriculum.

The loose and fluid state of the high school program was viewed with alarm by the colleges and universities. Some of them instituted a process of accrediting certain high schools which, in turn, would be likely to send them students who had a more uniform background. Regional accrediting began to be implemented. National committees were formed to analyze the situation. One such group, the Committee on College Entrance Requirements, recommended in 1899 that all college-going youth should have four years of foreign language, two years of mathematics, two years of English, one year of history, and one year of science. "Apparently, in the view of the colleges, foreign languages were twice as important as English and mathematics and four times as important as history or science."[5] This committee clearly had in mind the traditional importance accorded to language which went back to the Latin grammar school.

Most high schools came to be co-educational and enrolled an ever-increasing proportion of the boys and girls of high school age. Attempts were made to make the teaching less formalized and less dependent upon sheer memorization. In imitation of the colleges, a large variety of clubs, societies, and athletic competitions appeared.

Even though the high school at the end of the nineteenth century enrolled only about ten per cent of the school age youth, it promised an increasing number of boys and girls the opportunity of education beyond the elementary grades. But before the ideal of universal public secondary education was to be realized, certain issues had to be resolved.

*Forces opposing early high schools.* Early expansion of the high school movement was opposed by a number of groups for a variety of motives. Many wealthy citizens could see no reason for the public high school since the academies were doing an adequate job of preparing their youth for college. Some church groups and private owners of academies had considerable sums of money committed in already operating academies. Taxpayers' groups opposed paying for the education of other people's children. The tradition of free public schools as pauper schools and the belief that the parents must accept full responsibility for providing an education for their own children was still strong, especially in the south. In addition, the legal issue of tax support for secondary schools was not yet resolved.

The Kalamazoo Case, which came before the Michigan supreme court in 1874, was the best known of the court decisions which clarified the issue of tax support for high schools. The suit before the courts sought to prevent the Kalamazoo schools from levying taxes for the support of the free, public high school. Those filing suit admitted the need to support the common schools through the elementary grades, but the high school was said to involve instruction in the classics in order to prepare students for college. This was education for a select group, and thus the use of tax money for its support was not justified. The ruling of the supreme court was in favor of the school district. The court pointed out that the state had established a system of education from elementary school through college. Consequently, secondary education was to be

---

[5] Butts, *op. cit.,* 514.

made available as a part of this system if the voters so decided. The right to tax in support of public, secondary schools was legally established. Following this ruling, the local school boards were encouraged to move ahead with plans for high schools, and states enacted laws which fostered the continuing expansion of the public high school.

*Significance of the early high school.*     The early period of the public high school is considered to be between 1821 and the turn of the nineteenth century. During this period, a number of significant advances were made.

1. The early public high school appeared as a result of strong social and political changes in American culture. It came to be supported and justified because it was in the best interests of a democratic society.

2. It supplanted the academy as the dominant form of secondary education in America.

3. It began as an institution which aimed primarily to teach the practical subjects but soon came to prepare its students for both college and for life.

4. It was firmly accepted as an integral part of the state system of education, and the legality of public tax support was established.

5. The curriculum was broadened and the elective system was introduced.

6. Colleges and regional accrediting associations sought to help standardize the curriculum of the early high school.

7. State systems of education from elementary school through the university were developed.

8. An increasing proportion of high school aged boys and girls began to enroll in secondary education.

In 1900, the public high school had begun its amazing growth, it enrolled over two-thirds of all the high school students, and it had established linkages with elementary education below and colleges and universities above. In short, it had become solidly established as the dominant secondary educational institution in America.

*Transition to Today's High School*

It was a great step from the early public high school to the high school of today. Many changes were made in curriculum, organization, and total services, and today we often find ourselves debating the wisdom of some of these changes.

The American people have lived through tremendous changes, experienced wars and a long depression, attempted to adjust to undreamed of technological developments, and faced the grinding, strength-sapping travail of a prolonged cold war. Such a period is bound to have had profound effects upon the public schools. School people also were not still; they were involved in significant research and improvement in educational psychology, philosophy of education, teaching procedures and materials, and curriculum development.

Some of the more notable areas in which the early high school has changed in its twentieth century evolution include the following:

*Enrollment.* Secondary education has experienced tremendous rates of growth. The number of secondary school pupils approximately doubled in size every ten years from 1880 until 1930. Between 1930 and 1940, pupil enrollment grew by fifty per cent. During the war years, there was no such increase, but since 1950 the growth in enrollment has resumed. Between 1900 and 1960, the private secondary school enrollment increased by more than 800 per cent. During this same period, the public secondary school enrollments grew by over 1400 per cent.[6]

This means that the high school is faced with considerable problems of sheer logistics in handling great numbers of boys and girls. It also means that an increasing majority of adolescents are in school. In 1900, about 11 per cent of the age group of fourteen to seventeen years was enrolled in secondary school. In 1960, over 83 per cent and in 1966, 84.6 per cent of this age group were estimated to be enrolled.[7] When some reasonable number of severely mentally retarded, the physically disabled, and emotionally handicapped is taken into consideration, it suggests that the high school of today deals with the great cross section of American youth. The high school is now a common school—a school for all youth. Thus, public secondary education has accepted a task which no other major nation has asked of its schools.

*Compulsory education.* Legal provisions for compelling boys and girls to attend some school were initiated in 1852, yet it wasn't until 1918 that every state had some sort of compulsory attendance law. At present, most states require attendance between ages seven to sixteen or until graduation from high school. A few states even set the upper limit at age eighteen. In this way, legislators have confirmed the abiding American belief that every youth should complete a substantial amount of edu-

---

[6] *Status and Trends: Vital Statistics, Education, and Public Finance* (Washington, D.C.: N.E.A. Research Division, August 1959), 9.

[7] *Rankings of the States,* 1967 (Washington, D.C.: N.E.A. Research Division, 1967), 18.

cation, and this has come to include secondary education. Such a situation has placed new and, to some, onerous obligations on the secondary school.

Compulsory secondary education caused the high school to face a situation which elementary teachers had met long before. Boys and girls who were not interested or suited for the typically abstract, academic training of the high school were forced by law to attend. The imperative implication of this must be faced—if all normal boys and girls are compelled to attend high school, the school must provide somewhere in the curriculum some satisfying experiences. To do less is to admit that the public secondary school has not met the great challenge put to it by the American people. If the high school cannot and does not offer educative experiences to all youth, at least some of which are perceived to be satisfying, then the only recourse is to change the laws or provide a new educative agency which will provide for these needs.

*Mass education.*     Public high schools are engaged in mass education. This is not something to be debated; it is something which exists. Secondary school personnel have accepted a mandate from the people and are in the process of attempting to handle attendant problems effectively.

When the great increase in enrollments began leading to the situation of mass secondary education, the schools sought an organization which would be efficient and orderly. They settled upon an organization suggested by the pattern of successful business and industry. The school board members no longer could handle the administration of the school as a part-time activity, so the development of the professional school administrator seemed inevitable. Actually, the flow of authority came from (a) its locus in the people of the state to (b) the school board, which usually is elected by the citizens in the district and which represents them, to (e) the superintendent who is hired by the board, to (d) the principal in each school and finally to (e) the teachers. The board sets policy within which the chief administrator works. He runs the organization to the board members' satisfaction or they replace him with a new superintendent. This system is quite efficient but also somewhat autocratic. As a result, in the 1960's, demands by organized classroom teachers for collective negotiation rights began to spread rapidly. A pattern, long utilized by labor in industry to make its demands heard, has been adopted by teacher groups (some affiliated with the N.E.A. and others affiliated with the A.F.T.) in order to more effectively gain a measure of participation in the district organization.

Other big business methods came to be utilized by secondary schools. Systems of bookkeeping, pupil personnel accounting, budgets, personnel, and reports were modified or imitated by the schools. Not all of these are viewed with enthusiasm at the present time. For example, the Carnegie Foundation for the Advancement of Teaching sought a neat, logical, businesslike structure for obtaining standardization in transferring high school work to college. In 1909, a "Carnegie Unit" was defined as including a year's work in any subject. This concept came to be interpreted as meaning one regular period a day, five days a week for the school year. The Carnegie unit[8] has provided standardized figures quite suitable for clerks and bookkeepers to carefully enter into the appropriate columns; yet, at the same time, this concept has fostered a curricular rigidity which has straitjacketed curriculum revision efforts ever since. Each subject must be taught one period a day, five days a week for a school year if it is to rate a full unit credit. Fractional credits are not popular. Therefore, it has been difficult to make the curriculum more flexible by providing some subjects more than standard daily and weekly allotments and reducing other subjects to less.

A number of recent innovations, notably modular and flexible scheduling, has enabled substantial breakthroughs in some schools.

Mass education has led to the goal of efficiency. This is interpreted as meaning that each class must be filled with at least twenty-five students under the direction of a teacher. Anything less is difficult to justify—on the basis of efficiency. This has come to mean that, unless the state provides special support money to make up the difference in cost, small, special classes for the mentally retarded or the highly gifted, for example, are not possible. It has also led to the typical, heavy teaching load of the secondary school instructor. Teachers often teach five or six classes each day and may deal with as many as two hundred different students daily. Two common problems which teachers express are (1) the difficulty of retaining enthusiasm, sparkle, and interest through six straight periods interrupted only by a half-hour lunch, and (2) the impossibility of really getting to know 150 to 200 different pupils.

*Curriculum development.* The high school has accepted an ever-increasing proportion of the adolescent group and has attempted to prepare some of them for college and some of them for life. By and large, the public high school has leaned toward the concept of the comprehensive high school. This type of education somehow has been more compatible with the democratic tradition to educate all youth in the

---

[8] See Ellsworth Tompkins and Walter Gaumnitz, "The Carnegie Unit: Its Origin, Status, and Trends," *NASSP Bulletin,* 48:1–78, January 1964.

same institution rather than to establish college preparatory schools separate from vocational or general high schools.

Early curricular developments led to parallel curricula. Most schools offered a sequence of courses which provided the background deemed right and proper by the colleges. They also offered practical courses in a number of areas. In the early 1900's, curricular areas such as commercial, homemaking, industrial arts, and general were identifiable. During the early period, curriculum was described and organized purely in terms of the logic of the subject matter.

Significant developments in educational philosophy and educational psychology led to a growing attention to the learner. It slowly became apparent that the most important element in the learning situation was the student, for only he could learn, no one could do it for him. A whole new approach to curriculum building resulted.

Aims of education were formulated which went beyond the simple coverage of various subjects. Committees and groups carefully developed aims and objectives of learning which focus upon desired changes in the learner; for example:

> The program of every secondary school should . . . [make] maximum contribution to the following objectives:
> a. loyal, intelligent citizenship, and morality in the broad sense of the word;
> b. effective home membership and leadership;
> c. the abilities and tastes which insure pleasurable and harmless employment of leisure time;
> d. the maximum development of abilities and interest in the best suited vocational activities;
> e. physical health;
> f. the development of the most healthy and satisfying personality and mind; and
> g. the development of interests and abilities insuring continued learning through life.[9]

Such aims were broad and inclusive. They reflected the expanding role of the secondary school in response to the increased demands placed upon it. These aims gave focus and orientation to the curricular offerings and provided a basis for evaluation. Thus the aims and objectives approach to curriculum construction and revision came into being.

School personnel developed increased understanding of group process and the importance of teacher involvement in curriculum build-

---

[9] Harl R. Douglass, *Secondary Education for Youth in Modern America* (Washington, D.C.: American Council on Education, 1937), 129.

ing. As a result, committees of teachers became the working unit within which curriculum was examined and revised. Classroom experimentation was encouraged and led to sound curriculum improvement. Whole school systems instituted coordinated curriculum planning based on an analysis of the total program of studies from kindergarten through the twelfth grade.

Our store of knowledge has grown at such a rapid rate that two developments seemed inevitable. Content has been pushed downward. College courses increasingly have been taught in secondary schools. The advanced placement program has enabled bright students to take college-level courses in high school and to qualify for advanced placement in college and/or college credit. At the same time, high schools are pushing courses down into the junior high schools. This whole movement resulted from the need to help some youngsters move more quickly into advanced work. The other development has come more reluctantly, but there has been some attention given to eliminating irrelevant material (for example, some mathematics teachers report that at least one-third of the material taught in solid geometry is not essential to the study of higher math) and some work toward reducing overlap and undesirable repetition. Committees in various subject areas at local, state, and national levels have been working on these problems and a variety of new curriculum materials have been developed.

*Expanding services.*    The public high school has expanded its services in order to attain its broadened educational objectives. The school library became established in order to enhance the teaching in the school. Books, pamphlets, newspapers, magazines and, more recently, recordings were made available as a school facility for use in classwork and for recreational and exploratory use. Basic reference materials were to be found. Professionally trained librarians were hired to direct this special service of the school.

The scientific movement of psychological testing provided useful tools for the secondary staff. Therefore, the high school began to administer a variety of tests and to make the results available to teachers. Records systems were revised in order to include such pertinent information in convenient form.

More recently, guidance and counseling services have become a part of the school. Trained personnel were sought; in-service training of teachers provided insights into the responsibilities and benefits which accrued. Students were apprised of the available services.

Hot lunch programs resulted from attention to the health needs of the students. Meals planned by dietitians were made available as a substitute for the cold sack lunch and the fare in the downtown hamburger shop. This service required kitchen and serving facilities, lunch rooms, and additional trained personnel.

Larger districts which resulted from consolidation and unification brought the need for transportation services. Where students were compelled to travel long distances to and from school, school boards were encouraged to provide bus service. The logic seemed to be that if society compelled boys and girls to attend school by law, the school must provide transportation to those students who must travel an excessive distance. In this way, the high school found itself in the transportation business.

Audio-visual materials and machines augmented the available instructional materials. Many high schools hired part-time audio-visual directors to supervise the program, keep the machines in repair, order and schedule audio-visual materials, maintain an audio-visual library of school-owned films, filmstrips and recordings, and assist teachers in their use of this resource to improved teaching. Comprehensive instructional resource centers were developed to bring all major teaching and learning resources together in a coordinated organization.

*Reorganization.*     The movement toward reorganization of the high school has been an important development. The early high school came to be a four-year institution built upon an eight-year elementary school. Thus, the 8-4 plan is considered the traditional organizational plan.

As a result of dissatisfaction with the traditional organization, several communities put into operation the first junior high schools during the period between 1909–1911. The movement has grown so that today the great majority of students are enrolled in some sort of reorganized high school system. The 6-6 plan is most prevalent, however, the 6-3-3 or some other organization involving a separate junior high school or middle school is also popular.

The junior high school movement stemmed from a belief that the early adolescent required a different kind of education than either the typical elementary or secondary schools provided. An additional consideration which gave great impetus to the growth of this movement was the expedient need for efficient use of school facilities within a school system. For example, sometimes the overcrowded high school building was made into a junior high school and a new senior high plant was constructed.

At the same time that secondary education was extended downward to include grades seven and eight, another movement expanded the conception of secondary education upward two years beyond high school. Communities established junior colleges with a locally elected school board in control. These junior colleges usually offered two years of college work and also a variety of terminal courses which sought to satisfy the practical needs of students in the community. Evening or "extended day" programs made education readily available to adults.

Reorganization of secondary education resulted in a variety of plans. In many states, it led to the extension of the concept of secondary education to include grades seven through fourteen.

A study of American secondary education shows clearly that the public school of today is a social institution which developed in response to the needs of a changing society. Such a culture requires an institution which is sufficiently flexible and sensitive to keep up with these changes. Though the Latin grammar school and the academy failed because of rigidity, the public high school has displayed considerable adaptability, especially in relation to the tremendous changes in the twentieth century.

It sometimes comes as somewhat of a shock for teachers to realize that the public high school as they know it is likely to be maintained only so long as it adequately meets the demands of the culture which supports it. Already a number of proposals have been made for other educative agencies which would handle the sizeable proportion of youth for whom the present high school is unsuited.

## REVIEW

Secondary education as it is known today seems to have evolved as a result of several important factors.

1. The high school is partially a product of the ideas brought to this country by generation after generation of immigrants. The first secondary schools were simply an importation of the Latin grammar school by the early colonists. This basic heritage has been added to by countless immigrants since. However, the American culture has a distinctly Western European flavor, and the schools have developed in this tradition.

2. The very evolution of this democratic nation colored and shaped the emerging educative institution. The great ideas which captured the imagination of this country gave direction to the nature and organization of the schools. The needs of a democracy, the long experience of great numbers of Americans on the moving frontier, the growing nationalistic pride, and the emerging pressures of the twentieth century have con-

tributed to the determination of today's high schools. The American vision has been toward universal secondary education, and the high schools are just now approaching this goal.

3. The needs of a young, virile country engaged in continuous and vigorous growth have placed great demands upon the schools. Insistent emphases upon practical education were important factors in the establishment of the academy and later the public high school. Practical, tangible outcomes of education have been powerfully supported by the American people and have profoundly affected the present curriculum. Today a major, pressing problem facing the high schools is how to provide all youth with the useful education which they and their parents feel they need.

4. The great shift in thinking from the dry, formalistic humanism of the Latin grammar school to the experimental, scientific emphases of today has caused significant changes in the secondary school. Discoveries in the psychology of learning, insights into the nature of child growth and development, applications of the scientific method to problem solving, knowledge of human intelligence and aptitudes, and a recognition of the primacy of the individual operating in his environment led to the use of new methods and materials.

Review the following questions.

1. Early colonial secondary education has to do with the establishment and development of the Latin grammar school. Where was the first such school established and what were its functions? Why is the Latin grammar school significant?

2. The academy resulted from changed conditions and new demands. What were the influences which led to its growth? In what ways was the academy important to the later development of secondary education in America?

3. The first public high school differed in many ways from today's high school. What are some of the greatest areas of contrast?

# Selected References

Butts, R. F. and Cremin, L. A. *History of Education in American Culture.* New York: Holt, Rinehart and Winston, Inc., 1953.

Davis, E. D. *Focus on Secondary Education.* Glenview, Ill.: Scott, Foresman and Company, 1966; Ch. 1 "Historical Development of Secondary Education."

Douglass, H. R. *Secondary Education in the United States.* 2nd ed. New York: The Ronald Press Company, 1964; Ch. 1 "The Current Challenge to American Secondary Education," Ch. 4 "Purposes and Services of American Secondary Schools," and Ch. 20 "Types of Secondary Schools."

Good, H. G. *A History of American Education.* New York: The Macmillan Company, 1956.

Goodlad, J. I., ed. *The Changing American School,* Sixty-fifth Yearbook of the National Society for the Study of Education, Part II. Chicago: University of Chicago Press, 1966.

Metcalf, L. E., DeBoer, J. J., and Koulfers, W. V. *Secondary Education: A Textbook of Readings.* Boston: Allyn and Bacon, Inc., 1966; Part I "The Commitment to Universal Secondary Education in the United States."

Meyer, A. E. *An Educational History of the American People.* New York: McGraw-Hill, Inc., 1957.

Nakosteen, M. *The History and Philosophy of Education.* New York: The Ronald Press Company, 1965.

Oliva, P. F. *The Secondary School Today.* Cleveland: The World Publishing Company, 1967; Ch. 1 "The Development of the Secondary School."

Popham, D. F. *Foundations of Secondary Education—Historical, Comparative and Curricular.* Minneapolis, Minn.: Burgess Publishing Company, 1969.

# Index